MUSLIM WOMEN AND MISOGYNY

SAMIA RAHMAN

Muslim Women and Misogyny

Myths and Misunderstandings

HURST & COMPANY, LONDON

First published in the United Kingdom in 2024 by
C. Hurst & Co. (Publishers) Ltd.,
New Wing, Somerset House, Strand, London WC2R 1LA
Copyright © Samia Rahman, 2024

A Cataloguing-in-Publication data record for this book
is available from the British Library.

This book is printed using paper from registered sustainable
and managed sources.

ISBN: 9781911723011

www.hurstpublishers.com

For Mum and Dad

CONTENTS

Some names and identities of interviewees have been changed.

INTRODUCTION

Those who know me will know I was reluctant to write this book. It had been breezily suggested some years ago that I 'write something on Muslim women', and you know what, there was an energy in that 'you're a woman, do a woman thing' which jarred. But it wasn't just that. The responsibility and pressure of doing justice to the diverse and vast experiences of a group subjected to the worst misogyny, Islamophobia, discrimination and marginalisation of any section of society[1] weighed heavily on me. Who was I to appoint myself a spokesperson? What gave me the right to collate, capture and frame all the myriad ways of being a Muslim woman that exist? I couldn't quite reconcile why it should be my place to fulfil this role, when surely so many others could do it far better. In my over-thinking, imposter-syndrome, never-quite-good-enough internal dialogue, I was being asked to lay bare the lives of women who are among the most fetishised, scrutinised and talked-about categories of people in the world.[2] Everyone has an opinion on how (un)covered my sisters choose or don't choose to be. There is such a clamouring to speak on behalf of Muslim women, to tell us why and how we form our life choices, how oppressed/empowered we are and what steps we must take to be liberated, or saved, or more pious, or more integrated, or more authentic, or more Muslim or less Muslim, and, most importantly, less difficult.[3]

So how could I dare to position myself as the voice for the voiceless, I asked myself. I was just another invisibly Muslim woman who navigates my contradictions and my ways of being in the messy way that every human being in this beautiful, wretched landscape of our global existence does. All this while being able to slip under the radar, to 'pass' because I don't wear hijab, because I get to play the 'good Muslim'[4] with my palatable ways, my inoffensive manner, my fears of being too much, of taking too much space, of being too grateful just for being allowed to be. As a woman, a person of colour, a second-generation child of immigrants, I was someone who grew up contorting myself to make myself acceptable to this patriarchal, Western-centric world, making myself small to fit in, to not be any trouble. Someone who sluiced away those parts of me that might make others uncomfortable, who tried to be the good Muslim, to absorb the negativity, to not react or spoil the mood or expect more than I should, who just wanted to find a place to be and to belong.

I felt uneasy that I, with all my privileges, should be grasping to 'lift the lid' on the lives of Muslim women, to be perceived as a native informant. Perhaps my sisters who experience material, emotional and systemic oppressions of poverty, anti-Blackness,[5] homophobia and gender injustice prefer not to have their intimate lives scrutinised for consumption by audiences already harbouring prejudices and biases.[6] I found this thought painful. I was mindful, even consumed with fear, of inadvertently creating an extractive and sensationalist exposé that demonises us and fuels Islamophobia or conversely denies the very real problem of misogyny that exists across all communities, including Muslim communities. I felt a tremendous responsibility to write this book well; it means so much to me to get it as right as possible. After all, an agonising feature of writing is the knowledge that, particularly in our digital age, once a piece of work is 'out there', there is no taking it back.

As I procrastinated and postponed, I struggled with personal and professional insecurity. I was not a trained Islamic scholar, and I was hardly an intellectual nor dared even to call myself a journalist or writer. This was magnified by work environments which manifested many subtler aspects of misogyny, chipping away at self-worth through incessant belittling and denigration. To be constantly told you are incompetent or incapable and would never manage to write a book and at the same time to be admonished because you haven't yet written the book was something I had normalised and even excused. A certain type of patronage infantilises women, but how many of us are brought up to show deference to patriarchs and to accept their berating manner? I, despite all my privileges, despite telling myself that I could never write a book on misogyny because what have I ever experienced of misogyny compared with my sisters, found myself locked in a cycle of convincing myself I would never be good enough, as I traced a path within misogynistic structures. In recent years, I felt myself gaining confidence, courage and self-belief. I released myself from patriarchal binds that sought to fix me in the place they had designated for me, and who viewed my self-determination as a terrible betrayal of their patronage. At that moment I knew I was finally ready to write this book.

Of course, there were still times when I hesitated. Moments when I asked myself, 'who am I to speak on behalf of Muslim women?' Being true to other people's lives has always been my intention. Yet the fetishist's desire to 'unveil' intimate and personal lives of Muslim women sought to pull its voyeuristic, cliched and exploitative chains. I solicited the advice of academic Dr Fauzia Ahmad, a pioneering voice on the lives of Muslim women in Britain.[7] She told me that writing about difficult issues as an 'insider' researcher is always daunting. It is a responsibility to navigate the personal relationships we have with our communities while recognising that we could be seen as 'sell-outs' for airing 'dirty linen'. At the same time, we have to recognise how any negative revelations might be used to further tarnish and pathologise our communities.

'The difference is your intention,' Fauzia told me. 'You are not doing a tabloidesque "exposé" but instead are coming from a place where you are aiming to privilege and elevate the voices of Muslim women from diverse perspectives. You've also included the voices of Muslim men too, highlighting that exploring misogyny is not an anti-man exercise, but coming from a Muslim gender empowerment perspective.' She reassured me that my trepidation illustrates my awareness of how easily this issue can be misconstrued. 'Your nervousness, your anxiety, is why your contribution is needed.'

I once wrote about the relationship a writer has with the text and how much I feared being written about, thought about and perceived by strangers, not because I didn't believe in the veracity and poetry of every word I wrote, but because I know that my words can easily be disregarded in favour of criticising my validity as a woman, as a Muslim woman.[8] I fear becoming a commodity for consumption outside my work. Why must marginalised people always operate within the framework of the race, gender, class, sexuality, disability, faith, that defines us? Such readings of our work only extend the colonial and aggressive consumption of self and body.[9] Later in the book, I write about how a Muslim woman who steps into the public gaze no longer owns her self.[10] She must become available for those who wish to unpack her and dismantle her and gaze at her and pick her apart.[11] Isn't it enough to write and let your work speak for itself?

What is this relationship with reading that renders the reader in denial of the capacity for the written word to embody space for growth? It's often assumed that an argument presented in print or online is a firmly held position, an immovable declaration of all that resides in the writer's mind and heart, not an engagement with discourse that invites interrogation. But the words that jump from the page and into our imagination were never meant to be passive. Reading is not designed to be a form of osmosis through which thoughts and opinions become imprinted. I chatted with my friend Nicholas Masterton of the Turner Prize–nominated research agency Forensic Architecture, an independent organisation that investigates human rights violations from Grenfell to Karachi to Gaza. He told me about how the findings of investigations are disseminated into the public realm through court cases, reports, exhibitions and social media. We discussed how the output forms the advocacy and how the work 'takes on a life of its own' through the conversations, feedback and criticism it generates. This is how I hope this book will be received. The production of knowledge necessarily involves a process of co-creation that involves you, the reader, and invites you to engage with the ideas and concepts in a process that is alive, constantly renewing, and that doesn't seek out definitive, easy and simplistic answers about what Muslim women think, do, believe and want.[12]

Often, it is assumed that a person must have a fixed position on an issue, or an idea that we will eternally clutch to. But to be liberated from patriarchal dogma, we must be open to having our minds expanded and our opinions challenged to a point where re-assessment is not an impossibility. A re-appraisal of an idea that we once held on to, perhaps even strongly, is a constructive way to navigate what it means to exist in our often-incomprehensible world. Yet, we live in a world where the lack of female representation exists across societies. There is a negation of Muslim women in Islamic scholarship,[13] in leadership positions and in public life, as I will explore later. At the same time, stereotypical tropes are rife when it comes to the discussion of

Muslim women in popular culture, while the West frequently positions itself as a saviour of Muslim women.[14] For 'white feminists',[15] as I will go on to discuss, Muslim female empowerment is to conform to their narrow definition of feminism. Audre Lorde's words ring in my ears: 'Those of us who stand outside the circle of this society's definition of acceptable women ... know that survival is not an academic skill. ... It is learning how to take our differences and make them strengths. For the master's tools will never dismantle the master's house.'[16]

We are all struggling against manifestations of oppression and inequalities. So how do we define misogyny, how do we define the path for reform, and who sets the agenda? What does it mean to be a feminist anyway? Are we talking about forced marriage and honour killing and men who compel women to cover, or uncover, against their will? These are the headline-grabbing examples. But misogyny also appears in myriad, subtle forms—in pervasive, everyday interactions that leave us with an undiscernibly uncomfortable feeling that is not always easy to define. Years ago, I was at a meeting with a Muslim male colleague, who was involved with a Muslim organisation I worked for. We were waiting for others to join us, and it was the first time I had spent any time with him alone. Out of nowhere, he made a sexually explicit joke. It sucked the air out of the room and I felt disorientated. I am no prude, but I was thrown by the sharp inappropriateness of what had, up until that moment, been a regular conversation about work-related matters. I assumed his humour was derived from the corporate world of immature banter that he might have normalised. For ages afterwards I couldn't shake the discomfort of that encounter. It felt like an attempt to control the space and assert his power. I told myself not to over-think it—it was just a harmless joke. Where's your sense of humour, Samia? Don't over-react, don't be difficult.[17] Some weeks later, we were on our way to meet clients to negotiate a deal. He told me I should play the part of the dumb bimbo and he'd do the actual negotiating. I half-laughed while secretly seething and made a mental note to myself that this was not a man I felt safe to be around.

Misogyny, according to a dictionary definition, is 'dislike of, contempt for, or ingrained prejudice against women'.[18] Patriarchy is 'a system of society or government in which men hold the power and women are largely excluded from it'.[19] Through the examples of Muslim women organising, uplifting and supporting each other that I write about, I see many spaces where women are quietly dismantling patriarchy where they find it, calling it out when they see it, and walking away from spaces that uphold it. Patriarchy can only be disrupted if misogyny is rooted out. And let's face it, misogyny is everywhere. Spewing out in social media channels of the Muslim manosphere,[20] in institutions, and in private spaces where women are told not to be difficult and where feminism is blamed for all the problems that afflict humanity.

I admit it: I went to see *Barbie* with my twelve-year-old niece. She said it was embarrassing to see me laughing my head off for the entire duration of the film. I loved it—that's what I told everyone as I came out of the cinema. And then I hated it. Because we were supposed to love it, weren't we? This slick marketing ploy rehabilitated the icon of sexism and spoon-fed it back to the masses, and we all bought in while the Mattel machine laid the foundations for a slew of films to come,[21] all expected to be multi-million-pound-grossing public spectacles. At the same time, I wanted to love it because of the people who wanted me to hate it. Right-wingers, including some conservative Muslim YouTubers like OnePath Network, were shrill in their accusations that *Barbie* was anti-men, politically motivated, pushing an extremist feminist agenda and corrupting innocent minds.[22] And feminism is not compatible with Islam, did you not get the memo? In a YouTube video advising on gender relations and marriage in Islam, Na'ima B. Robert declares that feminism has caused 'being a man' to come to be seen as a problem.[23] She also implores her Muslim sisters to stop emulating so-called masculine traits. Let women be 'feminine', let men be 'masculine', and above all, submit and let men take care of you.

Writing about and researching Islamic positions on gender for my chapter 'Is Islam Feminist?' led me to ask whether Muslim female empowerment must necessarily be rooted in Islamic scholarship. The Qur'an encourages critical thinking to enrich debates, seek clarity and refine practices, while the Sunnah (the life and example of the Prophet Muhammad) includes questions raised by women of the first generation of Muslims that were answered directly by God.[24] Yet we all know that isn't the entire story. Islamic scripture is also cited as justification for much misogynistic rhetoric, which in turn is often used to justify misogynistic behaviour. Can we find answers in our religious traditions, or does seeking to do so mean trying to use the master's tools to dismantle the master's house?

Where does all this leave misogyny perpetrated against Muslim women by wider society? How does that get to be justified? The notion that the respectability of entire families is tied to the inferred actions of their female members is hardly restricted to Muslim communities.[25] I cringed at popular assumptions about gender roles in Islam while I was growing up. Since developing a youngster's innocent, awe-struck and tentative awareness of what it means to be a Muslim, I was always quick to counter accusations that Islam is a misogynistic religion. My own upbringing seemed so firmly removed from the stories of oppression and inequality that many people have come to associate with Islam, and it just did not occur to me that Islam and misogyny could be linked. In fact, for a long time I was even convinced that my inability to connect the two might have been because my experience of being a Muslim woman was not particularly run-of-the-mill. As I got older, I realised that there is

INTRODUCTION

no 'run-of-the mill' Muslim female experience, other than the lazy stereotypes of orientalist fantasy. I hope this book will be a testament to that. It is not just about being angry about misogyny and how it stagnates our communities and stifles Muslim women. It is not just about railing at injustice and offering quick fixes. This book is about expressing our multiple, messy, contradictory and complicated truths as we navigate misogyny, sometimes with success, and other times less so. After all, as Audre Lorde said, 'if I didn't define myself for myself, I would be crunched into other people's fantasies for me and eaten alive'.[26] This book is about how Muslim women move beyond the tropes and the stereotypes and the oppressions and the injustice. Not past it but beyond, to find beauty in the 'woman thing'.

1

IS ISLAM FEMINIST?

Dr Sofia Rehman is the author of *A Treasury of 'A'ishah*, an exquisitely bound book compiling forty insights and statements from Aishah bint Abi Bakr, the Prophet Muhammad's third wife and the youngest woman he married. Much has been narrated and discussed about Aishah,[1] from her age at marriage to her temperament, to the salacious gossip that she endured during her lifetime and that dogged her legacy after death. Sofia's collection covers everything from Qur'anic exegesis (*tafsir*), jurisprudence (*fiqh*), theology (*'aqidah*), politics, (*siyasah*), and heart-softeners (*al-raqa'iq*), interspersed with soulful commentary 'for the contemporary Muslim seeking spiritual and moral direction as they traverse through daily life and its challenges and possibilities'.[2] As I devoured the book, it occurred to me that the serenity and wisdom emanating from the pages could only be mediated by a woman whose wealth of knowledge and thirst for learning encapsulated the very spirit of Aishah. Sofia is an author, educator and independent scholar of Islam who trained in traditional seminaries in Syria, Turkey and Wales. Her PhD thesis is published as a monograph, titled *Gendering the*

Hadith Tradition: Recentering the Authority of Aisha, Mother of the Believers, and looks at the statements of Aishah bint Abi Bakr as recorded in the work of the fourteenth-century scholar Imam Zarkashi. These statements are mainly correcting and refuting, but sometimes corroborating, hadiths (recorded sayings of the Prophet Muhammad) that male companions of the Prophet attributed to him.

Disapproval of interpretation of the Qur'an beyond the confines of traditional exegesis meant that voices of women like Aishah were pushed to the margins.[3] Traditional and patriarchal interpretations gained prominence, because society was, frankly, patriarchal. Other voices did exist but were drowned out or ignored. The distorting effect of this omission is illustrated by this collection of sayings of the Prophet's wife Aishah. Similarly, the erasure of Shi'i narratives has further relegated figures such as the Prophet Muhammad's granddaughter Sayyidah Zaynab,[4] who along with her brother Imam Husayn is 'perhaps the most commonly cited religiohistorical role models in Shi'i Muslim communities', according to anthropologist Lara Deeb.[5] In Deeb's analysis, 'Looking to role models from Islamic history is a crucial element in formulations of what it means to be a moral and pious person', in Shi'i communities.[6] When the Umayyad caliph Yazid ibn Muawiyah massacred most of Zaynab's male relatives, including her brother Husayn, at the Battle of Karbala, she courageously took on a leadership role to reassure and rally the women, children and men who had survived. This version of womanhood remains potent in Shi'i communities today, as participation in social and political affairs is a foundation of piety, and women are encouraged to be like Zaynab and strive to live up to her example. Husayn offers an example of mortal sacrifice, while the continued struggle against oppression is entrusted to women, who hold the key to the future of Shi'i communities through their activism, organising and leadership.

When I first met Sofia, it was very briefly at the Bradford Literature Festival.[7] I had heard about the Leeds Lit Club,[8] which she founded almost a decade before, and also about her Islam and Gender Read-Along, which had set social media alight and offered a sanctuary for a global audience during lockdowns and the Covid pandemic. We met again after I sent her what in hindsight I realise was a rather garbled DM on Instagram. She was gracious enough to overlook my incoherence, and we arranged to meet when she was next in London. Amongst Uber dashes and arriving at Rumi's Kitchen, where she was scheduled to speak, to a welcome sign which would make anyone's heart dance, we found a cute cafe in Willesden Green and chatted like old friends, setting the world and its patriarchal structures to rights.

During a Zoom catch-up a couple of months later, I asked Sofia to tell me more about her journey. She described embracing a very conservative practice of Islam in her younger days and over the years deepening her understanding to find peace and liberation in an Islam that wasn't immersed solely in outward pieties. 'As a woman,' she said, 'it's very difficult to resist the urge and pull to go toward something that identifies, acknowledges and promotes your full humanity.' Sofia grew up in a middle-class British-Pakistani Muslim family, where 'Allah was always around'. She was full of questions about life, religion and everything, and had an insatiable appetite for reading. Her parents' attempts to send her and her brother to the local mosque reminded me of my own parents' short-lived and thwarted efforts to engage me, my brother and my sister in formal Islamic schooling. My parents resorted to teaching us at home, and like Sofia it was in my teens that my siblings and I took the initiative, after resisting the madrasahs and Saturday schools, and developed an independent interest in Islamic scholarship, much to our parents' relief.

Sofia's trajectory as a second-generation British Muslim is, she says, in line with the considerable research looking at British

Muslim identity formation and belonging. Islam not only fulfilled a spiritual void for her from the age of fifteen onwards, but
also provided community and friendships. She took the decision
to wear hijab at the age of seventeen, the first in her extended
family to do so, and soon after adopted the abaya. Within a
couple of years, she was regularly wearing the niqab, although
not all the time.[9] Her new friends at the masjid quickly displaced
her previous friendship circle, and although her parents were
delighted that she had 'found *deen* [religion]' and they could send
her to university without worrying about boyfriends, alcohol or
clubbing, they worried instead about her safety wearing hijab in
the shadow of 9/11.[10]

Sofia's first friends at the masjid were members of the Islamist
political group Hizb ut-Tahrir (HT). After attending a few HT
meetings, she became frustrated with the quality of discourse.
All the hot air and polemic was a world away from the intellectual substance that she was seeking. She attended a gathering
that took place in one of the largest conference venues in
London, and the sheer number of Muslims in attendance was
powerful, yet, despite searching, she found the event to be void
of any real exchange of knowledge. She continued to read widely
but found that the diversity of thought represented in Islamic
bookshops, where works by Ahmed Deedat, Hamza Yusuf and
Abu Hamza had once been side by side, had been supplanted by
books published almost exclusively by the Saudi publisher
Darussalam. This influenced the direction of Sofia's own learning
and led her to take a more Salafi approach to religion, as this
ideological instruction was all that was available, and preachers
doing the circuit were also that way inclined.

A couple of years of reading left Sofia still deeply dissatisfied.
Due to the reduction of diversity on the shelves of Islamic bookshops at this point, it felt as though she had read every book
available in Islamic bookshops but was still unstimulated. She

travelled across the UK to talks but found the repetition and superficiality of the preachers' sermons uninspiring. 'It got to the point where I would go to talks and I would sit there with my friends, bored and finishing off the sentences of the speakers because it was so predictable. Everyone was saying the same thing. And I kept thinking, how could a religion that is over 1,400 years old and that I believe is genuinely of a divine source, how can I at age twenty have already managed to learn everything that there is to learn—it's impossible!' Sofia had the humility to know that this couldn't be correct, and she determined to study Arabic. Soon after graduating, she got married and travelled to Syria, where her husband was already studying. They had both pledged to embark on a lifelong journey of learning and serious study, but until that point she had only ever experienced a representation of Islam in the UK that was narrowly defined and dogmatic. Those who were teaching Islam were all coming from the same institutes of learning.[11] In the Syria of the mid-2000s, Sofia became exposed to Sufi influences. Her Salafi sensibilities balked at this, but her quest for knowledge overcame any reticence. 'I thank Allah that at the core of it all I just wanted to submit to knowledge. I was prepared to be led by information that was rooted in our tradition legitimately.'

It was while in a bookshop in Damascus that her husband picked up Zarkashi's book about Aishah and said, 'One day you're going to translate this!' She would end up doing more than translating the book, and fifteen years later carried out a critical study and an entire PhD examining the work. Unaware of what the future held, Sofia quickly started to become aware of interpretations of Islamic scripture, 'and all interpretation is a form of human endeavour which is going to be limited by societal, economic, political, gender, race and many other systems'. Having that understanding of knowledge production enabled her to separate what was divine from what was man-made, and she was able to recognise 'that there are approaches to the Qur'an ... that are contingent, and those which are eternal. This all really opened up my mind'.

Sofia tussled with the education she had now immersed herself in, as it challenged the learning of her formative years. But her probing questions and engagement with her teachers meant not only that she excelled as a student but also that her world was opened up to a plurality of thought and critical thinking. She felt a spark that the preachers of her youth had never ignited. An expansion of her horizons beyond Salafi Islam, while to this day remaining cognisant of the role it played in making her a confident Muslim and putting her on the path of learning, something that was always encouraged. By the time Sofia and her husband returned from Syria to continue their studies at a centre in Wales, she was willing to accept that alternatives such as Sufism were not the corrupting innovations that some of her more firebrand Salafi preachers had warned. With inspiring teachers who challenged and encouraged discussion, Sofia felt enriched by what she regarded as 'pedagogy in action'.

One transformative occasion occurred when a fellow student suggested after congregational prayers that the entire school come together to partake in a recitation of the Qasidat al-Burdah, a thirteenth-century poem written by Sufi mystic Imam al-Busiri in praise of the Prophet. There was some protest from the Salafi-oriented students, including Sofia, who considered this to be *bid'ah* (heretical innovation). Sofia looked over to an Algerian teacher, a strict and fierce Salafi committed to upholding the truth, who had fought in the Algerian war of independence and who she was sure would not stand for this. 'This huge man didn't say anything. He just sat cross-legged in the masjid, eyes closed, swaying, singing the Burdah from memory in his unmistakable lion's voice. And I just looked at him and remember thinking, "wait, what?"' Having teachers who continually disrupted her binary, black-and-white thinking was pivotal for Sofia's under-standing of Islam. All that they embodied as Muslims proved crucial to her intellectual and spiritual development.

Sofia and her husband moved from Wales to Turkey, where her husband was carrying out research for his PhD. He had joined a critical reading group with local scholars and students from the nearby university. Sofia had reached a stage where she was committed to taking truth from wherever she found it, whatever drew her closer to Allah and brought her the content-ment of the heart of which the Prophet had spoken. However, when her husband came home one day with a copy of amina wadud's *Inside the Gender Jihad*,[12] Sofia was furious. She had heard all about amina wadud's work and had decided nothing good could come of such teachings. After a while, being a vora-cious reader and unable to resist a book, she picked it up and started to read. To her amazement, she couldn't find anything objectionable. She described this to me as 'a crack in the veneer'. Although she still felt resistance to amina wadud's teachings, this was the beginning of a demystification of so-called feminist or progressive scholars of Islam that Sofia had previously been convinced were absolutely beyond the pale. Some time later, her husband brought home Fatima Mernissi's *The Veil and the Male Elite*.[13] Sofia struggled with parts of the book and yet found that she was not able to disagree with much of the substance of what Mernissi had written—it was the tone and language that put her off.

As the years passed, Sofia became more open to works such as these, as did her husband. When they again returned to the UK, she felt her views on salvation and pluralism in Islam altering. With their youngest child approaching school age, Sofia decided to return to higher education, embarking on an MA in Middle East and Islamic Studies at the University of Leeds, after which she began her PhD. Her studies meant she was further exposed to different ways of thinking and a broader view of what it means to be a Muslim. To me, her openness to learning is indicative of her willingness to submit and remain humble and to embrace knowledge as a channel to help maintain her humility as she continues to seek out proof wherever it may be found. 'Intellectual curiosity can feed into our spiritual experiences and what we then go on to deliver to our communities,' she said. 'It's individual and communal.' Sofia's PhD is intrinsic to her journey. It is as if the text that forms the basis for her research were made for her. Both the text and the subject of the book, Aishah, embody the ways that patriarchal readings of Islamic scripture marginalise the role of women in our understanding of Islamic history and tradition. 'Here is a woman I have grown up only hearing about as a wife of the Prophet,' Sofia remarked. 'Now I was seeing her as this three-dimensional individual in her own right who was actually a politician, a scholar, an army commander, a strategist, an advisor. How is this not out in the public domain? How many ways could young women imagine their own futures other than simply as mother and wife, if we had Aishah represented to us in a way that truly honoured her?'

Of course, Sofia's point is not to say that the exalted roles of wife and mother should not be revered. Women for whom these most vital undertakings bring all the fulfilment they need should be celebrated and admired. What her words and the example of Aishah illustrate to me is how patriarchal interpretations of Islam have reduced complex and multi-talented women such as Aishah, fierce, feisty, provocative, argumentative, sometimes difficult women, to limited versions of themselves. Aishah, a role model for millions of women around the world, has had her complexity stripped away, and her role as wife and mother supersedes every other aspect of her identity.

In 2008, I wrote an opinion piece for *The Guardian*[14] to mark the launch by the Muslim Institute of the Muslim Marriage

Contract, created to protect the rights enshrined under Shariah law by the Islamic marriage contract, or *nikkah*, which is not legally recognised in the UK. By the time the contract was relaunched in 2011, I had joined the newly reconstituted Muslim Institute and was working there as deputy director. One of the architects of the contract, the late Cassandra Balchin,[15] a pioneering women's rights activist specialising in family law and parallel legal systems, encouraged me to attend the launch, where she spoke passionately about the abuses many married Muslim women experience by men who refuse to adhere to the obligations laid out in a *nikkah* because these obligations cannot be legally enforced. Some years later, Myriam François would present an excellent Channel 4 documentary detailing the findings of a survey that revealed the extent to which Muslim women were entering into religious marriages without civil registry, often entirely unaware that these contracts were not recognised under UK law and afforded them no legal protection.[16] I knew many women in this predicament, some quite unknowingly, others by design. But I wasn't about to admit to Cassandra, or to Myriam, that I was one of them—and would be for a total of ten years.

When I got married in 2004, my husband decided he wasn't keen on a big wedding and wanted a small ceremony, with immediate family and close friends only. He didn't like being the centre of attention, he said, or perhaps, in the nicest possible way, didn't relish the effort that went into organising weddings of any size. I'm no Bridezilla, but I had my heart set on a party to remember, and to convince him naively said I would organise and pay for the entire shebang. Still wanting to give him some sense of ownership over our nuptials, however, I suggested he sort out the registry. What could go wrong? Fast forward to a few days before the wedding, and every little detail had been excitedly attended to by my family and me. My husband-to-be, however, had not factored in that in order to legally marry in the UK, a couple had to give notice at their local wedding registry office at least twenty-eight days prior to their special day. The wedding was imminent, and he was only just beginning to make frantic enquiries about how to go about organising it. 'You had *one* job,' I thought, as it began to dawn on me how my future was likely to look. Much to my family's consternation, and with various eyebrows raised at the precarity of the life I was destined to share with this man, we went ahead. We were married in a beautiful ceremony at the Battersea Arts Centre in London, presided over by Imam Luqman Ali of Khayaal Theatre who performed a moving *nikkah*. But the marriage was not legally binding, and when arguments occurred, as is inevitable in the trials and tribulations that are par for the course of any marriage, it became very easy to threaten to utter '*talaq, talaq, talaq*' (I divorce you, I divorce you, I divorce you) and instantly terminate our union.

Ten years later, we were still together, and our marriage still was not registered. It had become a bit of an issue for me, not dissimilar to someone waiting for their boyfriend of ten years to propose: 'When will he actually *commit*?' A *nikkah* offered all the advantages of halal marriage but none of the legal responsibilities, so my Islamically sanctioned but not lawfully recognised husband was perfectly happy to keep things as they were. My moment came when he was trying to persuade me that we should go travelling for a few months to Southeast Asia. I hardly wished to burst his bubble but pointed out that there was a mortgage and bills to pay, and I didn't have the luxury of being able to leave my job for a few months and on my return pick up where I left off, in the way that he, a teacher, could do. So I suggested he should go and have his adventure, on the condition that we book our registry marriage for when he returned. He agreed, but was adamant that there would be no soiree and it would just be the two of us.

We gave notice at Lewisham Registry Office and picked a date three months later for our civil marriage ceremony. We asked if, when the time came, we would be able to grab a couple of people from the office to be our witnesses, and the officials laughed and said sure. Upon our arrival at the registry office at the appointed time to be legally wed, the receptionist greeted us and asked if our witnesses were on their way. We mumbled something about whether the staff at the office might act as our witnesses. The receptionist laughed and asked again when our witnesses were arriving. Realising that we actually definitely did need to organise our own witnesses, my husband suggested we forget it and arrange the registry for another day. 'No way,' I said firmly, 'I've waited ten years for this.' The receptionist explained that we had fifteen minutes to find two witnesses, mentioning that there was an addiction clinic next door and a mental health clinic on the other side, and that we should avoid embroiling vulnerable people in our chaos. I immediately ran outside and started flagging people down. After many strange looks and rejections from just about everyone we approached, a young student from nearby Goldsmiths University, emerging out of Lewisham Hospital's A&E department a little dazed, agreed instantly, apparently very cheered up by the randomness of our request. Soon after, a gallant man, long retired and on holiday from Jamaica where he now lived, asked some searching questions, checked everything was above board, and voilà—we had our witnesses! Very little was conformist about our marriage, and I chuckled to myself that this would be a great story I would tell the children we would go on to (never) have.

The pitfalls of being Islamically married without civil recognition have been widely researched.[17] Lacking recourse to state protection, many Muslim couples in crisis have turned to Shariah courts, where ugly divorces, abuse, mental illness, family feuds, and the most intimate and devastating family secrets have been laid bare to be disentangled.[18] In 2014, legal expert Aina Khan OBE started a campaign titled 'Register Our Marriage', which

seeks to raise awareness about the lack of protection of unregis-
tered faith-based marriages and advocates for reforms to register
these marriages under UK law.[19] Khan argues that the absence of
legal rights for couples married in Muslim, Sikh and Hindu religious ceremonies leaves women especially vulnerable to great
injustices. All the same, not everyone agrees that changing the
law is the answer. Rania Hafez, an associate professor of education at the University of Greenwich, believes that by deferring to
the power of the state instead of empowering and liberating
women, campaigns to enshrine faith marriages in law only serve
to infantilise women. 'Give men and women information to make
informed choices instead of invoking the law. It is not for the law
to police women,' she told me.

I had evidently tangled myself up in confused notions of what
it means to uphold Muslim women's rights, declaring in my
so-so *Guardian* piece that the contract seeks to 'address the pervasive gender inequality in marriages across the UK—inequalities
based not in theology, but in culture'. What was I thinking? The
argument that 'culture' is separate from 'Islam' is so simplistic. It
is a view that appeals to the binary thinking of those conservative Muslims who insist the Islam of the Prophet's time is the
'true' Islam that future generations must seek to emulate in minute detail. In another *Guardian* article responding to the Open
Society Institute's 2009 report on Muslims in Europe, I had
argued that the development of a British Muslim identity
enabled Muslims 'to cast aside restrictive cultural practices and
reclaim their Islamic rights in harmony with being rooted in
Britain'.[20] It is a writer's prerogative to slightly cringe at the
naivety of writings from over a decade ago, and when I look back
at my *Guardian* opinion pieces, this may well be the case. Just
like Sofia, my understanding of the constructedness of Islamic
practice was developing fast.

In his comprehensive tome *What Is Islam?*,[21] the late Shahab
Ahmed takes issue with the idea that the culture of Muslims and

Islam are separate sets of values. The common imposition of such a clean distinction often leads to the rather disingenuous argument that misogyny in Muslim societies, communities and homes is a result of the polluting impact of 'culture' on the 'pure' religion of Islam as derived from the Qur'an and Sunnah. After all, Islam was first established in a society with its own cultural context, and many of the Prophet's teachings responded to the pre-Islamic mores and rituals of that time and place. What does this mean for misogynistic practices that are justified as being in accordance with Islam? Are they evidence that Islam teaches misogyny and is indeed a misogynistic religion? If we wish to argue that it isn't, is it necessary that pro-woman—or, if we choose to define it so, 'feminist'—re-readings of Islam be rooted in Islamic scholarship? If so, who exactly gets to decide what constitutes normative Islamic scholarship, what falls outside of it, and what is therefore inadmissible in any case for gender equity in Islam?

Unfortunately, despite the vast and thorough examination of Islamic scholarship in Ahmed's exposition, he is disappointing in his analysis of existing female scholarship and defers to male scholars at this opportunity. His is a rich and ambitious book, which seeks to problematise the idea that what it means to be a Muslim can only be drawn from specific textual sources. This makes it all the more surprising that he marginalises contemporary female scholarship and the overall field of women and gender in Islam. At one point, Ahmed quotes my former colleague Professor Ebrahim Moosa, who describes Muslim women seeking a pro-woman reading of the Qur'an as making 'too much of a few verses of the Qur'an'.[22] I asked Ebrahim whether he would mind elaborating on this position, and he readily agreed. He explained his view that 'a historically informed practice of the tradition' of Islam 'does not get imprisoned in verses of the Qur'an or individual hadiths, but rather by an interpretive framework', and that 'placing the entire salvation of Muslims on verses of the Qur'an is a new thing.' I respect Ebrahim's work greatly, but I didn't feel convinced by this perspective. When I asked anthropologist Ziba Mir-Hosseini what she thought, she agreed that this was unsatisfactory and referred me to amina wadud's response to Ebrahim's argument in her book *Inside the Gender Jihad*:

> This circular argument, with its feigned perspective as an objective critique, draws no attention to the significance of gender as a category thought by reducing the overall agenda of Islamic feminist research and theories to 'a few verses.' Meanwhile, it unabashedly reinscribes the male privilege of 'generations of scholars' despite their being exclusively male and with their specific 'patriarchal norms.'[23]

wadud argues that many privileged Muslim male reformists possess a blind spot when it comes to class and gender. (I would also add race to this list).[24] Of course, wadud continues, this blind spot has been entrenched by generations of dominance by male scholars of religion, who remain ever-present in surveys of the literature derived from mainstream Islamic scholarship that one finds in most pious households today. Women in these works are routinely depicted as a separate, inferior species, infantile and in need of proper management. Consider a classic: *Perfecting Women* by Maulana Ashraf Ali Thanawi, a book still given as a present to new brides.[25] The Maulana makes it clear that women must be socially subordinate to men—this is the demand of so-called 'Islamic law'. The moral decline and degeneracy of Muslim civilisation is largely attributed to female misbehaviour. Indeed, it was concern about the 'ruination of the religion' caused by women, which had gone 'beyond the women and their children and in many respects even had its effects on their husbands', that forced the Maulana to write a guide to good behaviour for the weaker sex in the first place. Women are prone to excesses—even at a wedding reception they can commit 103 different sins, such as celebrating by dancing. Perhaps this explains why my husband was against a big wedding—to save me from all things haram. The Maulana urges strict seclusion of women, who he insists must be controlled and managed. *Perfecting Women* is not so much a guide to etiquette as an insight into the paranoid world of conservative male scholars.

Another equally distinguished and widely read Maulana, Abul Ala Maududi, goes even further. In his *Purdah and the Status of Women in Islam*, the founder of the Jamaat-e-Islami movement calls for the urgent need to police sexual morality: 'The free intermingling of the sexes brings in its wake a flood of obscenity, licentiousness and sexual perversion.'[26] He describes a 'wrong concept of equality' that has 'led women astray and made them unmindful of their natural functions on the performance of which depends the very existence of human race and civilization'.[27] Motherhood, obviously, is women's sole function, and the hijab—or purdah—is the lonely but solid institution standing between women and a moral abyss: 'The whole superstructure of the Social System of Islam rests only on one pillar ... let us not weaken Purdah, which is a bulwark against the sex anarchy, especially of the current age.'[28]

What is less well known about Maududi is that much of his thinking is not derived from an exhaustive analysis of Islamic texts. In an essay on Islamic scholars whose penchant for 'cherry-picking' is absorbed into religious tradition as received dogma, Shanon Shah explains that Maududi 'arrived at these conclusions by relying upon anti-feminist Western literature that painted a picture of moral decay ... If anything, these sources reflected the patriarchal underpinnings of Victorian and post-Victorian sexual morality'.[29]

Sofia told me that one of her dreams is for every Muslim household to possess a copy of her book about Aishah in the same way that many have abridged versions of al-Bukhari and al-Muslim on their shelves. 'I want Aishah to be tugging at their hearts in the same way she did for me and for everyone to see how much she, a woman, did for the first generation of Muslims.' Such knowledge would have saved me from a great deal of anguish as I was entering adolescence. My experience was that the more I read about 'women in Islam' in the books I found at Islamic bookshops (the same bookshops that Sofia correctly remembers almost exclusively stocked publications from Saudi), the more I began to worry that misogyny was indeed integral to Islam. Maududi believed in the restoration of seventh-century Islamic society and was a fierce critic of modernity. The contemporary preacher Zakir Naik came a few decades later and espoused a similar ideal in there being a 'true' original Islam, which must be preserved from the corrupting influences of anything that fell outside the narrowest norms. Fair enough that men and women are equal in the sight of God, preachers would say, but when it came to the crunch, women were always dangerous, not to be trusted, not very intelligent, and under no circumstance to be allowed away from the watchful eye of a male guardian.

As an example of the infantilisation of women in Islamic literature, consider this gem from the celebrated eleventh-century religious thinker al-Ghazali, revered by one and all as one of the great scholars of Islam. In his *Counsel for Kings*, al-Ghazali devotes a whole chapter to 'Women and their Good and Bad Points', in which he writes:[30]

> The race of women consists of ten species, and the character of each (of these) corresponds and is related to the distinctive quality of one of the animals. One (species) resembles the pig, another the ape, another the dog, another the snake, another the mule, another the scorpion, another the mouse, another the pigeon, another the fox, and another the sheep.

Which one am I, I ask myself. 'The woman who resembles the pig in character knows full well how to eat, break (crockery), and cram her stomach ... She is heedless of her husband's rights ... She always wears filthy clothes, and an unpleasant smell issues from her.' I quickly discount this species, along with the ape who is overly concerned with how she looks and whose 'secret (self) is not the same as her (outward) appearance'. Probably not the dog either, 'who, whenever her husband speaks, jumps at his face and shouts at him and snarls at him', though it's probably for my husband to answer this one. I wouldn't categorise myself as the scorpion either, who 'does her utmost to cause enmity and hatred', or the mouse, who 'is a thief', or even the pigeon, who 'flits about all day' and 'does not speak affectionately' to her husband. The fox seems to have some sort of compulsion to eat everything in the house when her husband is out and start a quarrel with him upon his return, saying, 'You left me (alone in the house) sick'. So that only leaves one option—the sheep, 'in which everything is useful. The good woman is the same. She is useful to her husband and to (his) family and the neighbours'. Al-Ghazali could have added, 'and very good for slaughtering'. Elsewhere in *Counsel for Kings*, he urges men to jealously separate their womenfolk from unrelated men, to the extent that if a woman is forced to speak to a man, she must imitate the voice of an old woman. She must also never lock gazes with a strange man even if he is blind.

At this juncture, I have to admit, Islam and I were on two different wavelengths. I mean, if al-Ghazali thinks the best a woman can be is a sheep, and Maududi and others engineer us behind lock and key, what could one expect from the average *ulama*, the so-called religious scholars, of the kind who populate YouTube and issue fatwas on numerous online forums? What is this perverse obsession with a woman's monthly cycle? Why is modesty and honour written on our bodies? Are we supposed to think of all Muslim men as latent rapists, unable to control their desires? And who appointed these brothers, who I thought were supposed to be averting their gaze anyway, as the fashion police, forcing and abusing women to 'dress properly', imposing the hijab as some sort of sacred relic, whether we want to wear one or not?

Al-Ghazali begins his chapter on women with the words: 'The Apostle, God bless him, stated that the best and most blessed of women are those who are most prolific in child-bearing, fairest in countenance, and least costly in dowry.'[31] Could the Prophet of Islam, often noted for promoting women's rights, have said such a thing, thus reducing women to mere commodities? It's a hard pill to swallow. Another hadith has been used to justify the control and abuse of women and is likely to be beloved by Muslim 'incels', entranced by Andrew Tate and his ilk.[32] I'll be talking about them in a later chapter, but for now let's look at how they justify their obnoxious anti-women views. Narrated by Usama ibn Zayd, it is said that the Prophet stated, 'I am not leaving behind me any tribulation that is more harmful to men than women'.[33] Is this to say that women are to blame for the evildoing of men, that women are responsible for tempting men to stray into sin?

I found it impossible to reconcile myself to these misogynistic ideas, so I sought out scholarship by female Islamic thinkers, such as amina wadud, Asma Barlas, Leila Ahmed, Ziba Mir-Hosseini, Kecia Ali, Fatima Mernissi and Sunera Thobani, many of whom also played a part in shaking up Sofia's Salafi world-view. I devoured their writings with a greedy appetite thick with gratitude, thoroughly relieved to find that the patriarchal religious teachings I had been subjected to were merely manufactured products of dubious male minds. Armed with the knowledge bestowed by these female scholars, I was able to confidently refuse to accept the Islamic dogma that I had been taught in my formative years, and which the likes of Al-Ghazali, Maududi, Thanawi and Naik espouse. Much of the conventional interpretation of the Qur'an that has remained unchanged for centuries consists of layers upon layers of accepted truth built on the interpretation of a long line of male scholars. Narratives steeped in patriarchy inevitably codify patriarchal definitions and understandings of Islamic pieties and rituals. This Islam of male supremacy was not an Islam I could recognise as an independently minded critical thinker who values autonomy. Beyond the rigid and narrow conservative notions of such groups as Wahhabis, Salafis and various traditionalists, there are other Islams—more amenable to new understandings.

How do so many Muslims embrace the concept that blind faith is a virtue? Even during my school days, I could detect that the Qur'an was there to be venerated. When I was a child, I remember how the Qur'an would be carefully wrapped in a delicate red silk scarf that smelled of incense and was placed on top of a wardrobe to emphasise its elevated status. We were only to touch it if we were in a state of cleansed purity (wudu), and it must never be dropped. It was sacred. I was taught to love this book and everything it symbolised. I was also a little fearful of it. I was terrified of not handling it correctly, or, heaven forbid, letting it fall to the floor in a clumsy moment of absent-mindedness. Worse still, I lived in perpetual anxiety of mispronouncing a letter or making a mistake as I recited from it. I particularly dreaded such an error, not just because I was told what a grave sin it was to recite the Qur'an incorrectly, but because I was warned that anyone who listened to your recitation would be punished even more severely if they failed to identify the mistake and correct you. I was petrified of condemning my mum or dad to languish in hellfire. Later, as I entered puberty, I would learn that I must never, ever, ever touch the Qur'an while menstruating. This led to a number of particularly excruciating situations.

I can still recall my abject horror when my Religious Education teacher asked me whether I would be able to bring in a copy of the Qur'an for a lesson she was preparing on Islam the next day. I was beside myself trying to think of a way I could transport the Qur'an to school and back without actually touching it. And what if my teacher was also on her period! The potential for sin was just too vast. In the end, I explained to her my dilemma, to which she was extremely sensitive, saying she would rearrange the lesson for the following week. (That same year, during a trip to Karachi, I was confidently told by an aunty that a menstruating woman should not sit next to a man. There was no explanation as to why. As it turns out, I was soon to realise that if you happened to commit the faux pas of sitting next to a man in Pakistan, whether he was a close relative or a stranger, he would immediately jump up and seat himself elsewhere anyway. Such was the taboo that the capacity for awkwardness during the monthly menses was a moot point.)

When a text is venerated, the assumption prevails that its content cannot possibly be questioned by mere mortals, for to do so would be to challenge the word of God. For the vast majority of Muslims, the Qur'an and the hadith provide a complete guide to living. Whether it concerns financial dealings or etiquette in the bathroom, every aspect of a person's life is covered. The sacred book is timeless, the message universal. To argue the contrary is to veer towards apostasy.

After reading literature at university, I found that passive, literalist absorption is an impoverished approach to text. Yet this is what the traditional scholars offer as their interpretation of the Qur'an. The valuable contribution of these scholars is not in any doubt, but their commentaries have often epitomised the phenomenon whereby prevailing culture is interpreted through the medium of religion. It is also important to note that these scholars were predominantly men. The inevitable consequence of this has been the creation of an Islamic exegesis that is devoid of female input and therefore heavily weighted in favour of patriarchal concerns. Male scholars had very little access to the lives of women during the classical period and so could not possibly justly illustrate the place of women in Islam. Women became subjects of commentary in translations and interpretations of the Qur'an and hadith with no way of representing themselves with an authentic voice. The classical scholars in turn influenced contemporary traditional commentaries by people like Maududi and Sayyid Qutb.[34] Thus Islamic scholarship became caught in a cycle of misogyny that seems to perpetuate itself endlessly.

Dr Shanon Shah is a trained sociologist of religion. His knowledge is grounded firmly in an academic perspective and in his own personal grappling, since his late teens, with Islamic texts, unlike Sofia, who received a traditional education in the Qur'an and hadith at seminaries in Syria and Turkey before embarking on her postgraduate studies. Shanon references amina wadud, saying, 'We all have a "prior text"[35] that we bring to the text.' He tells me about his own prior text as a mixed-race Malaysian: 'If you go to a state school in Malaysia and you are Muslim, you have to go through eleven years of Islamic Studies, and it's a particular type of Islam that's taught to you, from the Shafi school of thought, but heavily circumscribed by the Malaysian Islamic authorities to erase anything politically sensitive.' Shanon was already beginning to question his Islamic education when he took up a scholarship to study in Australia, at a time when he was also coming to terms with his sexuality as a gay man. His experience of racism and xenophobia had not yet become full-blown Islamophobia, but coming of age against the backdrop of the imprisonment of Islamist Malaysian Prime Minister Anwar Ibrahim on charges of sodomy—as damaging a charge as could be brought—left Shanon unable to locate his authentic self in the religion that he had been taught. Fearing that he had no place in traditional Islam, late into his studies in Australia, Shanon chanced upon an organisation of women in Malaysia that would change his life. 'I discovered the work of Sisters in Islam, a group of very intelligent women who identified as both Muslim and feminist.[36] And I thought to myself, okay, so how do they do this?' Not long after, he was back in Malaysia working as a journalist and decided to do a feature on Islamic feminism based on interviews with these women. 'I was so fascinated. They were so fascinated—for them it was like, a Muslim man wants to interview us. And he says he's an Islamic feminist! This never happens! The only Muslim men that ever want to interview us want to tell us that we're wrong!'

Through Sisters in Islam, Shanon read amina wadud's *Qur'an and Woman*, after someone told him that when wadud converted to Islam, she said that if she found anything in the Qur'an that didn't sit well with her conscience, then she would no longer continue to be a Muslim, and that day had never arrived. Her seminal book blew Shanon's mind, and he committed to re-reading the Qur'an for himself. He picked up Abdullah Yusuf Ali's translation and did exactly that. 'When I got to the end, I thought to myself, okay, this is not so bad. This is the prior text stuff. I expected to find myself in it, reading it as a gay man, and I think this is the first thing people realise: the Qur'an is not written in a homophobic way.' Shanon also consulted the works of Ziba Mir-Hosseini, Scott Kugle[37] and other scholars and discovered interpretive tools such as thematic analysis and semantic analysis. He was also impressed by amina wadud's questioning of how it is possible to find violent and unjust meanings in a book whose general worldview is about liberation and justice. When taken in isolation, certain verses of the Qur'an might seem to point to something patriarchal, but within this larger system of liberation, wadud argued they must mean something else. 'When I first started reading the Qur'an for myself, I was struck by

Surah Baqarah,' Shanon said. 'Even those parts which Islamic feminists say are more egalitarian seem to address men.' This bothered Shanon, but accepting that there is a patriarchal world-view that has shaped how the Qur'an is organised was key. Leila Ahmed writes about how patriarchy pre-existed Islam, how Muslim women resisted it, what Islam has inherited and rejected from these traditions, and how liberatory struggles were written out via the politics of occupation and patriarchal governance as Islam became an empire. She also writes about the jostling for power between the establishment voice in Islam and the ethical voice in Islam, something that not only runs through Islamic texts but also is played out in Muslim societies, traditions and histories.[38] The struggle has never been resolved, and we are yet to ascertain which voice has gained the upper hand.

Reverence for traditional scholars has become an instrument for suppressing criticism that could inspire gender reformist re-readings. Who would dare criticise al-Ghazali today? Or other venerated luminaries such as the fourteenth-century Syrian scholar Ibn Kathir, or Abu Bakr al-Razi and al-Tabari of ninth-century Iran? Criticism is made even more difficult when the dominant thinking forbids any attempt to offer a personal per-spective on the Qur'an. The seventh-century jurist Said ibn Jubayr quotes a hadith attributed to the Prophet's cousin Ibn Abbas, who recalls the Prophet saying, 'Whoever speaks con-cerning the Qur'an according to his own opinion, let him expect his seat in the fire.'[39] So there you have it: keep your mouth shut—particularly if you are a woman.

There are numerous examples of how misogynistic interpreta-tion has become part of Islamic theology. For example, in the Qur'an, Adam's wife is not named; she is not held responsible for the transgression that leads to the couple's temptation by Satan to sample fruit from the forbidden tree. Both Adam and his wife share the blame for this action, and there is no charge that original sin lies solely at the feet of the woman. Yet in the exegesis of traditional Islamic scholars, Adam's wife becomes Hawa (Eve), and thus to some extent the story recorded in Genesis is appropriated. The classical hadith collections recorded by the ninth-century Persian scholars al-Bukhari and al-Muslim, which are regarded as two of the most authentic and respected compilations of hadith, make frequent reference to Eve and depict her as the guilty party in the act of disobedience. Some go even further and present Eve's alleged lead role in the act as symbolic of the capacity of women for weakness and betrayal. Despite having no sanction in the Qur'an, this episode has become accepted in traditional scholarship and is used by a strand of followers of Islam to support the misogynistic notion that oppressive restrictions are there to save women from themselves.

Another example relates to the interpretation of a Qur'anic verse about male and female witnesses. In Surah Baqarah, in discussing contractual debts, the Qur'an states:

> And get two witnesses out of your own men. And if there are not two men (available), then a man and two women, such as you agree for witnesses, so that if one of them (two women) errs, the other can remind her.[40]

The classical scholars have engineered a patriarchal reading of this verse to infer that a woman's testimony is worth half that of a man, thus perpetuating the stereotype of the intellectually impaired, emotionally fragile and unreliable female. I cannot believe this is what God intended. The message here is obviously contextual. During the era of the Qur'an's revelation in seventh-century Arabia, women were not involved in judicial, political and public affairs. They were subjugated and considered inferior. Islam set out to instil equality in society, and the Prophet was an exemplar of this. He viewed women as equal in all senses to men. In light of his example and the spirit in which the Qur'an was

revealed, it seems obvious that the discussion of female testimony in financial transactions in this verse is a technical solution
to redress social norms, not a universal comment on a woman's
reliability as a witness.[41] In fact, Islam set about encouraging
women to step forward and give legal testimony. By calling on
two women to bear witness, Islam pushed for women in society
to be engaged in greater numbers, to represent themselves and
support each other. When considered in relation to the Prophet's
overall attitude towards women, this interpretation seems to be
the only sensible and fitting one.[42]

Reading Islamic literature on women, one could be forgiven
for assuming that Islam has produced no female scholars and
that there are no historical accounts of women in Islam by
Muslim women. However, there are significant examples of
female scholars and students of Islam at the time of the Prophet,
and so-called 'alternate' perspectives presented by women were
also part of the original body of work from which *fiqh*, Islamic
jurisprudence, was derived. A comparative reading of hadith
alongside the prevailing attitudes held in society lay bare the lie
that the Prophet was in any way misogynistic. Women attended
consultations held by the Prophet in mosques and argued and
debated with him.[43] The level of openness to women and the
seeking out of female intellectual input was unprecedented for
the time. Sadly, this was never matched in subsequent centuries.
We only have to look at the dearth of facilities for women in
contemporary mosques to illustrate how far today's Muslims have
deviated from the example of the Prophet.[44] The mosque was
intended to be much more than a place of worship. The Prophet
worked to create a space accessible to both men and women that
would disseminate advice and guidance. Philosophical and theological discussions, education, and the settling of disagreements
were to be made available to all within its four walls. The idea
that the mosque should become a male-only domain with no

provision for women is in contradiction with the Prophet's aims. It seems that with the Prophet no longer alive to assert a pro-woman position, the prevailing cultural attitudes of the day meant that scholarship by women—works that are only latterly being rediscovered—became side-lined.

Prolific and influential women scholars of early Islam included Umm Darda, wife of the Prophet's well-known companion Abu Darda. She is one female luminary who is mentioned in al-Bukhari as possessing a vigorous intellect and producing great scholarly work. Ibn Kathir writes of her superior knowledge in matters of Islamic law and jurisprudence. Karimah al-Marwazi-yyah was one of the later female scholars, and widely regarded as the singular authority on the interpretation of al-Bukhari during her lifetime. Despite her example she was, unfortunately, to herald the dwindling of female influence in the exegesis of the Qur'an as the list of women scholars diminished after her. The most abundant period of female scholarship was undoubtedly during and immediately after the Prophet's lifetime—proof of his rejection of misogyny and nurturing of female education, a tradition exemplified by his wives, all culminating in a blow for any Muslim who denies women an education on the basis of religious teachings. For example, Umrah bint Abd al-Rahman was an eminent figure and an authority on the hadith reported by the Prophet's wife Aishah, under whose aegis she had studied since childhood.

Furthermore, according to the eighth-century commentary of Ibn Kathir, Khawlah bint Thalabah's husband had declared a form of divorce that would leave him free to remarry but not allow her to do the same. He justified his behaviour as being acceptable according to the pre-Islamic traditions of the time. Khawlah refused to accept this injustice and complained to the Prophet, who inferred that existing societal norms could not be challenged unless God revealed a specific new ruling. Khawlah did not give up and prayed that Allah would intercede on her behalf, convinced that a benevolent God would not force women like her to suffer such oppression. She was proved right, and in Surah Mujadilah, Allah revealed that this form of divorce was impermissible.[45] This is how one of the Prophet's female companions came to be known as *al-mujadilah*: 'the woman who disputes' or 'the woman who complains'. Here was a difficult woman who in the time of the Prophet was seeking to disrupt and subvert the patriarchal order. The Prophet was humble enough to accept that he, too, might be influenced by the patriarchal norms of his day, and he listened to the woman's complaint and learned from it.

It is when women claim space and don't contort themselves to fit the prevailing order, when they don't give up in their battle to be heard, that patriarchal injustice can be tackled. But what if this means stepping out into the public realm, with all the vulnerability and expectation that involves? Ingrid Mattson, a Canadian Muslim activist and scholar, writes about the necessity for women to take up leadership roles. She argues that however well-meaning or mindful men may be, often the erasure of women's rights and the reinforcement of patriarchal structures come about because of an absence of women speaking for women in positions of power and authority. Women in religious leadership positions are particularly to be welcomed, she contends, to challenge the resistance to a deconstruction of orthodox traditions and practices that have become codified as 'true' Islam. Mattson speaks of Ibn Rushd and his theory of 'renewal' and references in the hadith where the Prophet says: 'At the beginning of every century, God will send to this community someone who will renew its religion.'[46]

As Sofia's research shows, early Islam's female scholars and the voices of the Prophet's wives, particularly Khadijah and Aishah, serve to reset the gender dynamic in the interpretation of Islam which had been so heavily weighted in favour of men. It has been argued, for example, that Aishah's narrative can be read as an illustration of the burdensome nature of polygamy. A growing body of opinion now points to a wealth of evidence indicating that polygamy is not in fact permissible in Islam. We may determine this by examining the historical context in which the Qur'an was revealed. Men in seventh-century Arabia thought nothing of taking tens, possibly even hundreds of wives, whether as a result of war, peace treaties, trade agreements or the acquisition of slaves. Women were treated very dismissively and were given few or no rights. The Prophet, directed by God, sought to alter this state of affairs. He did this by permitting the taking of more than one wife, up to a maximum of four, only if certain conditions were met. Leila Ahmed writes extensively on how polygyny as a practice evolved into a political economic institution that propped up a benign patriarchy.[47] Yet the requirements for polygamy dictate that each of a man's wives must be equal in every respect, down to the tiniest detail. Financially and emotionally, a man must treat each wife with unfaltering precision— he must love each woman absolutely equally and is to spend the exact same amount on each woman in material terms. These conditions are unmeetable. However much anyone may seek to attest to the contrary, I simply cannot believe that it is possible for any man to love more than one woman equally. This watertight prerequisite renders the feat outside the spirit of Islam. I am sure many husbands, including my own, would concede that, in fact, one wife is quite enough!

The Prophet remained monogamously committed to his first wife Khadijah for almost a quarter of a century. She was fifteen years older than him and already a widow, which made their marriage unconventional for that era. The Prophet was evidently comfortable in a non-patriarchal union, opting to move into the home his wife already owned. He was slow to partake in the pervasive practice of polygamy and only took further wives after Khadijah's death. These were marriages designed to strengthen alliances and establish peace. His devotion to Khadijah was unquestionable, yet Aishah is considered by some commentators to have been his favourite wife. There is a great deal of controversy surrounding Aishah's age upon marriage, which has been estimated between nine and fifteen years old. Through twenty-first-century eyes, it is shocking to think that the Prophet Muhammad, by now fifty, could be betrothed to a child. However, during the Prophet's time, marriage at such a young age was unremarkable, and Aishah had already been engaged to someone else. It is important to consider the social mores and culture of the society into which the Prophet was born before passing judgement on his actions or even before blindly imitating them.

But there remains more to the dynamics of the Prophet's two most scrutinised marriages—to Aishah and Khadijah—than most mainstream scholars appreciate. These marriages were far removed from any notion of sexual power over women, something we should remind ourselves of in the discussions on toxic masculinity in the later chapter 'Red Pilled'. Furthermore, the Prophet's wives were not typically virgins. In fact, it was Aishah's and Mariam's virginity on marriage that were not the norm. Although there are some scholars who claim Khadijah was a virgin when she married the Prophet, this is highly disputed. But what is clear in depictions of these two wives of the Prophet is that Khadijah is presented as belonging to a pre-Islamic era, whereas Aishah, who is a virgin, is seen as representing the Islamic age. It is interesting to explore the extent to which these depictions have been shaped by patriarchal narratives. Reducing Aishah's age to pre-pubescence could be one way that Sunni scholars sanitised her personality, rendering her as innocent as possible and beyond reproach (particularly from the criticism of her in Shia narratives), when in actual fact, Aishah was likely to have been feisty, argumentative and sharp-tongued.

What better way to diminish the scandalous aspersions upon Aishah's fidelity? A pure, innocent child subjected to wicked rumour-mongering and bad-faith insinuation. This leads us neatly to the much-maligned ruling on adultery. The Qur'an is presented as being unequivocal in its assertion that sexual relations should be conducted within the boundaries of marriage. And what of those who express their sexuality outside marriage? The punishment detailed in the Shariah, or Islamic law, is horribly barbaric. Could the Qur'an really sanction the stoning to death of women and men who commit adultery? Modern-day examples from Iran and Afghanistan would suggest that usually it is only the woman who is punished; and in Pakistan, it seems even if a woman is raped, she is still considered guilty. Here we see the hypocritical corruption of the text. Revealed at a time when fornication and sexual promiscuity were unbridled, the Qur'an considers adultery, referred to as *zina*, to be heinous. It seeks to deter chaotic behaviour, particularly because seventh-century Arabian society was tribal, with great importance placed on bloodlines. Children and women were dependent on men, so regulating sexual activity would increase the likelihood that a man would take responsibility for them. Yet the Qur'an's method of dissuasion does not translate into actual punishment. This is because a successful conviction for adultery carries impossible conditions. In a similar vein to the appearance of permitting polygamy, punishment for adultery becomes hypothetical. Four witnesses of sound mind must bear witness to the act of sexual intercourse for a charge of adultery to be upheld, or a confession from both parties must be obtained. The punishment was simply never meant to be realised.

The 2021 film *Lingui, the Sacred Bonds*, written and directed by Chadian filmmaker Mahamat Saleh Haroun, is one of the most beautiful pieces of cinema capturing the way that Muslim women's lives are defined by moral policing. 'You have to watch it,' I told my friend Dr Raha Rafii, a historian and specialist in Islamic jurisprudence. She did. We discussed how we were mesmerised by the stunning visuals, the colours and the phenomenal acting that erupted in the emergence of rich female characters, strong sisterhood and mother–daughter bonds, estranged family ties, and the lengths men will go to in order to take control of the lives of women. Amina, a single mother, is confronted with the hypocrisy of patriarchal rituals and empty piety when her only child, Maria, a teenager who is still at school, becomes pregnant. The women are punished for transgressing social and religious convention. 'A subtle verdict on the hypocrisy of patriarchy, where women are subject to punitive patriarchal control,' Raha observed. The imam at Amina's local mosque is only interested in whether she attends congregational prayers regularly. After all, as a single mother, she is a woman who must dedicate herself to expiating her sins. A pious and wealthy neighbour whom she looks to for assistance is only concerned with persuading Amina to become his wife, and his seemingly sincere attempts to woo her obscure an ugly and catastrophic truth. Pregnancy outside marriage is a terrible sin, and now both mother and daughter confront the burden of shame. But whereas Amina surrendered to her fate as an outcast woman, Maria, who has been expelled from school, will not endure the same ignominy and seeks an abortion, demanding the right to take control of her own body. Abortion is apparently forbidden, yet female genital mutilation is an accepted ritual. Men dictate what should happen to a woman's body, and seemingly pious men violate women's bodies any way they decide. It is the women who circumvent these acts of violence against them and who resist misogynist norms that are justified as Islamic. Whether through fake FGM ceremonies, backstreet abortions or vigilante justice against rapists, the women in this film work together to claw back power and dignity.

Raha described the film as a depiction of women in solidarity with women, something I explore in greater detail in the chapter 'Solidarity with My Sisters'. 'The female abortionist reassured Amina that as far as she is concerned, they are sisters, and to not worry about paying for the abortion,' Raha said. 'Pregnancy out of wedlock has already left Amina and her daughter outcast, consigned to abject poverty. They're desperate for the cycle to break, and it is other women who support them.' For Raha, tackling issues such as FGM and rape head-on unravels some of the complexity of how these issues are navigated in women's actual lives. The women in the film are successful in taking care of each other, and justice is served in a way that is complicated and messy. One thing we both noted was that head covering was not the all-or-nothing signifier that it has become in more Salafi-influenced societies. In the film, women put a piece of cloth over their head when the context rendered it suitable to do so. Other times, they would not. Yet that didn't stop Amina from being chastised by the imam for not covering up according to his expectations.

I spoke to a friend who had worn hijab for decades, ever since she was a teenager, but after a journey of introspection, religious training and study of Islam was no longer convinced of the theological imperative for women to cover their hair and so decided to stop. She had first put hijab on because she firmly believed it was a commandment from Allah. When she later concluded that this was not the case, she felt she couldn't in good conscience continue to wear it, because to do so would be to act out of fear of what people might say if she took it off, rather than out of fear of Allah. Her decision to stop wearing hijab was for the sake of Allah, not because she was worried about judgement, discrimination or the violence of Islamophobia from other people. She had experienced these hardships as a visibly Muslim woman wearing hijab, but she told me they would never have been reason enough for her to stop. Her only reason was that she could no longer see the hijab as a divine commandment.[48] 'I started wearing hijab as an act of worship of Allah, and I took it off as an act of worship of Allah,' she said. She enjoyed being the disrupter in events or situations where she was often invited as a scholar of Islam. Not wearing hijab would surprise, confuse or unsettle some people. 'I liked being that mental jolt that some people got, that here's a woman who is speaking about Islam with authority. Who is claiming Islam and is not afraid to do so.'

How do women and their allies challenge misogyny when they are told, 'ah, but this is what we Muslims believe'? The imam in *Lingui* is clear when talking to Amina that Islam is resolute. To liberate much that goes under the rubric of 'Islam', and to challenge those who tell us what Islam decided, we need to read the Qur'an and the life of the Prophet Muhammad in the context of the time it was revealed. Throughout history, both the basic sources of Islam have been read through the lens of cultural practices of a seventh-century society. A casual examination and consideration of the historical context upholds the perspective that the original sources themselves are free from misogyny, certainly misogynistic intent. The Qur'an was never supposed to be approached as a superficial legal code. Yet those who interpret the Qur'an in this manner do so to uphold their own agendas of patriarchal control and the oppression of women, or to fuel the Islamophobic fire that brands all Muslim men misogynists and all Muslim women oppressed.

This is not to say that there is nothing uncomplicated about Islamic scripture. There are more than a few contemporary scholars of Islam who struggle to find enough evidence to be convinced that a progressive reading is possible, however much they would like to. I spent an afternoon with Aysha Hidayatullah, author of *Feminist Edges of the Qur'an*,[49] at a Shoreditch cafe with Berlinesque techno overtures. The setting was incongruous with our conversation, as I took the opportunity to probe Aysha about the fall-out from her exegetical focus on anti-patriarchal readings of the Qur'an. Her analysis encompasses the contemporary giants— Riffat Hassan, Azizah al-Hibri, amina wadud, Asma Barlas, Sa'diyya Shaikh and Kecia Ali—and what she produces is a considered and honest confession. It comes through from our conversation that for Aysha, this is a deeply personal project. Her findings are painful but, as far as she is concerned, undeniable. She assesses the verses in the Qur'an that generate the most unease for pro-woman interpretations and sometimes finds herself unable to reconcile them. With regard to the notorious 4:34, for example, she cannot arrive at any conclusion other than that the verse speaks of a context in which men may hit their wives. amina wadud rejects this verse utterly, but however much Aysha wishes to, she cannot. She explains the personal toll that publishing this book took, and her fear that it would fuel patriarchal and misogynistic interpretations of Islam. She also laments the book's impact on some of her professional relationships with women she holds in great esteem.[50] She questions whether it was worth publishing something that would prove so detrimental to her well-being and would create distance within the community of scholars of Islam in which she found belonging. But ultimately, citing intellectual honesty, she stands by her work, and suggests that we engage with the Qur'an in a process of co-creation, while acknowledging it to be a divine text. That doesn't mean that this is the end of any conversation on inclusivity in Islam. It is just that, for her, answers may not be found in Qur'anic text, but located in Islamic tradition and practices instead.

A little later that summer, over a coffee in my favourite cafe in Southeast London, Shanon and I spoke about what it might mean to engage with the Qur'an in a process of co-creation. Maryam, the mother of Jesus, has an interaction with God, after all. For Shanon, 'trying to beat a confession out of the Qur'an to tell us it's not homophobic or it's not misogynistic is the less interesting discussion now. The more interesting discussion is, what were these other themes in other traditions that the Qur'an was actively engaging in as well, and what was everyone thinking about gender at that time?' Many stories from texts in Judaism and Christianity that were circulated in the ancient world but never canonised can be found in the Qur'an. As Muslims, we have not been encouraged to explore these scriptural worlds from other traditions. We are taught that the Qur'an has perfected everything that came before it and that Muslims don't need anything else. Shanon and other contemporary thinkers are questioning this.[51] 'In the same Qur'anic surah, you have two different verses saying two different things about how many women a man is permitted to marry,' he said to me. He cited the example of Jewish rabbis who, because of the way they read Genesis, decided that, actually, there are many androgynes in the world, and therefore there must be six, seven or eight genders.[52] 'Scholars of Islam had these similar discussions; however, their aims were ultimately conservative. It was to uphold a patriarchal order,' Shanon explained. 'If they had discussions about the possibility of six or seven genders, it would be to discuss how they must comply with the patriarchal heteronormative system.' Even so, the point Shanon was making was that religious scholars of the past were open to having these discussions in the first place. Although it is a written scripture, the Qur'an is not read from page 1 through to the end; it circulated as an oral text, and people would meditate on certain passages and uncover layers of meaning that could be personal or developed collectively to derive rules for a community. It is this kind of reading that we are no longer encouraged to undertake as Muslims.

A decade ago, amina wadud, wrote a short blog post discussing the symbolism of Hajar, a slavewoman, 'some say of African origins', who became Abraham's 'concubine' or second wife for the sole purpose of providing an heir.[53] Abraham's first wife, Sarah, was assumed to no longer be fertile because of her age, and the couple were childless. Hajar, who previously worked as a servant for Sarah, bears Abraham a son. This child is celebrated as the first son of what wadud describes as Abraham's 'patriarchal household'. By a miracle of God, Sarah too later becomes pregnant and gives birth to a son. The stories of the two brothers and their father are related in Christian and Jewish scripture, but in the Qur'an, we witness the erasure of Hajar (and also of Sarah), according to wadud, and a rendering of events that is incomplete. Abraham is ordered by Allah to abandon Hajar and their son in the desert, seemingly an inevitable death sentence. He does so, and both he and Hajar place their trust in God's will. Slowly overcome by dehydration, and unable to bear her baby son's tortured cries, Hajar, in desperation, runs between two foothills separated by half a kilometre in an attempt to attract the attention of anyone who might be travelling through. The chances of there being anyone around are almost zero. Seven times she runs back and forth, before a miracle befalls her. A spring spurts water to quench the mother's and baby's thirst, and before long a passing tribe discover them and take them in.

wadud ponders on how this single forsaken mother's frantic search is re-enacted all these centuries later in a ritual that forms part of the Hajj pilgrimage: 'the central theme of this story is white-washed. Here is the ultimate expression of the inter-sectionality of race, class and gender made barren by our lack of commemoration'.[54] Hajar was called upon to uphold patriarchal structures, and she submitted fully to what was required of her, perhaps with little choice. The circumstances that led her and her child to be subjected to the ultimate sacrifice or test are unclear, but what could be argued is that once patriarchy no longer required her services, she became disposable. Yet, her story is brought to life in the Hajj, a pilgrimage widely considered obligatory for every Muslim who can afford to make it. 'How then do we reconcile with Abraham, the dead beat dad, Sarah the selfish bitch, and even God, the benevolent?'[55] This sentence caused a social media furore, with angry commenters furious at what they considered wadud's disrespectful and insulting language. But they were missing the point of her provocative message: 'a single black female, head of household not only makes this ritual necessary but also makes it possible by her tenacity of survival in spite of gross race, class and gender inequality.'[56] It is the patriarchal process that wadud is referring to—the deadbeat dad is a failure in the eyes of patriarchal structures for not protecting his child and the woman who bore him. Yet, it is also patriarchy that celebrates him in the Qur'anic story of these events. Herein lies the tension, pointing to the lenses through which hadith and Qur'anic commentary are cultivated, the stories that are erased, the actions that are elevated, and the intertwining of Islamic, Christian and Judaic religious stories and traditions.

Not long after I met with Aysha Hidayatullah, the industrious team at Kantara Press asked me to organise a launch of amina wadud's 2022 book, *Once in a Lifetime*, which had just come out. The book is inspired by a series of blogs wadud wrote while undertaking a journey to Makkah and shines a spotlight on the entrenched patriarchal and exclusivist views that prevail. The launch was a huge success, with every seat at the Yunus Emre Institute filled with curious Muslims, a diverse and vibrant cohort of critical thinkers bursting with questions for The Lady Imam. I had always been awed by wadud, much like Shanon, who described how his first encounter with her works had blown his mind. Despite the good fortune of having various opportunities at events where she was speaking, I had always felt shy and too tongue-tied to speak to her beyond pleasantries. I knew I was not a match for her vast knowledge and fierce intellect and simply could not persuade myself to engage her in any meaningful conversation out of fear that I would say something ridiculous. This time, I promised myself I would speak with her after the event and perhaps, if I was brave enough, raise some of the thoughts that had emerged from my conversation with Aysha. However, I became completely distracted by an unpleasant incident. One of the organisers, a young woman publisher, was invited by her colleague to join him on stage at the end to make closing remarks. She laughingly and a little nervously declined and said she would leave the presenting to him. That unremarkable exchange then became a scene of humiliation when an older man, a well-known Muslim public figure, sitting in front of her, span around in his chair and said: 'How are you going to be a publisher if you can't do public speaking?' He then kept mumbling, although I didn't catch quite what he said.

Some minutes later, the event finished, and the young woman immediately left the room, visibly upset. I felt so sorry and angry for her. I had also been nervous about speaking publicly early in my career, and there are many brilliant and successful people who never conquer this fear. For an established and powerful man to humiliate a young woman in this way was shocking and awful to witness. But what I saw next was heartening. A young man, who had been sitting next to the woman, looked angry, but I could see he was trying to remain calm. As the well-known male public figure queued for the book signing, the young man approached him. 'You don't talk to people like that,' he said, politely but firmly. 'She's been looking forward to this for months and the way you spoke to her ... You just don't do that.' The older man mumbled some self-justification and dismissed any accusations of wrongdoing, saying he was just encouraging her for her own good. I was furious for the young woman but inspired by this young man's willingness to call this behaviour out. It turned out he was the woman's husband, and it occurred to me that certain misogynistic behaviours normalised and accepted by my generation, and, I am sad to admit, even normalised by me, were no longer tolerated by young British Muslims. This young woman had been disempowered and belittled at an event she should have been proud of, and her husband stepped up in solidarity to say this was unacceptable. This, at least, was something to celebrate.

There was a lot to reflect on as I made my way home after the event. I took a hard look at the ways that I myself was inadvertently enabling misogynistic behaviour by excusing it as harmless or just a quirk of someone's character. A few months later, I recalled an incident at a conference I had organised on the topic of Muslims and Europe. It was one of the most enjoyable, stimulating and vibrant conferences I had ever had the privilege of organising, and I had never felt so content, relieved and, dare I say it, actually proud. Each panel, mostly made up of early-career female academics, creatives and emerging thinkers, was a hit. I remember feeling euphoric that it had gone so well, even fretting about how I would be able to top this next year. Then, at one point, a guest who regularly attended these annual conferences, and with whom I had always had pleasant interactions, came up to me and congratulated me on the positive energy, the thought-provoking sessions, the engaging speakers, the critical vibrancy and the quality of intellectual discussion. He ended, 'I was talking to [one of the trustees] the other day, and we were saying, you're not really a leader are you, but I have to hand it to you, you've done a brilliant job this weekend'. I looked at him. I can't really remember what I replied, but I know it was a little sharp, because that's unlike me, and I could see he was surprised. I wanted to cry. I couldn't understand why he felt entitled to say that to me, what it even meant, and who he thought he was to make such a casual and derisory uninvited assessment of my capabilities based on his limited contact with me. It upset me greatly, and I couldn't quite shake off the negativity I felt when I really should have been on a high. It occurred to me that amongst the many collegiate, supportive and highly professional colleagues I had the privilege to work with, there were a handful of men who thought nothing of denigrating and belittling women, however successful our achievements, and who were eager to undermine women to further their own agendas and thirst for power. And they would never change. And I knew that this was misogyny.

A few days after the amina wadud event, I felt inspired to re-read wadud's seminal book *Qur'an and Woman: Rereading the Sacred Text from a Woman's Perspective.* I pulled out my much-thumbed copy from my bookshelf and smiled at the extensive notes I had scribbled in the margins and my enthusiastic under-linings on my first reading. I remembered how I had pored over her teachings and had been thrilled to hear her speak on various platforms such as at Musawah and Inclusive Mosque Initiative.[57] For wadud, as well as locating the liberatory worldview of the Qur'an as Shanon described, the key in challenging patriarchal readings of the Qur'an, and the subsequent patriarchal practice of Islam, is to understand that Allah is beyond gender. Pronouns are a point of moral panic these days. Yet it was before the abundance of bad-faith, wilful misunderstanding of the notion of misgendering that wadud began arguing that to exclusively use the masculine pronoun negates the Islamic concept of *tawhid*, or the oneness of God. Instead, using feminine or plural pronouns for Allah recognises that rigid gender binaries are a construction of our contemporary context that has become hardened since the onset of modernity. This makes sense to me, even if it remains uncertain for Hidayatullah. Michael Muhammad Knight doesn't dance around this uncertainty either. In a 2012 article, he discusses how much he wants to believe in progressive iterations of Islam, such as a queer-friendly interpretation of the story of Lut, but says that he needs something more concrete.[58] Nonetheless, in his 2020 study *Muhammad's Body*, Knight looks at how the semantics of Arabic grammar have prioritised masculine pronouns, as there simply is no gender-neutral pronoun in Arabic, bringing him much closer to wadud's view.[59]

Mohammad Fadel, in his seminal paper 'Two Women, One Man', offers another perspective.[60] Along with amina wadud, he takes the works of Leila Ahmed and Fatima Mernissi, who also very much inform my own reading of the Qur'an, and analyses their argument that Islam is at its essence 'a gender-neutral belief system that has been obscured by a centuries-long tradition of male-dominated interpretation'. Fadel introduces the concept of political versus normative discourse to illustrate the tension between feminist readings of the Qur'an, which appear to suggest there is a 'true' objective interpretation that promotes gender equality, and an array of postmodern readings that are subjective and therefore to be discounted. My discomfort with this position is that it disregards what cultural anthropologist Leyla Jagiella has discussed in her writings and talks—that it is the traditions of Muslim societies that offer the missing pieces of the jigsaw puzzle which, in its completion, points to a framework of equity and justice as inherent to what it means to be a Muslim. To reduce Islam to texts is to miss the essence of what it is to be a Muslim. Islam is more than a series of texts—it is a series of histories.

It is hugely seductive to regard the very first believers as the original and authentic Muslims, untainted by cultural baggage. In a world where many Muslims feel disaffected and demonised by the dominant global narratives and trapped in the cycle of capitalist dehumanisation of our spiritual selves, it is tempting to find a way to reject contemporary culture and everything it stands for and to seek solace, direction and validation in a way of life utterly removed from all that is around us. Looking to a romanticised 'perfect' past is by no means exclusive to Muslims. British politicians have long banged this drum, whether by shouting empty slogans such as 'Back to Basics' or by evoking a rose-tinted, post-war era where community spirit resounded and no one was yet moaning on the *Daily Mail* website that 'it's PC gawn mad'. However, this yearning by Muslims to mirror life as it was lived in the Prophet's time seems undermined by a point rarely acknowledged: the Prophet and his companions, indeed the entirety of the early Muslim community, lived in a society in which customs and culture were already in existence. They did not live in a vacuum, and even as Islam was revealed and practised it would hardly have been feasible for them to insulate themselves from the pre-Islamic culture into which they were born.

Islam was revealed in an era and context vastly different from the ones in which we live today. We can only discover its mean-ing and relevance for contemporary times by lifting it out of the seventh century and understanding how it was shaped by its times, culture and contact with the mores of surrounding civili-sations, including patriarchal norms prevalent in the Sassanid Empire, among the Byzantines and so on. Revisiting how we engage with the text is also crucial. As Muslims, many of us grew up being discouraged from questioning or engaging with Islamic texts in any kind of critical or interpretive way. We look for easy, two-dimensional answers rather than building compli-cated truths. Shanon tells me that when he decided to read the Qur'an starting from the very first page, Surah Fatihah, he finally understood what it means to study and engage with the text. If we want to discover whether the Qur'an upholds patriarchy or enables misogyny, perhaps we need to ask questions of the text. We should be bold enough to ask, 'what does this really mean?' and to be honest with ourselves and admit when we're not get-ting to the heart of it or when we feel uncomfortable with its interpretation. 'Is it not enough to sit with that discomfort for a while, and on a separate day reflect on another portion of the text that troubles you?' Shanon asks. 'And you might eventually feel you have an insight, and in this way you answered a question you had, for now. And other questions will inevitably arise.' This is how one embodies Islam as part of a lived experience rather than reading the text passively or trying to bend it out of shape. This is how we locate feminism, whatever feminism means to us, in Islam.

2

THE GAZE OF OTHERS

Where Muslim women have sought to grasp power and effect change, they face a myriad of pressures and challenges. Visibly Muslim women of colour, catapulted into the public eye, face the task of taking space reluctantly offered to them.[1] How many times have events been advertised with a programme of all-male speakers? More recently, this has been called out, and Muslim organisations are getting wise to the bad PR that might ensue. Don't worry, we'll get an attractive young woman to recite a verse from the Qur'an before our annual event. Box ticked. Nobody can accuse us of misogyny now. Here's a picture of a woman, a token. As long as she doesn't take up too much space, as long as she isn't a difficult woman. As long as she doesn't demand a seat at the table.[2]

From blockbuster films to reality television to women taking to the stage to give keynote speeches later uploaded onto social media, the on-screen imagery that envelops our lives is created for a male gaze. The hierarchy of consumption places the priorities of this gaze at the centre, even behind the lens, directing the action, manipulating the message. Devouring every sexual detail of the female form for basic pleasure, objectification diminishes each and every woman, however covered or uncovered she may be. It strips away her tumultuous depth and simmering humanity to a husk, a mere commodity. Insidiously, the gaze can become something that is turned inward. Young girls and women internalise society's insistence that their value is measured according to their physical attributes over the multitude of complex, contradictory, dizzying and wondrous non-observable attributes that make up their fulsome being.

In an interview with Anita Rani for BBC Radio 4's *Woman's Hour*, the *Great British Bake-Off* winner Nadiya Hussain talks about the moments in her career when she has felt that she doesn't belong, or when people have said that this isn't her space to claim, or perhaps her face doesn't quite fit. She talks about being made to feel very uncomfortable, having what she calls 'crying in the toilet–type moments' before pulling herself together for the camera.[3] The camera itself creates an endless tension between image and reality when its renderings are consumed by a variety of gazes. For Susan Sontag, photography inevitably objectifies and commodifies its subject, numbing us to a person's essential humanity and placing the viewer in a predatory interpretive role.[4] In our contemporary times, the phenomenon of the selfie is one that seemingly erases the distance between subject and photographer. Distance is severed and, as such, so is connection, because by turning people into objects, the gaze claims to know the person in the selfie in a way that they could never fully know themselves.

How do Muslim women endure, knowing that so much of their self is rendered invisible? Nadiya has since learned she has the right to take up space, and she is doing exactly this. Inspiration to be proudly visible, for her, comes from the unseen women. She raises her voice to acknowledge and pay homage to women from whom she learned strength, resilience and all the skills that contributed to her success, using her platform to make them visible. This is what motivates her to continue: celebrating the women who came before, like her mum and her grandma. She claims space in the public domain for all of us who would otherwise be rendered invisible. People may see her on TV or at publicity appearances, with her body and aesthetic held up against pre-determined standards of how a woman in the public eye should be perceived and objectified by the power of its gaze. But she refuses to be a tick-box, a token, window-dressing to mask misogyny.

Dr Aminul Hoque writes that Nadiya is 'a symbol of hope and a role model for the voiceless' as a hijab-wearing Muslim woman who has spoken openly about social justice issues and mental health struggles.[5] Her celebrity status makes her, as far as he is concerned, perhaps the most famous Bangladeshi in the world. She calls out racism and challenges those who question her right to partake in traditional British rituals, such as making a cake fit for the Queen in 2016 and daring to replace swede with apple when making a Cornish pasty in 2017. For Hoque, she is a great Muslim leader, an inspiration. Yet, even Nadiya is haunted by the fear of being labelled what Sara Ahmed describes as a 'difficult woman'. Of finding that her complaints mean no one wants to work with her, because her dark-skinned presence disrupts their uncomplicated, comfortable, homogeneous whiteness.

Being visible, having a platform like Nadiya, is like carrying a torch for the women who aren't offered an opportunity to put their head above the parapet yet feel the violence of having their bodies watched, scrutinised and objectified every single day. For Hodan Yusuf, intentionality is the premise of all action. When it comes to spirituality it is second nature, something she describes as 'a muscle that you exercise'. A Black, visibly Muslim woman who has been a journalist, Hodan is an actor, but she considers herself first and foremost a poet and a writer. The issue of speaking and writing publicly is about weighing up repercussions. Perhaps we can ask ourselves why it is that Muslim women are hesitant to speak up. Notwithstanding the silencing of women's voices, those who overcome obstacles to make themselves heard are forced to consider the implications for their online or physical safety. 'If I say what I want to say, what are the possible outcomes?' Hodan asks herself. 'I don't want to wake up and be representing the entirety of faith or gender or race or an ethnic group, but these things are imposed upon us.' Tuned in to the potential consequences of things she might do or say, Hodan 'might decide to do or say these things anyway. I weigh the risks against the need to say this or the need to write that in this particular way. Like a journalism risk assessment, you're constantly filling out the form in your mind'.

It's not just the imposed responsibilities or projections put upon Muslim women by mainstream society and how our words may be used to fuel Islamophobia. Hodan is alert to the reality that anything she may say has the potential to be misunderstood by people who have an agenda against Muslims and Islam, but equally, her concern is how misogynistic Muslim men will use her words and actions against her. 'I have female friends who have been harassed online and they do a little investigating and find that the IP address of the accounts that are abusing them can be traced to Muslim men they know in real life. People who will greet them in the street with a "salaam, sister", and then go online and actively harass Muslim women.'

The insidious influence of social media presents options of either conformity or failure. Filters, photo-editing and all manner of duplicity are employed to make a person more idealised than they could possibly aspire to be IRL (in real life). IRL, a person is flawed. Now that our lives are lived through the medium of virtual reality, it feels inevitable to be objectified, judged and subjected to abuse. Brushed and sculpted, using all the latest guides and trends and YouTube tutorials, you can gaze out from the black mirror and expect to be blisteringly picked apart. You can even opt out of real life altogether and use technology to project an unreal, exemplary image of yourself. Many times, I have come across high-profile social media personalities, from all spectrums of the Muslim world, perhaps at an event or meeting. The way they go on to present events that I witnessed IRL to their followers is so divorced from the mundane reality of what was said or how things happened. A simulacrum, a hyper-reality to quench their followers' thirst for content that reinforces their carefully curated persona.

I was at an event at the Houses of Parliament a few months ago and met a British female Islamic scholar whom I had heard much about over the years. Known for her particularly hardline, conservative perspective, she has a huge social media following. I didn't recognise her as she only ever appears on public platforms wearing niqab, but her name badge caught my eye. This was a small event for invited Muslim women, so I assume that she felt comfortable taking off her niqab in a rather more private context, even though a handful of men were present. I went over and introduced myself and told her I had been following her work for some time and was pleased to finally meet her in person. She wasn't easy to engage, so we had a brief chat where I did most of the talking, and that was that. She hovered on the fringes of the meeting, and I was struck by how shy she seemed IRL, not at all the confident, strident advocate for traditional Islam that her online presence conveys. The following day, I was scrolling on social media and saw she had posted something about attending the event. As I read on, I was amazed. She had recounted our conversation, almost word for word, and attributed it to someone far more important and high-profile than me. She said this person had come up to her (I had), seemed to know all about her work (which I said I did), and was keen to speak with her (as I had tried to do). The entire time, she said, the person had been surrounded by people clamouring to speak with her. Our friend had in fact been nowhere near the throng of attendees throughout, so I knew this had not happened. I am probably naive about the highly curated nature of social media content, but the embellishment of events, bordering on fabrication, took me entirely by surprise.

A person becomes reduced to an aesthetic in today's social media age as the inverted gaze becomes a medium ripe for self-objectification, a compulsion to author our own story and reveal our best self to the world. Defiant and confident faces beam down from Instagram to declare they are reversing the process of objectification. What a persuasive conceit, for what else is a selfie other than full disclosure, while a female protagonist is left without anchor, inevitably shamed by the expectations of convention into which she contorts and contracts but can never comfortably fit? The emancipatory ideal falls short, and we are left with a complicated gendering in pursuit of internal truth. Yet, what is this truth that we speak of? As we turn the gaze back on ourselves, are we finally taking ownership of our projected selves? Is the online persona really a democratising tool that enables everyday individuals to sculpt and fashion their image exactly as they would like?

Perhaps it is the sense of unreality encouraged by social media platforms that emboldens men to dehumanise the online versions of the women they know IRL. Humanity becomes located in the imagination of men and women via the patriarchal matrix in which we are constructed. Do you dare to be authentic? Your fantasy projection may score you an objectified 10 in the gaze of our society, but when you're relegated to a 6.5 by impatient social media followers, then you know you've fallen victim to the impossible pressures imposed by an uneven playing field obsessed with digital exhibitionism and narcissism.

THE GAZE OF OTHERS

I ask Hodan why anyone would hide behind an avatar or an anonymous social media account to harass a woman for expressing herself in public. Hodan replies that though she may have searched for meaning in the intentions of others in the past, she refuses to expend her energy on these questions anymore. 'It's not for me to do the emotional meta-homework of why this section of the community of Muslim men is behaving in this way. I have now got to the point where I would respond in the same way as when someone might ask me why white people are racist.' Disengaging from thinking on behalf of men is a form of self-preservation. 'It's hard enough to be thinking about protecting yourself and the women you care about. It is hard to thrive in your life and function if you are constantly putting out small fires everywhere. It is exhausting, especially when you come across these people in your own networks.'

Violent, misogynistic societies exist throughout the world, everywhere. But there is a deep disappointment in knowing that there are Muslim men who have disconnected from the true spirit of the Prophet's teachings. 'It angers me as a Muslim woman who tries (even if I fall short) to live by the teachings of Allah, conscious of Allah, the Almighty Being who sees everything, who knows our intention, who has given us guidelines on how to interact with one another, and with society,' Hodan says. To see misogyny proliferate in Muslim communities upsets Hodan, 'because the teachings are right there and yet they have co-opted and misrepresented certain teachings to justify their behaviour, and that is where it is really painful.'

Hodan acknowledges the violence visited upon Muslim men in our securitised political landscape, 'because the truth is, I still care deeply for my brothers in faith. Of course, not for individual men who may perpetuate harm. But Muslim men as a collective are our families and the families of our friends. They are our brothers, fathers, uncles, husbands, sons, nephews, etc. My ask is that other men, the silent majority, actively hold their fellow brothers more accountable for their behaviour against women.' To see Muslim men directing hostility toward Muslim women on social media platforms is unbearable. 'This is a frightening time as a Black person, as a Muslim, as a woman, as a visible Muslim. To be openly out there articulating your thoughts, writing what you think, saying what you want to say, it's not easy, you're constantly weighing up the repercussions.'

Some of the most horrific racism that Hodan has experienced has been from non-Black Muslim women. 'What is a Muslim community to me when I am experiencing physical racist violence at the hands of Muslim women for just existing. This is my experience. As a Black Muslim woman, the intersect is a painful one, but it shouldn't be, it really shouldn't. You don't want to be forced to justify your life, your existence constantly. There is a reason why the friends I feel the most safe with are often Black Muslimahs [Muslim women].' One of Hodan's grandfathers comes from an area near the Somali city of Zeila, which has a mosque with two *qiblahs*, or directions for prayer. What this means is that Islam came to Somalia even before the *qiblah* was changed from Jerusalem to Makkah—within the Prophet's lifetime. Yet the anti-Blackness rife in Muslim communities means Hodan is constantly asked by other Muslims if she is really Muslim and challenged to prove her Islam. It is beyond wearying. 'This is my experience as a Black Muslim woman, and it's not a pleasant one,' Hodan says. 'Some of the most ardent defenders of white supremacy are not white people.' There has been very little moving of the needle, and Black Muslim people continue to be subjected to the same questions and experiences of racism in mosques.[6]

Having long been involved in grassroots activism, Hodan describes having an ambivalent relationship with the term 'activist', explaining that she has always been drawn to being an advocate for justice in any capacity. 'I'm just trying to live my life. I'm trying to just be me and do the good I can in the few years we have on this earth.' Her feelings of vulnerability and responsibility inform her poetry, writing, acting and previous work in journalism. 'I've just tried to live my life and not be smothered by the labels.' Muslim actors, like any non-white, non-heteronormative and non-male actors, are always in danger of being typecast, with roles tending to be set in one time and place with a tragic backstory. When you're a jobbing actor, you take what you can. 'But the next time you get the call, you hope the person you're being cast for is a three-dimensional person that isn't always wrapped in a history of grief and trauma, that offers the capacity for love beyond pain. That's what I wish for.'

I ask Hodan whether she feels objectified in the acting world. Her reply is profound. 'As an actor, I don't think it's any different to how I am objectified by someone sitting opposite me on a train. Because society objectifies Muslim women, period. Orientalism has done its damage. There might be a camera lens in front of you, but the people behind the lens are the same.' During the disorienting months of the Covid lockdown, Hodan wrote, directed and acted in a play called *Refu(ge)Tree*, which was chosen to be featured online in a theatre festival.[7] She found taking control of the narrative, writing, and acting in her own work to be empowering, 'because even if there was trauma, there was love outside of it. Even if there was a backstory and certain experiences I was trying to capture of dehumanised migrant communities, having to wade through the state violences that borders and immigration policing impose on people, I was still able to capture the essence of the woman who was the main character, and the love she had'. Drawn to drama and acting since she was a child, Hodan didn't pursue theatre upon finishing secondary school, although it never really left the horizon of what she wanted to do. It was in 2019, before Covid, that she got her first television role, and with the experience of presenting her work at the theatre festival, she has found that even if she is in a production where she doesn't have total free rein, she has an opportunity to enter into dialogue with people who do have control in order to bring ideas, emotions and experiences to the characters being represented. These dialogues can be important to minimise the process of objectification, even though she finds that 'the objectification of Muslim women is so profoundly a part of our societies'.

Differences in perception in the public context go beyond binaries. It is the embrace of the binary that denies more pluralistic responses, engulfing Muslim women entirely and leaving them diminished. Modern popular culture offers no respite; Muslim women are either oppressed or realise their agency through acts of radicalisation, becoming the bloody trope that the world fears their authentic selves must truly be or gaining emancipation through the rejection of religiosity. Within those binaries, where does the complex Muslim woman in the limelight stand? To be invisible or even remotely outside mainstream conventions—whether that be a Eurocentric ideal or the ideal of the uncomplicatedly pious Muslimah—can stifle self-esteem, self-worth and self-value. Add to this the conflict between the inner and outer self, as individuals struggle to find their place in the world of increasingly homogeneous aesthetic ideals and the pressure to have a curated public persona. To be relentlessly rendered a representative for all Muslims in a manner that is excluding and alienating can only accentuate anxiety, as those in the public eye struggle under the gaze of others. On the other hand, if society's gaze decides you don't quite fit its expectations, the assumption is implicit that, as a consequence, you have no right to claim space.

Taking to the stage or screen to perform an acting role exists in the same landscape, for Hodan, as expressing herself through her poetry and writing. 'I've always done public speaking and poetry, and whether its social justice activism or performing, it's always been one form of stage or another. I've just been myself whatever platform I've chosen. The process is the process.' Fleshing out and building a character you're getting to know and have to embody requires drawing on lived experiences, 'but that character is not me'. All good acting requires pulling from something you know, whether that's from experience or research. 'It's important to remember that that is a character. Muslim women, and Muslim people generally, should be allowed to create fiction. We're talking about storytelling, and people should be allowed to do fiction, even if that's a story you don't like. If you don't like it, don't watch it. But let fellow Muslim people breathe, let them do different forms of art, let them express themselves in the ways they choose.'

Perhaps that space to let others breathe is lacking in our communities. Instead, like Hodan, we find ourselves navigating daily anxieties, asking what the implications might be, what will happen if we act this character or are quoted in a newspaper about that topic or publish a poem of our innermost thoughts, how will it impact our life? For Muslim women, this can be a constant struggle. It's a complex responsibility of protecting our faith or our faith community. 'But actually, Allah protects his faith, He is more than capable of doing that,' Hodan points out. 'What I have a responsibility for is not feeding malicious intent, not feeding the cycle of violence that is perpetuated by states against Muslims and Muslim-majority countries. Beyond that, I just want to live my life, to be. I am in the public eye, but also I am my private self, and I protect who I am, because I feel so much of a person's private life is not safe because it can easily fall into the hands of people who might weaponise it. It's important to me that we save some things for ourselves. Things that remain between us, our Lord and our loved ones. In an era of hyperconsumption and over-production of "content" on social media, very little is held back. And it's important to me, in order to maintain my sense of self, that most of my precious personal, familial and private life remains exactly that: private.'

When Syima Aslam considers what led to the creation of the Bradford Literature Festival,[8] she realises that the journey began with her own personal and professional life experiences. She grew up in Halifax, which she describes as a microcosm of Bradford, with similar dynamics of the South Asian community played out, but on a smaller scale. When she and I first met in 2005, Syima was running a restaurant in the centre of Bradford. She had moved to London to attend university, and when she returned to the North felt that she had stepped back ten years. 'I had moved on, and you make this automatic assumption that the world has moved in the direction that you have.' What she found was that the Muslim South Asian community remained conservative. The city had been one of the wealthiest in the UK but was by Syima's return in post-manufacturing decline. It felt to Syima as if it were constantly on the cusp of regeneration but never seemed to manage to reclaim its past glory. 'I often describe Bradford as a doughnut, because it isn't that Bradford doesn't have wealth. It's just that its wealth is concentrated in the outer circle.' The inner circle, where the Pakistani community and minorities were concentrated, experienced none of this wealth and lived in stark poverty.[9] Syima had lived through the Bradford race riots and along with running the restaurant saw that the centre was no longer a place that those in the wealthier outskirts of Bradford thought to travel to. For the city to be buoyant again, she realised it needed an inward investment strategy. After the restaurant closed, she worked to develop the local further education college's marketing strategy and saw that population growth was coming from areas of high deprivation and low levels of educational attainment. She knew that without intervention, the children from these areas were never going to be able to walk into the jobs that were forecast to be in high demand in the coming decade. For her, education was key to addressing economic deprivation and the social ills that it triggers.[10]

As a second-generation British-Pakistani who travelled back and forth between the UK and Pakistan from a young age, Syima spent months at a time in Pakistan. When back in the UK, her mother took her to the library every Saturday where she would read voraciously and was able to recover her English language skills. 'This is the reason why it's a literature festival. Without literacy, you don't have access to the curriculum and if you want to create that kind of change, that's what you need to target.' It was when writing a strategy for a film festival at Bradford's iconic museum that Syima came up with the idea of the literature festival. 'People create artificial boundaries, and as human beings we don't experience the world with those boundaries—in fact everyone goes seamlessly from a book to a film or whatever.' Syima's urge to do something worthwhile was also motivated by a diagnosis of advanced breast cancer soon after the birth of her only child, a daughter. Facing mortality while breastfeeding her baby was a painful experience. And when her marriage ended just a few years later, she found herself the head of an all-female household, with both her small baby and her own mother entirely dependent on her. Just as Hajar was driven to protect her family, Syima found the impetus not just to empower her immediate charges but to do something for her community.

Syima forged ahead putting together Bradford's first ever literature festival, along with her co-director, Irna Qureshi, who was also Bradford-born and -bred. The two women suddenly found themselves figureheads for a city that for a long time had been labelled a failure in the multicultural experiment. They were simultaneously charged with the responsibility of rehabilitating a city's reputation and forced to justify their credentials for representing it—the burden of representation that Muslim women are weighed down by. Motivated by the epiphany that she had at that time, Syima says she never asked for permission; she just set about securing funding and garnering support for her idea. She found herself stepping into spaces where she was the only brown, female, Muslim person and refused to be made to feel that she couldn't demand a seat at the table. Once, someone said that an English literature festival, which was popular among white, middle-class audiences, already existed in the district and that a festival focusing on Urdu and Punjabi literature would be a great idea for Bradford. Syima refused to be pigeonholed. 'I read, write, speak Urdu and Punjabi fluently. Most people of my generation don't,' she said. 'I'm an avid reader, and despite my fluency, my consumption of Urdu literature is probably 1 per cent. If you drop down a generation, you will struggle to find many youngsters proficient in reading Urdu and Punjabi literature, particularly as many of them now have parents who primarily spoke English growing up. The whole point of this festival is to create a change around literacy as well. You will certainly not be doing that by creating a South Asian literature festival. That will just be a tick-box exercise.'

Syima and Irna recognised that there was something of a novelty factor in the way that their endeavour was received. Although Irna was far more embedded in the arts and culture sector, the idea that two South Asian Muslim women could curate and create a mainstream literature festival was enough to get them noticed. But everyone who knows how the machinery of PR works will recognise that the novelty factor has no longevity. Certainly, you can be flavour of the month, but only if you promise not to disrupt or render uncomfortable those who have deigned to give you their attention, and even if you play by all the rules, there is always a shelf life. Over the years, the festival has grown beyond the benevolence and indulgence of those who

enjoyed the novelty factor. Support for the festival has strength-
ened even as it has confounded its critics. But what Syima has
been told along the way is that she's too ambitious, she has set
her sights too high, the festival is too big and is trying to achieve
too much, 'possibly because these are not the expectations people
would have of someone from a city like Bradford,' she says. It is
only with the success of the festival that such mutterings have
been silenced.

Syima also had support from within the community, with key
political and publicly active figures in Bradford championing her
vision. There were still those who were suspicious of her aims,
asking whose agenda she was serving and what the intentions of
the festival really were, but Syima was resolute. 'In the graphic
novel *V for Vendetta* by Alan Moore, V tells Evey, "I didn't put
you in prison, I just showed you the bars."[11] I was determined not
to do that to myself,' she says. 'The festival is meant to be positive for the city. It's designed to be a platform for nuanced debate
and dialogue, and to bring communities together, and challenge
the negative perceptions around Bradford, which are often tied
to its Muslim population.' The national media frequently come
to Bradford to take the pulse of the Muslim communities in
Britain on any issue that was the headline of the day. Syima's
vision is to take ownership of those debates, because otherwise,
they'll just take place without us. 'I chose not to engage with
certain negativity, because I knew that what I had set up was
about creating aspiration and lifting communities out of illiteracy
and poverty.' However, the festival aims to engage with all communities, and Syima acknowledges the burden of representation,
which means that not everyone will engage with, or get, or be
happy with every aspect of any programme she curates. 'But then
the festival wouldn't be doing what it is meant to do if that was
the case.' Managing expectations of the Muslim communities of
Bradford as well as external observers was always in the fore-

ground, but that couldn't compromise the vision for the festival to create change.

From a culture sector point of view, the festival was far from the received wisdom of what a literary festival should look like, but Syima says clearly that BLF was never meant to replicate Hay or Cheltenham or the other big literature festivals of the UK, other than in terms of quality and recognition. The socioeconomic backgrounds of the audiences that BLF wishes to engage are given paramount importance, and these considerations are built in, meaning that initiatives like going into schools and the implementation of an ethical ticketing policy are integral. 'People aren't hard to reach—they're easy to ignore. You can't talk about cultural inclusivity and wanting to engage people with culture without providing them the means to do so, and for a lot of people that means free access.' Syima's yardstick is to ask whether a single mother living on a council estate would be able to bring her children to the festival. She thinks people get hung up on ethnicity and believes class is a far more divisive factor. 'It is the people who don't have the money who don't engage.' Bradford is an international city with communities from across the world, including refugees and migrants bringing rich traditions and cultures with them.

When the festival first took off, Syima and her team set up an education programme that saw speakers go into local schools and communities where they engaged with Muslim women and children who otherwise might not have had the chance to visit the festival itself. Now that the festival has become part of the fabric of the UK's arts and culture landscape, schools across the district are keen to come to the festival and take an active part in the programme, which also now attracts a diverse group of volunteers. The festival still arranges for female Muslim authors to go into schools and meet with pupils, often influencing and inspiring them greatly in their learning and development, and it still quietly continues with this form of outreach. 'A few years ago, the festival organised an event at a community centre known to be particularly conservative. Teenage girls who were from families who frequent the centre were volunteering, and it was evidently a huge point of pride for them.' What's more, although the community centre is a twenty-minute walk from the centre of Bradford, these youngsters had never visited the library in the city, so it prompted many of them to travel there for the first time.

This level of effort to engage the so-called 'hard-to-reach' groups is an extremely labour-intensive, 'micro-through-to-macro' kind of work, which funders, who are often output-oriented, are not always built to understand. It was only five years into the festival that Syima was given funding specifically to go into communities; beforehand they had done this legwork with their existing shoestring resources. Ironically, this funding was awarded by the Building a Stronger Britain Together initiative set up in 2016 by the Home Office as part of the government's counter-extremism policy. BLF was heavily criticised for accepting such funding, and some key speakers who had been booked to take part in the festival pulled out in protest. 'I think there's a bit of me that's become cynical of cancel culture, because it's a good way for people to make a name for themselves,' says Syima. 'Everybody wants the work done, but nobody wants to pay for it, and somehow you're just expected to make these things happen. And then despite the size of the festival, they have the gall to turn around after the festival is over and ask, "so what do you do for the rest of the year?" Unrealistic expectations and naivety exist around this space and in this work.' Syima has found that there is a focus either on communities or high-quality work, and often the two don't always gel. 'There are times when you have people who do "high-quality work" doing community work, but often, although not always, it is a tick-box. Actually having a model that melds it all together is not the norm, but it's what BLF tries to do. We're the most diverse literary festival in Europe, maybe even beyond. When we talk about diverse-led organisations, we talk about organisations led by diverse people for diverse communities, of that community. The kind of diversity where you have every community together doesn't exist that much. And when you talk about that, there is a bit of "stay in your lane".'

The traditionally patriarchal and Eurocentric definitions of diversity, community, and who gets to occupy which lane have long been imposed on the rest of the world. Absorbing the limitations of this model of perfection, we now have a global culture that stubbornly refuses plurality. This is despite the fact that other societies have historically managed, successfully, to incorporate diversity into their perception of perfection. Today, the objectification of people into commodities to be consumed is teetering out of control, along with the echo chambers, confirmation bias and rabbit-holes of conspiracy that are a worrying by-product of social media. The unresolved problem remains an inability to dethrone the concept of who is allowed to claim space, and how much. Remember: men are brave; women are submissive. The West is drowning in a quagmire of individualism, and the binary perceptions it projects deny the more pluralistic responses to gender that exist elsewhere. Muslim tradition has long celebrated self-definition, and it is tiresome to presuppose Islam carries the burden of misogyny alone. Rather, what informs our opinion of ourselves is the burden of responsibility. The result? When faced with a stereotype or idealised beauty or behaviour, we all declare that we don't adhere to that model, we are unique, we are worth it, we are individual, while in reality, the self-help, beauty, influencer and public intellectual industries have rendered us all mass-marketed clones, desperately trying to uphold a certain version of what we have constructed our public image to be. Individualism in relation to the collective is seen to lie at the heart of all understanding of ourselves. It is here that we are afforded the ability to speak in terms of me, of I, oblivious that we are projecting an outdated homogeneous trope via our blinkered gaze that negates the flexibility to be different, to be flawed, to change our minds.

When Julie Siddiqi's local mosque re-opened after the easing of Covid restrictions, its committee announced that *tarawih* prayers (night prayers during Ramadan) would only be open to men. Julie couldn't understand the justification for this, a culmination of many years of feeling that women had been excluded, disempowered and overlooked by the members of the mosque committee, many of whom were deeply misogynistic in their attitudes.[12] She was angered by the decision, which she felt was without reason and made out of complacency rather than a concern for health and safety. She asked the mosque to reconsider and said she would make her objection public if they refused. However, the committee dug their heels in, so she remained true to her word and spoke to her local newspaper. The story was picked up by the *Daily Mail*, and even though Julie never spoke to the right-wing tabloid, she suffered a huge local backlash, which became particularly vicious on social media. 'People were saying, "who does she think she is?" ... "she's made it all about her," and accusing me of using this to create a platform for myself,' Julie tells me. She had been prepared for a cool reception from the mosque thanks to her stand, but she was utterly shocked by the vitriol and hostility she was attracting from her local community. Her attempt to call out patriarchy and highlight the marginalisation of women led to vicious accusations that she was motivated by a hunger for power and a disdain for Islam, not by a desire to stand up for justice and equity. Many times I have seen women who attempt to subvert the patriarchal order subjected to the most awful assassinations of their character by men. What better way to distract from a woman's valid message than by casting aspersions and saying she is difficult or hysterical?

MUSLIM WOMEN AND MISOGYNY

This is not to say that there aren't times when exposing the shortcomings of our communities can be manipulated by those seeking to fuel Islamophobia. But turning a blind eye to injustice is the height of naivety. Any issue that is suppressed will erupt onto the surface and reactionary solutions may well be imposed. 'It carries on because no one wants to talk about it,' says Julie, 'because we're bringing shame upon the community. But I'm not bringing shame on the community—you who are behaving in patriarchal and misogynistic ways are bringing shame on the community'.

The local mosque published a letter signed by women refuting the claims Julie had made, even though the patriarchal attitudes of the men in charge were well known throughout the community. One of the local women even called Julie up and 'went for' her, such was her fury. Julie felt gaslighted and suspected that some of the women had been pressured into siding against her and signing the counter-claims, perhaps after being convinced that this was important in order to defend Islam or Muslims. The tide of fury was unrelenting. 'I tried for about two days to reason with people online and explain that we can do better and need to set an example to our young people and practise inclusion.' But every single time, the responses she received were horrendous personal attacks, prompting Julie to come off social media completely, something which, ultimately, she found utterly liberating.

From that moment, Julie made a conscious decision to keep away from online spaces and forums. She had sworn off Twitter (now X) from the outset, because, she says, she knew that there she would be targeted and trolled by random people, 'from the far right, but also Muslims.' Friends and family who are regular users tell her that the toxicity of the platform has just got worse, and she feels sure that she made the right decision. Even though she is on Facebook, her account is private, so at least she knows that complete strangers can't message her. Her gratitude for this

74

filter is not without reason. 'Whenever I have put a post up and made it public, even on Facebook, I very quickly see people, predominantly Muslim men, piling in and making comments,' she says. 'I used to try to engage with people, but I would get nowhere. They would be impossible to reason with. Instead, they took great joy in belittling me and would encourage their networks to join in. It was relentless, pointless and a huge waste of my energy.'

Why is Julie so disproportionately targeted? Her Jewish–Muslim interfaith work is one of the main reasons,[13] as well as her involvement in the government counter-terrorism policy Prevent[14]—involvement which, she says, has been heavily exaggerated and distorted. There are many sensitive subjects she would like to speak about and debates she feels she could make a positive contribution to, but with the backlash she has experienced already, she knows it would end up being intolerably exhausting. 'And it is misogyny,' she says. 'It is wrapped up in patriarchal attitudes towards women. The way they go for me, and other women, they don't go for men in the same way at all. There is something about not wanting women to speak up and have their opinion. It really feels like that.' Julie has even had moments where she has felt unsafe and taken police advice. On one occasion, when Israel was bombing Gaza, passions were understandably inflamed, and Julie became a focus for heightened emotions expressed online. She found herself being described in increasingly ugly language, labelled a traitor and worse.

In 2013, Julie was president of the Islamic Society of Britain, one of the largest national membership organisations of Muslims in the UK.[15] That spring, British soldier Lee Rigby was brutally murdered by two Muslim extremists, and the atrocity plunged Julie into the spotlight. Yet even then, she faced a struggle with people within her organisation who preferred she remain silent. As the horror of what had happened unfolded, Julie was contacted by BBC *Newsnight* and *Channel 4 News*, who asked her for interviews. Her instincts told her she should do it, even though she felt the immense pressure and burden of representation. 'It felt like there was a lack of space for other voices to speak up for the Muslim communities,' she says. At that point, the Islamist extremist Anjem Choudary was still being given disproportionate airtime on mainstream TV, even though he represented only a tiny minority of Muslim opinion. Julie knew that if she didn't agree to the interviews, people like Choudary would seize control of the narrative and perpetuate damaging myths about Muslim communities. 'The sort of stuff he would say was so divisive and ugly, yet he was so confident in himself, so calmly cultivating this impression that he was speaking for the majority.'

Julie decided to do the interviews, despite her fear of the reactions from not only elements of the Muslim community but also the far right. 'I was doing it for people like my mum. I was doing it for the general public, who may never have seen a hijab-wearing Muslim woman speak.' Julie was well aware of the construction of relatability and of how her privilege as a white woman would impact how her message was likely to be received.[16] But she also felt there was something powerful about a visibly Muslim, female spokesperson publicly articulating their opinions with nuance and thoughtfulness. 'I just didn't want people to see Anjem Choudary sitting there and hear his awful rhetoric.' One of the men from the ISB's broader scene, who also had a media profile, called Julie up and told her not to do it. He suggested that if she ended up speaking on the same platform as Anjem Choudary, she would be giving him credibility. Julie was appalled by this advice. How was she suddenly responsible for giving someone like Choudary credibility, when mainstream media channels had been doing just that, unchallenged, for years? 'I really felt it was the right thing to do,' she says. 'It was frustrating that only extreme perspectives were aired, and it just didn't feel right to be offered this platform and not use it constructively.'[17]

After her television appearance, Julie set about petitioning the BBC to stop giving Anjem Choudary a monopoly on commentating on Muslim-related news events. She has made many other media appearances since, but she knows that she does not have the capacity, or inclination, to appear on television constantly. 'It sounds obvious, but if I am asked to make media appearances, it has to feel right in my heart. It has to feel that I really do have something to add to the conversation.' Julie knows there have been times when she has been invited to appear on a platform as a token Muslim woman for the optics, but she became attuned to when this was the case and made sure she wasn't manipulated or used. What was important to her was that she would not be dissuaded from doing something if it felt to her that it was the right thing to do. 'There is an element of feeling there is a need for different voices. But unfortunately, there are also elements within the Muslim communities that really would rather that I kept quiet. But I know the scene well, and the issues.' Appearing on the media, working in interfaith activism with Jewish groups, being involved in anti-terror initiatives, some of them government-led, and being a woman have all made Julie a target, and this doesn't come without an emotional toll. But Julie feels that as long as she is authentic to herself, refuses to get embroiled in agendas and manipulation, is straightforward and careful to make sure she isn't pushed into speaking about things she isn't well informed about, and avoids being everything to everyone, then her conscience is clear.

It is her faith which brings Julie peace in the midst of such tumult. 'I take it back to my prayers and pray to God. People say all sorts of things, but God knows why I do what I do, and that's all that matters.' When Julie spoke up about her local mosque, she knew that she was saying what many other people had been saying, but she describes the level of abuse she endured, as well as the fact that very few people were willing to speak out in her support, as representing a pivotal moment. It made her realise that the toll of being a public figure, particularly as a visibly Muslim woman, can be enormous. And it highlighted to her why so few people are willing to take a stand, because the fall-out can be overwhelming. This didn't deter her; in fact, it galvanised her conviction that she had to continue speaking up about the erasure of women in religious spaces, because she knew how hard it was. She also knew she needed to continue her activism, because although she was subjected to many vicious and highly personal attacks, hundreds of others would contact her to tell her how much they empathised with her and related to what she had to say, and how it had given them the courage to challenge the injustices they were seeing or experiencing themselves.

Being a hijab-wearing Muslim activist disarms many people, who don't know how to categorise Julie. She first started wearing a headscarf because she believed it was her Islamic duty. Her thoughts on this, thirty years later, are less dogmatic, and she certainly doesn't believe that women who don't wear hijab are condemned to an eternity in hell. However, hijab is integral to Julie's identity as a Muslim woman, yet it confuses many who don't expect it to align with her outspokenness. I'm reminded of comments made by a non-hijab-wearing, classically trained female scholar of Islam, who said her profile helps to legitimise those women who do not fit expectations of what an Islamic scholar should look like. She encourages women to claim Islam and take their seat at the table. For too long, women have been told they cannot expect to be in positions of power because they don't look the part, don't dress the part, don't have the right connections, don't come from the right family, don't have the right ideas. Similarly, Julie confounds expectations as a white,

Muslim, hijab-wearing activist who refuses to conform to patriarchal stereotypes. She isn't a naturally confrontational person
and doesn't set out to stoke fires, but age has made her less
concerned about what people think of her. What drives her forward is her sincere passion for her faith and genuine desire to
help Muslim women, women of faith, and all women.

Around the world, people are strangled by the burden of
speaking out and of becoming involuntary spokespeople for their
faith, gender or community. Conformist societies render group-
thinking the norm. Non-conformism travels from the fringes
only to become commodified and neutralised, breeding further
social conformism and leading to the surreal, inevitable conclusion that to be unconventional, you only need to place your
online Amazon order and purchase your required 'look', as if it
were a fancy-dress costume. Which identity hat must you wear
today? And has the empowered status of the wise and respected
older matriarch been relegated to the footnotes of history? With
experience should come agency, whether in the home or the
community or elsewhere. Julie Siddiqi has found empowerment
with age, but the burden of representation doesn't cease.

The journalist and broadcaster Remona Aly knows what it
means to be a visible Muslim thrust into the role of spokesperson for her faith, whether she likes it or not. Interviewed by
national television media outlets in the aftermath of seismic
events that led the world's gaze to seek out Muslim perspectives,
she describes feeling 'not only a burden of representation but a
necessity of representation'. She says, 'I never sought out speaking on television or radio following atrocities such as the Paris
attacks or *Charlie Hebdo* [Islamist terrorist attacks carried out in
2015], as I felt I had no authority to do so. But I recognised the
necessity of speaking out, especially when so few Muslim women
are willing to go into the public space as it is such a vulnerable
position to be in. I ended up going on BBC *Newsnight* in the

tense aftermath of the *Charlie Hebdo* attacks, alongside Julie Siddiqi and Nabila Ramdani.[18] During the burkini ban fiasco [in France], I was getting five television requests in one day. This puts even more pressure on those of us who are available and willing to speak publicly, all this while simultaneously managing the pressures of your own work and daily life. There's also the anxiety of having your words scrutinised—they say words are your weapons, but they can also be weaponised against you. So there is a fear of saying something that could be used against your community or that could be seen by your community as a betrayal of them.'

The sound-bite era of news consumption means only a very short and pressurised window exists to speak on a media platform in the aftermath of, for example, a terrorist atrocity. In that brief moment, Remona has to convince the burning gaze that fixes upon her that she is a human being, that her fellow Muslims are human beings. She wants to show sympathy for the victims and convey she isn't an outsider but a fellow Westerner, a European, a Brit. Muslim women in the media are pushed into a binary that dictates that you're either against extremism or you're for extremism. This framework is damaging and, as Remona points out, can reinforce the polarising rhetoric of the extremists. There's very little opportunity for nuance when the media machine is just set up for hot takes. The struggle to satisfy the expectations of everyone is overwhelming. 'You can't say everything you think or feel within minutes, even seconds, but I try my best to be authentic,' Remona says. 'And I have realised, you get judged whatever you say. Some people will call you out for not saying what they wanted you to say, and some hostile Islamophobic voices have already decided you're the enemy, imposing collective responsibility upon you.' Muslims don't have the privilege of having a mainstream profile, Remona tells me. Existing as minorities in the West, you're constantly aware of being a minority and have to be more mindful of how you articulate your views. The task can feel urgent, because if you're not speaking out, who might they get instead?

As Julie Siddiqi also mentions, a compelling reason to agree to take on such a stressful role is that some segments of the media have historically gone to sensational fringe community leaders for the shock factor. Reactionary Muslims were wheeled in as spokespeople for Muslims even though their views were not particularly representative, simply because this would pull in viewers. The damage to the perception of Muslim communities has been long-lasting. 'As a woman you are judged; as a person of colour, you are judged; as a Muslim you are judged; and for me, as a hijab wearer, you are judged,' says Remona. 'All these things are working against you or working for you ... as a visible racialised Muslim. Some people are rooting for you, of course. But this is the immense pressure upon you as you are speaking on behalf of your communities at a highly emotive time. You don't want to appear on TV always reacting to world events, often dramatic and negative. You also wish to be normalised, to appear on TV talking about regular everyday things to create relatability, empathy, and convey our humanity.' Remona's work has been centred around building a more nuanced and broader understanding of lived faith experiences, and she has received opportunities to carve a window to those existences that rarely get seen. In her regular slot for the national BBC radio series *Pause for Thought*, in which contributors offer short spiritual reflections, Remona feels she has been given space to speak more personally and authentically as a Muslim. She has had work published that highlights 'a spectrum of lived faith experiences in constructive, relatable ways, not via reductive, reactionary frameworks'. She also remarks on the challenges of dealing with the shrinking of media space around religion, belief and ethics, noting how areas like religious programming are always operating under the threat of precarity if they don't fulfil commercial interests. The under-investment in this hugely misunderstood area is a missed opportunity. 'The answer is to increase the accommodation of religious literacy, not push it into a corner.'

Of course, there are those who desire to appear as media spokespeople to feed their ego, to gatekeep access to their communities and to make a name for themselves. But such naked opportunism is easy to identify, and more often the charge is wielded against women unfairly (usually by men) to uphold patriarchal structures of power and vested interests. There are men who take issue with Muslim women who appear in the public sphere ready to meet the gaze that falls upon them. Yet in Islam, the responsibility of being confronted with the objectifying potency of others' assessments is not for women to bear alone. Islamic teaching advises us not to look at people as objects but as a sum of all their humanity. Both men and women have been granted the ability to gaze and are compelled to look upon others conscionably in a manner that is not reductive. The totality of the Qur'anic message about the objectifying gaze is thus not contained in the conclusion that it is women's responsibility to avoid objectification, although it is the right of any woman to veil herself of her own volition if this is what she wishes to do. Nor is it the point to be preoccupied with averting one's eyes when interacting with a member of the opposite sex, which as well as being awkward and impractical could itself foment objectification. The point is, rather, that the gaze itself is anathema. *Purdah*, or the segregation of the sexes, is routinely interpreted as the optimal path to thwart objectification, but barriers, whether they manifest in the form of veiling, lowering the eyes or physical separation of the sexes, are a misapprehension of Islam's wisdom. It is the gaze itself that we must erase from our psyches in order to create a healthy and respectful dynamic of interaction and appreciation between human beings. The Muslim

woman, weighed down by the burden of the gaze, struggles to be
an exemplary female in reaction to the gaze she is subjected to.
Wearied and re-imagined, she is unable to escape objectification
even in Muslim societies, which are often so very removed from
Islamic ideals. Our own misinterpretations of the gaze in Islam
are rife, regardless of cultural or religious tradition. Muslim
communities and nations have only served to imbibe the worst
aspects of the Western concept of the neoliberal gaze and embody
its meaning without question. Without critically re-thinking the
Qur'anic construction of the gaze, we will never get past the
distractions of veiling and segregation.

But what if society, your community, men who insert themselves in positions of power, and the women you thought would
uplift you decide they are entitled to tell you how you should
meet the othering gaze? Kinsi Abdulleh has lived and worked in
East London for thirty years, running the Somali-led, Africa-
inspired culture and heritage organisation NUMBI Arts.[19]
NUMBI's first exhibition, Somali Museum: Any-Space-
Whatever, which was crowdfunded during the Covid pandemic,
recently exhibited at the Whitechapel Art Gallery.[20] Kinsi was at
the forefront of the project, which seeks to claim space for Black
British Somali communities in the UK's cultural landscape and
history, as well as connecting with diaspora around the world.
The exhibition, *to be oriented by divine inspiration and ancestral
knowledge*, has rooted Kinsi prominently in the visors of the art
establishment, but her journey to this point was not without
struggle. Kinsi was told she was too much, too loud, too emotional, and was often not taken seriously by those who sought to
extract her visionary energy but only as long as she didn't take
up too much space or spill out of the box in which she had been
placed. The gaze turned in on the marginalised Black women she
represents, the minorities and the disenfranchised. Operating
within the hierarchy of power, she found her efforts were some-

times subjugated through the structures of injustice that limit us all. Women are subject to demands that they be pliant to the whims of their objectification, regardless of the specific form that it might take. For Muslim women such as Kinsi, it is through the prism of the Western obsession with the veil that they are imagined, and in a wry effort to subvert this, Kinsi created *SCARF*, an arts magazine celebrating Black British Islam.

The gaze objectifies and dismisses Muslim women and girls as disempowered creatures. It seeks to save them from themselves and liberate them from their garb. Fetishised and deconstructed in the minds of those who pass judgement from a watchful distance, Muslim women are among the most closely observed and scrutinised groups in the Western imagination. Nor are they free from policing gazes in Muslim societies. Locating Muslim women's bodies as a site of ideological and political battle is hardly unheard of in many Muslim countries as well as beyond. Freedom from the gaze of voyeurs will not be derived from a piece of cloth, whether one chooses to cover or uncover. Neither is it dependent on someone else lowering their gaze. Instead, Muslims are urged in Islam not to be so utterly consumed by the gaze. Believers are counselled to recover the moral principle and use it as a buffer against the pervasive neoliberal gaze that objectifies, commodifies and sexualises. In Islamic tradition, what is celebrated instead is an equalising gaze, with the Qur'an first stating the obligations upon men with regard to perceiving others before mentioning the same obligations for women.

Sometimes a gaze can fix a woman firmly on the edges, and any journey inwards along the concentric circles of society is discouraged. What's interesting about being from the 'margins of society' is that self-perception is a necessary process to make sense of one's own work, renowned author Ayisha Malik tells me. She explains that the expectation we have of ourselves, as well as what we presume others to have of us, leads many things to be left unsaid. Muslim women absorb much of the social discourse about representation and ideas of authenticity that takes place around us. The extent to which that then manifests in the work we produce is another story. Ayisha herself has been on a journey. 'When I first wrote *Sofia Khan* in 2015,'[21] she says, 'I think I was living in a literary vacuum and didn't feel the pressure at that time, and the conversation around representation was quite different. It was still fairly novel. I essentially wrote what I wanted to write—a Muslim *Bridget Jones*.'

After writing a book with a main character who isn't widely represented, Ayisha found she became a go-to person. Initially she felt obliged to say yes to everything—diversity panels, writers' panels, all wanting to hear what it was like for her 'writing as a Muslim woman'. She was not entirely comfortable with being packaged so neatly. 'On the one hand there is this idea of representation, and on the other there's also baulking against that. The expectation to then not talk about the Muslim aspect of having written a rom-com would have been slightly miscalculated, because how can you write characters and then not want to talk about the subject matter that arises as a result of that character's creation? Then there's this idea of authenticity. I think even framing it as "what is authentic and what is inauthentic?" is problematic in itself.'

For Ayisha, falling out of love with an identity that forefronts 'writing as a Muslim woman' meant breaking out of contrived boxes and understanding the flaws of writing for a certain gaze. 'The idea that there is any one authentic story is ridiculous. From my gleaning of conversations with people and my own personal bugbears, what irks a lot of Muslim women and men is falling into Western tropes of being a subversive Muslim woman or writing characters that don't invoke hard-hitting issues, as if that's something that's refreshing. Moving away from that is seen as an original take on issues that were widely held in the hands of people from different backgrounds, and so I think claiming that space is really important, because one is telling another side of a story and how these are characters placed within the remit of literature and other storytelling mediums.'

If authenticity is understanding the different strands of lived realities, the gaze defines who is being centred, how they are being perceived and what their own perception is. There are debates in the publishing industry around who is allowed to write about whom. On this question, Ayisha is clear that if people are writing characters from backgrounds that are alien to them, then they must be able to fully immerse themselves in the perception of that world and ask searching questions of themselves. 'These are the questions I was asking myself when I was writing white English characters in *This Green and Pleasant Land*,'[22] she says. 'The difference is, I am in a society where I was brought up surrounded by white people, so I didn't find it to be too much discomfort. I brought in my observational skills and all that I've witnessed and seen of a nation and people, and that came out in the characterisation. Would I have been as confident writing a Chinese character or a Black character? People are multi-faceted, so how are you meant to create a character without being immersed in an environment in which you have so much evidence of actions, reaction, histories and background of people you wish to write about?'

The pressure that writers might put on themselves to write authentically is relative to how much they seek to yield to those expectations from without. Ayisha isn't certain that her latest book, *The Movement*,[23] holds the subjects of identity and belonging to the same extent as her first three. She can't help but wonder if the reception to the book would have been better if it had been more similar to her previous writing. 'I want to write whatever I want to write about, and I don't want to write about what people expect. If life, and we, are ever evolving and changing, then surely what one writes about should reflect that?' But being true to your calling can cause difficulties. It may mean it is more difficult to be published, or it may limit what kind of advance you can negotiate. The publishing world is very much about books of the moment, and what is the next best thing. 'I think it's about whether you want to be part of that fray and literary rat race, or if you want to take a step back and ask why it is you're writing what you're writing, and what is it that you want to create in your body of work,' says Ayisha. 'Part of that has to do with characters on the page that are nuanced and of a certain background which we don't often see in books—moving away from their identity being the main thing to do with their story and narrative, and just having those characters act as they are, and be who they are, without bringing in issues to do with identity politics. People have been saying that for a while now, yet publishing doesn't seem to want to listen.'

When writing her *Sofia Khan* books, Ayisha found that people took umbrage at the fact that her main character smokes and swears. Ayisha was accused of trying to create a hijabi character that panders to the Western gaze, with critics naively claiming that no hijabi girl would ever behave in such a manner. 'I just think that's an example of how we bring our own biases and prejudices and desires for what kind of person we want represented on the page,' Ayisha remarks. 'We forget that an author is creating a fictional character, and part of the problem is that we perhaps conflate what we expect in real life and what we expect a character should be allowed to do within the pages of a story. Criticism of *This Green and Pleasant Land* has been as superficial as lamenting that only a South Asian family is represented in that story because other types of Muslims exist. Well, yes, but I won't do a tick-box exercise of representing everybody on the page all the time. One is expected to address the problems of the world within the framework of a single story, which feels like an impossible task. My goal is to be sensitive, do my research, and write what I want.'

Speaking with Ayisha, I thought back to a conversation I had about photography being a form of death, because it captures a moment, an object, a person or a context that no longer exists. Words, once written, typed, printed, are also a form of death, but out of the disruption emerges something new. It is similar to a television appearance or a photo shared on social media—a gaze has faltered as we lock eyes with the person in the photo or on television. They invite us to let them contribute to our story before we have even had a chance to internalise our own perception of what we have looked at in that moment. What is key is that this form of self-objectification is not done on one's own terms but seeks approval from the viewer in a desperate soliciting of likes, reposts, comments and follows. An influencer on social media seeks affirmation for the image, the persona, the brand that is being projected, which has been constructed purely for the objectification of others. It is the only way it will remain alive in the consciousness of those who view it. Our idealised self, representing how we wish to be perceived, consumed and realised, can be validated solely by the external gaze, via a reaction from others. Instead of energising a diversity of self-representation, the internal gaze is a slave to the norms of neoliberal discourse. Turning the gaze inward is a state of mind, we are constantly told, and that's why authors are subjected to demands to be all the things that we imagine they should be.

Society stakes its claim on feminine aesthetics and privileges the right to scrutinise. Our visual encounters are resolutely gendered as we search female faces and bodies for the covered-up truth. The mask is more than just foundations and concealers and contouring and strobing, hijabs, niqabs and *dupattas*.[24] Men need only be bare, authentic. What is that I hear them say? A woman employs trickery to enhance? The objectifying gaze will see through her 'mask', her layers, every attempt to present the best possible version of her 'self'. Instead, we should understand the best and purest kind of gaze to mean treating people as equal beings and honouring far more than the superficial mask they present to the world. Let us not reduce the complexity and vibrancy of our finite selves to objectification based on transient and fleeting external attributes or a demand for only the authenticity we approve. As we gaze upon others, let the experience be expansive as we quench the thirst of our eyes. The gaze is powerful. The gaze is anathema. Let us make the gaze benign. All societies have an aversion to the gaze, but as we soak in the entirety of every person we observe, we are reminded that not all gazes are the same. Each of us is our own landscape.

3

SOLIDARITY WITH MY SISTERS

A teenage girl paces up and down a narrow alleyway speaking Bengali into a mobile phone. The walls of the dark, claustrophobic building are pretty-fied by colourful decorations and posters of flowers and adorable babies. We glimpse small rooms on either side, decorated in a similar cutesy way. Now and then, women come into view. Are they chatting, gossiping, waiting for something? Some are fixing their hair, applying make-up, tidying. Others look like mannequins with bright-red lips and empty expressions. The rooms resemble bedrooms. Very few men are around. How innocent this youngster looks. Her petite frame is swathed in a dark, glittering *lehenga*,[1] and her thick, raven hair, parted in the centre, falls loosely around her shoulders. A *teep*[2] adorns her forehead. 'Aren't you coming? You don't want to fuck me anymore?' she asks. 'You're probably tired of my pussy. You fucked me so many times ... Come see me and I'll do you good like I always do ... Have I ever disappointed you in bed? Don't you like fucking me anymore?' The scene cuts to a view from the outside of this walled community in Bangladesh, one of few Muslim-majority countries where prostitution is legal. It is dawn, and the call to prayer reverberates and soothes across the skies. The imam's tremulous voice fades into Maike Rosa Vogel's hypnotic rendition of 'Where We Meet', featuring Konstantin Gropper,[3] its lyrics inspired by a poem penned by the late Austrian documentary filmmaker Michael Glawogger.

Glawogger's documentary *Whores' Glory* (2011)[4] was released three years before he died from untreated malaria while filming in Liberia. It is an eye-opening glimpse into the worlds in which prostitutes in Thailand, Bangladesh and Mexico exist and thrive. A cornerstone of the women's lives is their adherence to faith—Buddhism, Islam and Catholicism respectively—and each segment articulates the comfort and strength that these sex workers draw from their belief in a higher power. Filming in Bangladesh takes place in a sprawling complex called City of Joy in Faridpur, central Bangladesh. Up to 800 women live and work in tiny rooms packed along cramped corridors. Occasionally, entire families occupy a single room; this is a profession often passed down along generations, after all. Madams 'own' the prostitutes and allocate them to the rooms they manage. The landlord, a man we never meet, arrives at dusk every night to collect the rent. The women use whatever tactics they can to lure clients to their rooms. They seduce with revealing clothes, cake themselves in make-up, cajole, beg, plead, harangue, haggle, and sometimes playfully—or even aggressively—grab at men who wander through the suffocating endless corridors looking to buy sex. Competition is fierce and the stakes are high. Women brawl over clients as the pressure to make money by selling their bodies heightens, particularly when footfall is slow.

A spindly woman with her hair in a tight, high bun sits cross-legged on a bed. A man reclines lazily with his head on a pillow. A baby girl plays blissfully next to them. The woman explains that she has worked in this industry for twenty years. Twelve years ago, she came to Faridpur and fell in love. As the woman speaks, the viewer realises the man is not a client but her husband, and the little girl their child. 'But love needs money. Without money, neither love nor lovers last.' Now she and her family live off her meagre income and the earnings of four prostitutes who work for her. She treats them like her own flesh and blood, she says. Without them the family would be homeless. She looks to her baby daughter. 'Because her mother is a whore, no one will want to marry her. If someone does marry her, it will only be for money. When there is money he will love her. If not, he will kick her out. And then what? She'll probably become a whore.' She speaks without emotion. There is no reaction from the wordless man lying motionless on the bed.

The oldest profession in the world locates the battle for power in the control of women's bodies. Are sex workers victims of misogynist structures created simply to please men, or are they empowered women choosing to express their sexuality as they wish? Some third-wave feminists argue that prostitution offers a means to economic empowerment and refuse to see sex workers as victims. In the iconic 1981 Bollywood classic *Umrao Jaan*, Amiran is a young girl kidnapped and sold to a brothel owner. Her pathway to a loss of innocence is accompanied by an education in poetry, dance, high culture and etiquette. Renamed Umrao Jaan, she grows into a highly desired courtesan, mesmerising men who frequent the *tawaif* or brothel. In an interview with *The Huffington Post*, Glawogger responds to the suggestion that the prostitutes in his documentary are victims, condemned to a life they did not choose and from which there is no way out, by saying, 'There is no *right* life. What's powerful is how they cope.'[5] I am struck by this. Life is, after all, a navigation of our own unique set of challenges. Perhaps it is patronising to dismiss women as pitiful victims simply because they don't conform to notions of Western feminism.

Later, however, I reflect more, considering the commodification of the women in the documentary and the inevitable male gaze of the director, perhaps even the production team, which provides the pathway through which the viewer can consume their lives. Interactions are transactions in this world of paying for sex. Glawogger admits to buying gifts and paying money to the workers in an effort to win their trust and co-operation in the making of the documentary. Yet still they manage to keep some versions of themselves far from consuming eyes. He talks of the many times they would lie to him and change their stories, 'but I made a contract to myself, whatever they say is truth, it's part of their job to fake it, so why shouldn't they fake it with me?'[6] When you feel that your voice is not heard, what relevance is the notion of truth anyway? Ultimately, this is a woman's world—men may purchase the women's bodies, but as one madam tells a new recruit: 'Don't do everything a client asks of you. Tell him, "I sell my body, not my soul." Politely say, "You may use me up to a certain point. I cannot go beyond my limits. I'm not a slave you can buy."' These are the negotiations women make to ensure a seemingly unbearable life is bearable. Brothels are designed for the pleasure of men, but, as Saba Dewan's research has revealed, they are households led by women.[7] In the *tawaif*, patriarchy is inverted, and the bonds that tie everyone together are between women—mothers and daughters, madams and those girls she 'owns', sisterhood between the prostitutes themselves.

My beloved friend, a sister to me, Leyla Jagiella, describes *Umrao Jaan* as a 'male fantasy'. Just like Dewan, she sees the film as negotiating a patriarchal society in an effort to attain agency. Women who ran *tawaifs* were entrepreneurial and self-made. Along with the courtesans in their household they were well educated and cultured, largely respected, and held their place in South Asian society's pre-colonial structures. The puritanical Christian impact of colonialism served to push these empowered women-led institutions from being on the fringes to beyond the pale. Just like all aspects of culture, patriarchy and patriarchal norms do not remain fixed, and it would be naive to claim that pre-colonial patriarchy was more liberal. But Muslim traditions around the world incorporated spaces that lay adjacent to patriarchal norms, and it was in these spaces that women-led communities such as *tawaifs* thrived. The impact of Victorian-era colonialism was to narrow what constituted accepted morality and values. The *tawaif* was no longer afforded a space in society and became associated with shame, corruption and an affront to the idealised monogamous family system that upheld patriarchy.[8]

In her 2020 book, Sunera Thobani writes:

> The ongoing feminist refusal to rethink the feminist tradition through sustained and substantive engagement with the divides of race, coloniality, nation and so on, keeps the orientation of feminist futures within the orbit of Westernity. Moreover, the feminist insistence on reading what are basically Western constructs of patriarchy and heteronormativity as transhistorical and transcultural allow[s] Western feminist appropriation of the historical experiences and struggles of Indigenous, Black and Third-World women to bolster hegemonic narratives of white gendered/sexed victimhood.[9]

Who can forget the cries from women such as then-US First Lady Laura Bush that the 2001 invasion of Afghanistan was an intervention by the 'civilised' world to free Afghan women?[10] The liberation of Muslim women from the oppression that Islamist terrorists had imposed—and 'would like to impose upon the rest of us'—was a front in the ideological war between the West and the Rest. The concept of feminism, as constructed through the colonial/occupying Western lens, is offered up as the only hope for salvation. The Muslim woman's default position is that she needs to be saved by white feminism because there is no other opportunity for her to free. White, Western-centric feminism defines what it means to be free, and therefore the negotiations and navigations enacted by the women in City of Joy or in the *tawaifs* of *Umrao Jaan* are only to be pitied.

I asked in my introduction, what does it mean to be a feminist anyway? Who gets to define what misogyny entails? I frequently wonder this and am far from the only one. Eyes wide open, in a nineteenth-century West London building that had formerly been a cinema, I was at the launch of a female artist's latest installation. It was a stunning, immersive and interactive show celebrating the age-old tradition of Islamic calligraphy through the prism of digital technology. Victorian fixtures were spread over the leather-bound furniture; dark panelling and austere por-traits christened the walls. I wandered in wonder at such a beau-tiful place.

'Everyone's a misogynist. Everyone exploits everyone. There is no female solidarity, because when it comes to misogyny, women are among the worst.' The scolding surprised me from a woman I had respected for decades, who was known for her feminist principles and work with grassroots Muslim communities. She had been at the forefront of challenging patriarchal attitudes since the 1980s, yet here she was seeming to excuse men's bad behaviour by instead laying the blame on women.

We had been talking with others about authoritarianism, patri-archy and nepotism in Muslim spaces. I had felt the release that comes with relaying experiences and incidents among people who just get it, who know exactly what you are talking about because they have been through the same thing, who see the injustices that others make light of or dismiss because to admit the truth would make them uncomfortable. Affirming and supportive sis-terhood is a balm in a spiky world in which each of us is trying to find our place. The conversation had touched on an event held by a Muslim organisation that had recently seen an exodus of female staff and board members. In an effort to manage the optics of the now all-male entity, a hijab-wearing, attractive, young

Muslim woman was to perform a five-minute role at the beginning. She was plastered all over the promotional material for the event to convey a female-friendly image, despite the reality of how women in the organisation had been treated. Dismay had been expressed among our group that this woman had agreed to be involved in the event even though she had known about the circumstances of the other women's departure.

Performative expressions of solidarity are commonplace in our meaningless tick-box culture. When the murder of George Floyd sparked the Black Lives Matter protests, corporations, organisations and institutions hastily switched their social media profiles to black, regardless of their records on diversity, equality and inclusion. Of course, it's easy to make superficial gestures, to be seen to be fighting against injustice, as long as it doesn't require conceding power. It is only when women and their allies are willing to speak up, to tear up the rule book and disrupt the order and the status quo, ready to let other women know of their experiences, good and bad, in public and in private, that solidarity can be tried and tested. I see solidarity in the brothels of City of Joy, and in the *tawaif* of *Umrao Jaan*. I also see brutality, manipulation and cruelty. But does this mean that women are the worst misogynists?

Let us consider the background to another incident: a Muslim woman of colour quit her job, in protest at bullying and undermining of female employees by Muslim men in charge. She confided a catalogue of appalling behaviour she had witnessed and experienced to a white, non-Muslim woman who also worked at the organisation, and who regarded herself as firmly on the side of social justice and inclusion. The white woman then sought out other versions of what had happened. She was desperate to source the 'other side of the story', so she wouldn't find herself in an uncomfortable situation. 'Oh, I spoke to so-and-so, and he contextualised things,' she said. Some weeks later, it transpired she had agreed to take on a new role, ostensibly to cover the work of the departed colleague, and was surprised that the women who had left in protest felt betrayed. Her argument was that she, a white woman, was engaged in challenging Islamophobia, and her personal experiences with the men involved had been positive, which left her reticent about taking a stand. She was convinced by her male colleagues' justifications and defences, which involved questioning the integrity and veracity of the aggrieved woman's experiences. She chose not to believe a Muslim woman. Muslim women are discarded, rendered unreliable when they are no longer compliant. The white woman will carry on regardless; she doesn't want to get involved. It's all just politics anyway, nothing more serious than a 'falling out'. She doesn't need to make herself uncomfortable.

I've been told this more times than I would have liked: 'I've heard the other side', which often means the character assassination of 'difficult' women, or 'it's all just politics', a reduction and erasure of patriarchal and misogynistic behaviour that feels like gaslighting. The suggestion that female solidarity is conditional is hard to hear. There are many who would argue that no one is compelled to take a stand or to call out misogynistic behaviour or involve themselves in something they don't wish to be involved in, or for that matter boycott something they don't wish to boycott. Yet I, and many women I know who believe in the fair and just treatment of others, would not think twice about turning down invitations and opportunities from those I have been informed do not behave ethically. I believe women when they tell me they have been marginalised, oppressed, mistreated. That's not to say I won't carry out my due diligence, but my default will always be solidarity.

I'm with my friend Irum Ali at a cafe in East London, and she pulls me up on this. She tells me she's come to a point in her life where she doesn't really believe in solidarity amongst women or solidarity amongst Muslims or solidarity amongst certain marginalised groups, because often identity-based solidarity is at the expense of someone else's marginalisation and means banding together to ignore that other people are being hurt. 'The category of women, to me, explains nothing,' she says. 'It's a very old school way of thinking.' A researcher and PhD holder, Irum tells me that although she is a Muslim woman of colour, as a cisgender person with class, education and financial privilege, she can't claim to be more oppressed than a trans white woman, or a working-class woman of colour.

'I find the category of woman really facile,' Irum tells me. 'And when anyone starts a sentence with, "As a woman ...", I immediately start asking questions about intersectionality, and that for me is where true liberation lies. It is not about women versus men, because that hasn't really worked in the past forty years of the first waves of feminism.' Intersectional feminism is inclusive in a way that white feminism never allowed, because now the category of 'woman' is bigger to incorporate all the different ways of being a woman and experiencing struggle. Female solidarity, Irum says, is used to gloss over issues. 'Many forms of subjugation are interrelated,' she says, 'and the politics of collective liberation demand that we understand how systemic forms of oppression work.' She asks how she can assume solidarity with a woman whose politics she finds problematic. How can our struggles be the same just because we share some forms of oppression, when they are in turn oppressing another category of people? 'The limits of representation politics are clear for us all to see, with women in power who clearly work against the interests of the majority of women. I don't want to stand in solidarity with other Muslim women who are not standing in solidarity with Black people, or with LGBT people. How can I stand in solidarity with women from immigrant backgrounds who position themselves as being from a "model minority" and don't stand in solidarity with migrants; who believe in this idea that we must be "good Muslims" and assimilate; or, and I say this as a non-practising Muslim, who believe we should only practise our Islam in a way that is deemed acceptable?'

Irum suggests that we find ourselves asking women for solidarity when they don't really deserve it, when their politics are toxic. She believes it's very easy to stand on a pulpit and say, 'I am oppressed,' but if we don't interrogate what that means, solidarity becomes problematic. 'I am not asking that we all have to constantly interrogate our solidarity, but that we don't make assumptions about people's politics based on categories alone,' she says. For Irum, a commitment to intersectionality need not descend into raking through a person's history to find one dubious Twitter spat or to highlight that one time they shared a platform with someone with hateful views. 'People's politics evolve,' she says. The point she foregrounds, however, is that where patriarchy is concerned, 'Muslim women can fall into the trap of assuming they are entitled to a special status that allows them to become perpetrators of oppression on another marginalised group'.

When it comes to misogyny, many are looking a little too eagerly for 'the other side' of the story. Let's hear 'the other side' so we can convince ourselves that nobody behaved so badly. So we don't have to feel uncomfortable or find ourselves in scenarios with difficult ethical stakes. Let's not rock the boat. As long as we're okay, as long as no one behaved badly towards us, it's okay, right? I'm reminded of the time when a senior media executive, a Muslim man not far from retirement, told me how a female colleague had accused him of misogyny. 'I thought my career was over,' he said. It was another female colleague who dismissed the accusation and told him this woman was a difficult woman and he had nothing to worry about. 'I've learned my lesson: you can't say anything anymore,' he told me, describing the impact the incident had on him. I wondered what he meant. What self-censorship was he claiming? What was it that he no longer dared to say or do? Was it something that might have made a woman uncomfortable and have led her to complain about sexist behaviour?

Humera Khan, co-founder of An-Nisa Network,[11] tells me that female solidarity is lacking among women in positions of power. 'There is a phenomenal amount of effort Muslim women are doing on the ground, supporting each other, but it is stuff they do without funding, they do it amongst themselves. But when it gets to the point of leadership, it gets more complicated.' Humera says that this is a difficulty not only faced by women, and everyone gets to a point where they need to make a decision about whether to go it alone or to be involved in something that they think they can influence. Humera has taken part in count-less projects and initiatives that had good intentions, even under difficult circumstances. 'But I just got disillusioned with it,' she says. 'In the early years there weren't so many women, just a handful. That's changed because women have made the effort.' Thirty or forty years ago, Humera remembers, independent women with agency were unheard of. 'My expectations of women remain different. So it always comes as a surprise when I see women playing by, what I call, the rules of men. Or they're choosing to be aggressive in a way that men are. Of course, I get affected and upset about certain patriarchal attitudes that are out there. But I'm more interested in saying I'm going to step back from that. Because confronting it doesn't seem to help or solve anything. I ask myself, what do I understand, what am I looking into, what can I offer, as another way of thinking about this? An-Nisa has always worked with the men, however frustrating it is. Because you have to.'

Having to work with men is not the only front where Muslim women must fight. The backdrop of this battleground is the history of white feminism, which has long caricatured the misogyny of brown men to carve a role for white women as part of a project to save brown women. In her fierce and thought-provoking book *Against White Feminism*, Rafia Zakaria argues that white feminism does not require its protagonist to be a white woman, but rather that they must be someone who sustains the white feminist agenda. 'A white feminist', she writes, 'is someone who refuses to consider the role that whiteness and the racial privilege attached to it have played, and continue to play, in universalizing white feminist concerns, agendas and beliefs as those of all of feminism and all feminists.'[12] As Irum argues, Muslim women, in turn, demand a level of solidarity and purity of purpose that no one demands of men. Women, are, after all, part of the patriarchal bargain, where they have gained power and suffered in the process. Why would they align themselves with weak and disempowered fellow Muslim women and lose that power? That's against human nature. Why do we feel so betrayed by the white woman who took the promotion created by the exodus of Muslim women who left an organisation they felt was misogynistic? Why aren't we holding men up to the same standard? Is this just another form of oppression women put on each other? Irum thinks so. She asks, 'where are our male allies? Interestingly, it is often queer Muslim men, rather than other women, who step up to advocate for Muslim women suffering under the patriarchy. Let that sink in'.

Zakaria relates an anecdote that illustrates the censoring of the self that women who do not conform to white feminism's vision of emancipation subject themselves to. The scene is set in a wine bar, where Zakaria is (not) drinking with a group of white, middle-class, US feminists, while simultaneously trying not to betray her faith-based reasons for being teetotal, as that wouldn't fit the *Sex and the City* vibe. Her personal history is traumatic—she fled an abusive arranged marriage—but she tries to gloss over the messiness, suspecting that her life story would only fuel white feminists' belief that they need to rescue oppressed non-Western women like her from their patriarchal contexts by liberating her from all her cultural baggage.

This is the crux of Muslim women's frustration with white feminism. When it comes to who gets to define what it means to be liberated, the assumption is that the Western-centric view of female emancipation is the only ideal, and any other mode of struggle is a compromise. Systematically analysing such assumptions, excavating their history, and then challenging the racism and class bias inherent in the ideology reveals exactly this. As I said earlier, this is not to blur the distinction between white feminism and white feminists. White women who happen to be feminists are not the issue. The challenge is to extricate the whiteness from feminism and to value the different ways in which feminism is a lived reality across global communities. To question white feminism's championing of acts of rebellion and dismissal of steady resistance, Fauzia Ahmad goes further, asking whether Black feminist writings adequately offer the spaces that Muslim women are seeking. 'Despite the existence of excellent black feminist scholarship and activity, the vast majority (not all) of these writers and activists ignore "Muslim women" or situate them within pathologized, victim-focused discourses,' she writes.[13] The rhetoric remains the same. Rebellion equals transgression, individualism, consumer capital and sexual promiscuity—all of which are valid life choices women must be free to make. But there are other paths that strong women tread, which involve endurance, resilience, collective political activism, and building and sustaining community rooted in faith. To conclude that white feminism is the only model for women's liberation and that non-white feminism offers no suitable alternatives or sanctuary only infantilises and negates the many achievements of women who follow a different trajectory.

Rakaya Esime Fetuga is a second-generation British Muslim in her mid-twenties who was born and grew up in London. Her family is from Ghana and Nigeria, and her parents, who were born in the UK, were from mixed religious backgrounds and embraced Sufi Islam in their twenties, bringing up Rakaya and her three brothers within the religion, with close guidance from Sufi sheikhs and teachers. Rakaya takes care of creative arts initiatives at Rumi's Cave, an arts and events venue in Northwest London which describes itself as a non-defined social space and alternative community hub, inspired by the legacy of the poet Jalaluddin Rumi.[14] A regular attendee and volunteer since the venue opened twelve years ago, Rakaya now organises open mic sessions and events which give musicians, poets, storytellers and performers the space to share their work. A programme of Islamic talks centring around the teachings of Sheikh Ahmed Babikir is also hosted at the venue, as well as a soup kitchen, food bank, night shelter and other charitable initiatives supporting vulnerable groups, elderly people and young members of the local community. Rumi's Cave has become a focal point for the local Sufi community, although it is also an inclusive space for all. A women's *mawlid* for worship and prayer draws a vibrant crowd, and fundraisers such as women-only raves with blacked-out windows allow women to enjoy themselves while also raising awareness and money for charitable causes.

Rakaya works as a creative freelancer and is involved in many women-focused projects. She is often invited to schools to teach schoolgirls how to use poetry to explore different topics and themes that are important to them, and she recently worked with St George's Hospital, in London, to encourage nurses, all of whom happened to be women, to use poetry to process their feelings, particularly in the aftermath of Covid. An annual slam competition in Tower Hamlets is also an opportunity for Rakaya to engage with youngsters and help them to use creativity to express themselves. In her work with young Muslim girls, she identifies recurrent themes. Islamophobia often comes up, along with worries about how they are perceived by the world as visibly Muslim girls and women. 'There is an energy of defence about the religion [Islam] and their choices,' which 'comes up a lot,' Rakaya says. 'And generally issues of self-confidence, but this is across the board and not exclusive to just Muslim girls.' Rakaya has observed that popular social media platforms such as TikTok are having a huge impact on how young people, particularly women, value themselves. They are often concerned with the ways they come across to their peer group, and how beauty is defined, as well as presenting themselves in a way that is acceptable and desirable. 'Muslim girls have the added pressure of living in a secular society, being judged for dressing modestly or wearing hijab, alongside the societal pressure to live up to unrealistic beauty standards, so it's a double-pressure,' Rakaya notes.

Rumi's Cave is an inclusive space, but women form the majority at most events, which is a testament to the fact that it is a women-friendly space and welcomes women and men who are respectful and empower each other. Glaiza Padulla, a young British-Filipino convert to Islam who is one of the two managers of Rumi's Cave, both of whom are female, said, 'I think that because this space is run by women, there's a certain type of guy who is comfortable coming here. And usually, they're the best type of guys.' Although she only has brothers, Rakaya was brought up surrounded by women from the community her parents were part of and had many female role models, particularly creative artists, who inspired her to take the career path she has chosen. She describes growing up free to make her own life choices, and her experiences of patriarchy were often in more abstract or removed situations, such as in a lecture by someone with a conservative position on Islamic teachings, or in the opinions of someone who was not a member of her immediate family or friends. She grew up empowered, although it was also a traditional upbringing, and her experience of patriarchy only manifested itself prominently in her lived reality when the topic of marriage came up. Rakaya sought solace in women-only spaces when she faced difficult encounters, particularly with men she was introduced to with a view to getting married. It was by retreating into women-only spaces and having conversations with other mutually supportive, nourishing and uplifting women that she was able to reflect and process what it means to be a Muslim woman in a patriarchal world. Through the sharing of stories and experiences in a safe and confidential space, women were able to show solidarity with their sisters and offer emotional, practical and spiritual comfort to each other.

Some time ago, I shared a video on Twitter of the all-female, teenage, hijab-wearing Indonesian heavy metal band Voice of Baceprot playing a cover of 'Sugar' by System of a Down.[15] I loved the video and revelled in the endless likes and retweets it elicited. However, there is no escaping that all the white liberal rejoicing at this 'rebellious' group of young Muslim women 'shattering stereotypes' and 'sticking it to the patriarchy' centres white feminism's image of liberation. Zakaria describes this as the great lie of relatability, with its implied claim that there is only one truly neutral perspective, which considers itself to be the original starting point against which all else should be measured. Subversion must take the form of what white feminism regards as rebellion. Anything else is a misguided enabling of the misogyny of brown and Black men perpetuated against brown and Black women. True liberation can only be realised through embracing, becoming and performing white feminism.

Shahed Ezaydi is a journalist in her early twenties who is currently researching a book on Muslim women and white feminism. When we meet, she reminisces about how she has always been intrigued by theories around society. While studying sociology modules on feminism at school, she noticed that all the feminists on the curriculum were white women. At the time, she thought perhaps this was what feminism was, and that the West must have been the pioneer of gender equality and women's rights. At university, there was not much more diversity to the reading lists, and Shahed began to wonder why she wasn't seeing herself reflected back in this field that interested her so greatly. Born in the UK to Libyan parents with traditional Islamic values, Shahed visited Libya with her family every summer and saw how, particularly in her wider family, men and women had more defined gender roles. Back in the UK, she began to receive jarring comments from friends who were repeating stereotypical assumptions about her faith and culture. All this fed back into Shahed's eighteen-year-old consciousness, and she started to consider the idea that perhaps Islam was not compatible with feminism after all.

At university, Shahed began to ask questions about the religion she believed in and practised and the Libyan community she was so proud to be part of. She looked for spaces in which her faith, culture and strong belief in gender equality could all co-exist. Her quest for knowledge proved fruitful, and she found stories and examples going back centuries of Muslim women who had been disruptive and fought for their rights. The fact that she had to seek out all this knowledge of her own accord, and that Muslim women's struggles were so absent from mainstream feminist discourse, made her realise this was a book she would have to write herself to challenge narratives around Islam and women. 'Friends at school would ask me if my dad was going to force me to get married, or force me to wear hijab. This is what they had picked up from the media and popular culture, particularly since 9/11, and so their ignorance was unsurprising.'

Years of seeing the stranglehold of white feminism over notions of empowerment and liberation left Shahed frustrated, particularly after her independent research proved that feminism was alive and well in communities from the 'global majority' (a term for non-white people, who collectively make up around 85 per cent of the world's population), but that these traditions and discourses had just been erased. After graduation, Shahed started working as a freelance journalist, and as she wrote more about these issues, a book exploring white feminism and Muslim women started taking shape. 'There was so little in current feminist literature that looked at how feminism could be inclusive or offer a seat at the table for everyone, or even talked about disrupting the entire table narrative.'

The construction of the goal of relatability is what compels Muslim women to contort for so many years in discomfort, having been presented with the illusion that apparently this is the only way to be a feminist, and thus to be emancipated. Relatability is just subjectivity dressed up as objectivity; it is exactly what Shahed seeks to subvert, and what Zakaria experienced as the reality of abuse and oppression. Zakaria was forced to run away from her home and seek the support of domestic violence services, finding herself in the position of a destitute single mother. Yet she did not find liberation in the spaces where white feminism expected her to gratefully reside. Those spaces, whether women's groups or the board of Amnesty International, expected her to conform to their narrow white feminist agenda where they always knew better. She writes:

> there is a division within feminism that is not spoken of but that has remained seething beneath the surface for years. It is the division between the women who write and speak feminism and the women who live it; the women who have a voice versus the women who have experience; the ones who make the theories and policies, and the ones who bear scars and sutures from the fight. While this dichotomy does not always trace racial divides, it is true that by and large, the women who are paid to write about feminism, lead feminist

organizations and make feminist policy in the Western world are white and middle-class.[16]

Irum would have asked her why she was surprised, reminding us of the patriarchal bargain. We are actively asking women with power to relinquish that power and stand in solidarity with those who have never been able to access it.

This division is part of a greater fallacy within liberal circles that it is enough to simply be well-intentioned, because this well-intentioned urge is the only way to save Black and brown women from Black and brown men, because only Black and brown communities harbour oppression and misogyny. White liberalism is the utopia in which Black and brown women may enjoy the heady freedom that white women in the West have fought so hard to achieve, and which women from other parts of the world can only dream of enjoying. A sobering one in three women in the US has experienced domestic violence,[17] yet there the offence is not viewed an 'honour crime'. Instead, honour crimes are perceived as faraway problems, not found in the West. This distortion fuels a desire to 'liberate' non-white women from the shackles of patriarchy, a ruse used to justify the post-9/11 invasion of Afghanistan under the pretext of helping women to throw off the burka and gleefully frolic in miniskirts. The policing of women's bodies knows no end of creativity, with the latest culture war that seeks to pit the rights of trans women, who are among the most marginalised groups in society, against women who deny their right to exist in spaces of chromosomal-designated exclusivity. Does this mean women with androgynous features, women who wear the face veil, and all women who don't fall within heteronormative boundaries carved out by white feminism will be required to constantly prove they are women? The transphobic moral panic of our contemporary times is yet another example of white feminists crowding out the many alternative ways of 'doing feminism' that exist.

109

Third-wave feminists criticised their second-wave sisters for their elitism and lack of intersectionality, but they continued the pattern of exclusion to the detriment of meaningful solidarity and allyship. To claim that women's rights began with Western suffragette movements denies the involvement of women in the Indian subcontinent in the fight for liberation from colonial occupation and other acts of political activism and agency. These were strong women who fought for the emancipation of their communities and were just as much feminist pioneers as Emmeline Pankhurst and the women who were pivotal in the UK suffrage movement.

Muslim women have strong traditions of organising them-selves for empowerment, beyond the *tawaifs* of *Umrao Jaan* or the brothels of City of Joy. In the late 1980s, a group of dynamic, young Muslim women in the UK identified a lack of facilities for Muslim women to be heard, supported and signposted to rele-vant social support services. They recognised the need to address mental health issues, trauma and abuse, in the face of reticence among Muslim communities to talk about so-called taboo sub-jects. They created a community phone-in service, which was then adapted to reflect increasing numbers of male callers. Three and a half decades of working in this field has convinced the veterans of this work that what we are witnessing is not a crisis of masculinities or an explosion of misogyny, but historical trauma which is being passed down through generations. They suggest that when we consider the subject of patriarchy, we should ask how it has come into existence and why. They believe we should move away from the idea that men hate women or that women hate men, but rather look at how patriarchy is pro-duced by the systems and structures which prop up society.

The origins of the phone-in service can be traced to a confer-ence held at Regent's Park Mosque in the 1980s on problems facing Muslim families and women in particular. Hearing stories of domestic violence and sexual abuse shocked attendees, who were unaware of the extent of these issues in Muslim communities. At that time, there was little understanding of mental health; nor was there much help for women suffering domestic violence or couples experiencing marriage breakdown, and the idea that sexual abuse was occurring was completely taboo. Such social problems were dismissed as Western ills that Muslim communities were utterly immune to. One of the conference attendees had spent time volunteering for Samaritans, an emotional support phone line, and it was she who suggested setting up a similar service for Muslims: it seemed the answer to the questions they were asking themselves, such as, where do people go with the anxiety and depression caused by abuse or discrimation? 'In Muslim communities we don't listen—we advise,' one of the group members told me. In her experience, our communities aren't inclined to listen to people and their problems but instead lean towards being advice-giving communities. There is a tendency to police the actions of others and assume we know their motivations; while this often comes from a well-meaning intention, it is disempowering. For the helpline group, it's clear that this is not an issue of pitting men against women. 'Men, for example, have themselves suffered trauma, such as from structural racism, and they don't know how to deal with it,' one of the women tells me. Disempowerment often leads these men to look to others for answers or solutions, so they seek out someone to tell them what to do. In this climate, many men and women don't have the confidence to look at the resources available and work out the best way to help themselves. When they contact the helpline, many are initially looking for someone to give them a fast solution to their issues.

The women's motivation for setting up the phone-in service also came from seeing a lack of support for Muslim women in mainstream spaces. When women would seek help for domestic violence or other issues, they would face the added ignominy of being told they were victims of an oppressive religion and culture. White feminism would offer these women salvation only if they chose rejection and rebellion. What couldn't be fathomed was that for many women suffering difficulty, it was faith that was giving them resilience and hope to overcome their challenges. The helpline was especially necessary because many women have been taught from a young age that obedience is an important quality. At the same time many Muslim men of that generation designated themselves as moral authorities and arbiters of social and personal justice. One of the women who set up the helpline had converted to Islam a short time before. She told me how much these ideas confused her because she understood that obedience should only be to Allah. The pressure to show the world that one's children are ideal young Muslims and not causing any trouble or bringing dishonour upon the family, or just expressing themselves in any way, encouraged further authoritarianism in Muslim families of that era. Her disquiet at the dynamics she was witnessing led to her dedicating herself to the work of the helpline. Decades later, she continues her tireless efforts, as well as engaging in proactive work to empower people to parent according to emotionally, psychologically and spiritually healthy Islamic practices based on the Qur'an and Sunnah. A lifetime of working with Muslim families has emphasised to her the necessity of empathetically addressing the needs of children to navigate from childhood to adolescence to adulthood.

The priority for many of the first generation of migrants to the UK was financial security, stability and academic achievement, which meant a lack of emphasis on emotional literacy. After five or six years, the founders of the helpline started inviting other organisations and also Muslim men to participate in their work. Through training exercises, they would illustrate how healthier families could result from learning about communication and understanding in personal relationships. *The Muslim News*, a newspaper set up by Ahmed Versi around that time, the first of its kind, was supportive of the helpline's aims and would include articles about the work being undertaken by the team that grew up around it. The women's intention was also to engage with local groups and individuals working in their communities to bring about change. Collaboratively, they would offer any support they could. This holistic approach led to training initiatives and co-operation with bodies with similar aims, sharing resources such as marriage workshops to help partners to understand themselves and each other before embarking upon a union. This was one example of how the phone-in service extended its efforts to help people to navigate conflict and difference, facilitating learning about human interaction and interpersonal relationships in Muslim communities.

Through their work with the helpline, the women realised that problems were being caused by the shutting down of anything that was uncomfortable, such as talk of sex or the alternative ideas of others, instead of educating young people to find their place and claim space in the secular society in which they lived. The helpline proved one of very few outlets for women to speak about emotional, psychological, sexual and spiritual abuse. Individuals who have spent decades battling to raise awareness of social issues within Muslim communities, often were met with denial or the turning of a blind eye, despite the evident damage and misery being caused. It is ironic that in this contemporary moment, some Muslims have suddenly been able to unite in their panic about LGBT issues in a way they were never willing to do about mental health, child abuse, domestic violence or misogyny. There were few sermons calling on men to treat their wives and children in exemplary ways in line with the Prophet's example. Imams were often quick to excuse bad behaviour by men and tell women who would come to them for advice that they should try harder not to make their husbands angry. Women who complained about abuse were even advised that they should put on make-up or lose weight and strive to be more attractive to their husbands to stop them from mistreating them or seeking a second wife.

Tané, in her late twenties, reflects on the disapproving attitudes of some Turkish-Cypriot relatives towards a couple in the family who were separating. 'These women themselves are languishing in relationships they are not fulfilled wholly by, or would rather not be in. You don't need to be a feminist, or call it feminism, to take a stance to improve your situation. If the assumption is that you are going to live in unhappiness because you don't identify with feminism, or you see it as undermining traditional values, what a detriment to you. It's not even about empowering yourself to make change; it's just about making yourself happy.'

When some women are empowered and healthy, there are other women who don't like this. Marriage prospects are often based on a woman not taking up too much space and not being too loud or assertive. Parents seeking a wife for their son might state that she should be a doctor, but she cannot be a doctor with opinions or be too confident. Some of the oppression that comes from mothers-in-law and sisters-in-law occurs because they themselves have normalised the idea that it is a woman's duty to 'fit in' with her in-laws. And policing a woman's behaviour, making sure she understands that she occupies the lowest rung in the ladder of the family's hierarchy, is seen as perfectly acceptable. Irum Ali, a sociologist, asks how Muslim mothers can expect their daughters to stand up for themselves against mothers-in-law or husbands after marriage or in the world of work if they are being bullied, when they have never been allowed to stand up to their parents or even an older brother. And the worst double standard is when a mother tells her daughter not to be too malleable when she marries, but she expects her own daughter-in-law to be exactly that.

I spoke to a friend who said that when she got married, she was desperate to make a good impression with her in-laws and be a perfect daughter-in-law, but she struggled with social anxiety, something she had revealed to her husband and which he had been very understanding of, but his family didn't show any empathy about. Her mother-in-law and sisters-in-law complained to her husband that she was cold, or standoffish, or had acted moody. Every interaction with them became stressful, and she felt under a microscope and misunderstood. It caused arguments with her husband, who began to see her as causing problems and bringing his family, particularly his mother, pain. She wasn't the right fit; she was difficult and awkward. Instead of supporting her to overcome her anxiety, the family made it all about themselves and how she made them feel. Her emotions and her pain were utterly irrelevant, and as a result, she would force herself into situations that made her deeply stressed and ill. She did this to try to make her mother-in-law happy, but whatever she tried wasn't good enough. She hadn't laughed at the jokes; she had hovered in the background and not made enough effort to join in the conversation; she was always sullen; she brought everyone down. There was never any allowance for the fact that she might need time to warm up in social situations. Her in-laws expected her to adapt her personality to suit their ways immediately, and when she was nervous and shy it was interpreted as being rude and lacking respect. It didn't occur to them that they might need to create space for her to ease into the family dynamic. I remember meeting her some months after her marriage and she was a nervous wreck, wracked with self-doubt and completely on edge. It was so sad. In such circumstances, why do some women seek to reinforce the patriarchy? When my friend was in this terrible situation, her sister-in-law said to her, 'You act like a stranger when you come to my house. Anyone else would just get the hoover out and start cleaning the house; they would just get stuck in.' She was stunned. She tried to explain she would hate it if someone came to her house and started cleaning and tidying without being asked. Everybody has their ways and behaviours, but her attempts to explain made things worse and she was made to feel like there was something wrong with her.

My friend's experience is not exceptional, but thankfully, expectations placed on new brides are less stifling than they were in the era in which the phone-in service was founded. What is clear, however, is that the service was ahead of its time. The founders decided early on to remain independent from existing Muslim organisations, and to only take money from specific sources that guaranteed a hands-off approach and would not interfere or try to influence their activities. They resolved to continue only by existing on the funds it takes to operate a communications system, and although they welcomed the involvement of 'brothers', these men would be handpicked to ensure they had emotional intelligence and did not harbour patriarchal or misogynistic attitudes. In this way, the phone-in service remained a small but powerful organisation that could not be manoeuvred to further any political, personal or sectarian agenda in the way that some Muslim organisations have been used. As the era of Prevent unfolded, mental health bodies were taking a keen interest in Muslim men's mental health and relating this to issues around radicalisation, so logging such data became politicised, something the founders of the helpline were wary of being involved in. The media narrative around radicalisation and Muslims in the aftermath of 9/11 left the helpline vulnerable. Journalists would call pretending to report suspected radicalisation or safeguarding issues, with the purpose of breaking a sensationalist story on how the helpline would respond and whether it chose to alert the authorities. Security services and police bodies were also keen to mine the experiences of the founders of the helpline, who in turn became very wary about whom they would permit to have an insight into their work in this securitised landscape.

Many women I have spoken to talk about seemingly intractable domestic situations and experiences of misogyny at the hands of fathers, brothers or husbands, that arise quite unexpectedly. The men in their lives are supportive and champion the rights of their female relatives as long as this does not disempower them as men. They tell women they are free to pursue whichever professional or personal life choice they desire, but the support is conditional on their choices not transgressing norms or bringing the family's reputation into disrepute. They may not even disagree with their daughter or wife or sister, but are reacting to an overwhelming pressure to uphold patriarchal norms in order to feel dignity and self-respect. Men in this way are just as much victims of the patriarchy. The phone-in service has fielded calls from women who tell them their husband treats them like a child, making sure they follow his rules—haram this, haram that. This harsh outward piety leaves no space for the heart, soul and mind or how Islam helps to alleviate mental illness and eases burdens, and how it offers nourishment and hope. The founders of the helpline noticed that daughters of parents who didn't berate, belittle and excessively police their behaviour thrived. Those who experienced emotionally intelligent parenting flourished in their academic, professional and personal lives. They weren't told that femininity had to be discarded to be successful. One of the founders talked about hearing a talk given by the late Merryl Wyn Davies, who asked why feminists required women to deny their femininity in order to be liberated.[18] Emulating masculinity and hardened, dictatorial and strident behaviour, was empowerment according to white feminism. It was decided anything beyond those parameters was not feminism. Unhealthy masculinity became the measurement of success.

The helpline was set up at a time when it seemed there were limited options open to Muslim women in distress. Often an issue would be at crisis point before a woman sought help. Now, Muslim women are looking to incorporate healing and wellbeing into their lives before reaching crisis, for example by embodying traditional holistic treatments and healing modalities to nourish their local communities. Aisha Beg lives in Keighley, a town in West Yorkshire with a sizeable Pakistani Muslim population. Until early 2023, she ran a clinic offering holistic therapy services. Her clients were almost entirely local women, and as her business grew over the years, it became the epicentre for wellbeing and support for Muslim women facing a multitude of issues. Aisha studied psychology to postgraduate level, inspired by her late mother who had worked as a psychologist in India. After her studies, she set about embarking upon a corporate career in human resources. By age twenty-three, Aisha was married, and as her husband's job involved a great deal of travelling, she decided to accompany him, which she describes as a wonderfully enjoyable period in her life where they saw the world. The downside, of course, was that she was unable to progress in her own career, and after returning to the UK nine years ago, she knew she was ready to develop an identity beyond being a stay-at-home wife and mother. She had grown up in a family where alternative therapies, such as homeopathy, herbs and acupuncture, were widely used to complement conventional medicine. This informed her decision to study psychology, and a period of secondary infertility, after the birth of her eldest daughter, also deepened her interest in this field. She started by offering therapeutic massages to women suffering from backache and other kinds of chronic pain. Then, at the age of thirty-nine, she embarked upon a one-year college course, and from there her holistic therapy journey began.

Aisha describes opening her clinic as a leap of faith, and as she had very little experience in running a business, there were trials and tribulations along the way. Nonetheless, her decision proved tremendously fruitful, and her clinic ended up being transformative for the well-being and health of Muslim women in Keighley. It became a hub providing mental and physical health support for local women, who would come for alternative therapies that are widespread in Asia and the Middle East. These include *hijamah*, or cupping, which is mentioned in the hadith as being practised by the Prophet,[19] energy healing, reflexology, massage, and eventually Mizan therapy.[20] 'The clinic touched the lives of many, helping them manage pain, trauma, generational trauma, fertility issues, depression and other issues,' she says. 'It is something that wasn't there before, and many of the women who came to me had been to their doctor but weren't taken seriously, or they had tried all manner of medical interventions without success, or had had their symptoms dismissed or ignored.' Aisha explains that because she trained in so many different modalities, she has been able to help a plethora of women who present with complaints of chronic pain, for example, to address underlying emotional issues that could be a root cause. 'When people have chronic pain and have been to their GP and tried different things or are on anti-anxiety medication or anti-depressants or strong painkillers, but nothing works, I look to emotional issues. Often it turns out there might be trauma from their childhood, sexual abuse, anything emotional that has happened to them. And that's where my energy healing and hypnotherapy comes into play. Trying to dig and peel away the layers to achieve healing by getting to the underlying source of the problem. Once we've done that work, very often the issue resolves itself.'

Aisha never set out to create a Muslim service, and although 90 per cent of her clients are Muslim, she does not incorporate spirituality into her treatments or in any way exclude non-Muslims. Hers is a women-only service, and clients are referred via word of mouth, often through family networks. News of Aisha's holistic services rippled through Keighley's tight-knit Pakistani community as clients who found the treatments benefitted them told cousins, sisters-in-law, aunties, mothers, daughters and nieces. As the practice grew organically, awareness of the connections between physical health, emotional health and mental health also grew among Muslim women in Keighley. The clinic became a safe space in which women could speak openly and honestly about their lives and their problems. Therapeutic services, where they did exist, had tended to be offered in the practitioner's home, or the service provider would offer home visits, which did not offer the privacy and confidentiality of the clinic. Aisha's background in psychology also helped her to work with her clients on well-being issues, and her multilingual skills in speaking Urdu and Punjabi, as well as the fact that she was embedded in the community, put the women at ease, particularly the older generation. Many women who came to the clinic had never before been able to express their emotions candidly in their mother tongue. Recognising the power of talking therapies alongside hypnotherapy and energy healing, Aisha pursued extra training in a range of techniques and practices to be able to help people with emotional and psychological ailments. Initially she was reticent about being too open about her work in energy healing, as it can be misunderstood as being associated with jinns and black magic. She would only introduce energy healing as a potential treatment after she had worked with a client for a little while and built up a level of trust. 'It's something that is difficult to explain to people—even I sometimes can't get my head around how effective it is. It's not something that is tangible or something that you can feel. It's the unseen world.' However, Aisha makes certain that her treatments remain within the boundaries of Islamic teachings, and therefore there are some practices she has avoided.

The sisterhood Aisha has experienced among fellow practitioners is nowhere more apparent than in the work she does using

Mizan therapy, a therapeutic practice with an emphasis on abdominal massage through the use of herbs and other traditional methods, such as castor oil packs, yoni steaming and sacred wrapping, all to bring the body back into balance. It is for both men and women and can help people to manage a multitude of conditions. '*Mizan*' in Arabic means 'balance', and this is at the core of Mizan therapy. 'In bonding together to improve the lives of women, from my training to my practice, I felt like I was part of a family of sisters that truly dedicates itself to healing women,' says Aisha. 'Having suffered from polycystic ovary syndrome for most of my adult life and suffered infertility for six years after the birth of my first child, this was something very close to my heart, which I wanted to do very much.' Such topics used to be taboo, and yet Muslim women are now finding a way to reach into their painful experiences and uplift each other with empathy or practical help and resources.

Being heard or being taken seriously in mainstream spaces has not always been a typical experience, and additionally, some Muslim women have found their female family members do not offer them the sanctuary they are seeking. I spoke to Muslim women who would tell me that however loving and devoted their mothers were, they would display an almost unconscious preference for their sons. As I walked along an inner-city canal pathway with Selina, she told me that there is a particularly endearing form of addressing someone in Bengali pronounced '*tui*'. Selina, one of a family of four sisters and one brother, said that her mother only spoke in this warm, loving tone with her brother. 'I've noticed it over the years, and although I wouldn't say it upsets me, it's just something I've picked up on.' I asked Selina whether she had ever thought about mentioning it to her mum, but she said she didn't want to make a big deal about it and that she didn't think it was deliberate. 'It's perhaps just a reflection of how she's been brought up to relate to the idea of a son. After all, he is an only son, and is so very cherished and wanted.' Selina did mention the matter to her brother, however. 'He was quite shocked,' she told me, 'and said he had never noticed. I think he felt quite bad and tried to play it down.'

Another young woman I spoke to said that her husband's mother had done everything for him his entire life, and she realised that this had left him unable to navigate conflict and have disagreements with other women. He expected his wife to emotionally interact with him in the same way that his mother did, which was to be very servile and to take his shouting and ranting as if it were an acceptable way to speak to someone. 'But of course, that is not a healthy way to communicate in a relation-ship,' the woman told me. 'Although his mother would do everything for him, almost acting like a martyr, she would use emotionally manipulative tactics to claw back some sense of power over her situation, such as refusing to talk to her son, sometimes for days, when she was upset or angry. This imma-ture way of interacting was normalised in the family and meant he himself was emotionally stunted.'

In Glawogger's documentary, women form solidarity networks and emulate power structures that give them some semblance of control in their lives. But there is still a compromise, and the structures they are emulating or navigating are patriarchal in nature or reality. However hard one attempts to break the cycle, there is a hangover that lingers. My friend's twelve-year-old daughter remarked to her one day that her nine-year-old brother was obviously their grandmother's favourite. My friend was upset to hear this, because while she herself was growing up, she had always felt that her brother was the favourite compared with her and her sister. It shook her that this feeling of being less loved was being passed on to her daughter. She gently brought it up with her mother, who was mortified that her granddaughter felt that way but was oblivious to the way she was treating the males in her family favourably.

SOLIDARITY WITH MY SISTERS

Showing solidarity with my sisters takes many forms. However flawed, compromised, earnest, intentional or coincidental our efforts, these efforts are ours. They are valid. We celebrate them. We create space, we give hope, and we honour those who came before, whose fight we continue. We seek out our networks where we can find them. We build, we fight, and we hold space. This is solidarity.

4

RED PILLED

In March 2021, the market town of Batley in West Yorkshire found itself splashed across UK national news headlines.[1] A teacher at a secondary school there had, as part of a lesson on free speech, allegedly shown his class a cartoon of the Prophet Muhammad. The image was taken from the controversial French satirical newspaper *Charlie Hebdo* and depicted the Prophet wearing a turban that was hiding a bomb. A Muslim parent complained, and the teacher was immediately suspended pending an inquiry. What should have been a matter for the school to investigate and resolve sensitively became a stage upon which actors of the so-called culture wars of our times played out their drama. Proponents of freedom of expression were in uproar, while hysterical media reporting led to burgeoning anti-blasphemy protests outside the school gate seemingly led by people with no direct connection to the incident. The teacher, warmly described by right-wing tabloids as a 'rugby-loving, burly, Yorkshire lad', was said to fear for his life after receiving death threats.[2] With a chill, thoughts turned to the horrific murder of teacher Samuel Paty in France, beheaded after a similar accusation that he had shown *Charlie Hebdo* images to his school pupils. The number of protesters, mostly young Muslim men from outside the area, began to swell. Commentators of all stripes and persuasions derided the group and swiftly conflated them with anyone expressing concern at the teacher's actions. This 'mob' and its tacit cheerleaders were dismissed as ignorant and reactionary, an affront to British values of free speech and tolerance. Hand-wringing at what must be done to counter the likes of such fanatics and their ilk rebounded. After all, weren't these crazed men letting the side down and feeding anti-Muslim sentiment with their emotive and irrational response?

Elsewhere, former Conservative Party co-chairwoman Baroness Warsi was tweeting her own response to the blasphemy furore. Having spoken to those involved, she indicated that objection to the use of the cartoons arose because it created 'a hostile atmosphere and led to Islamophobic discourse and language'.[3] Pupils had been left upset. 'Islamophobic bullying in the playground is well documented and taunts such as "terrorist" are regularly used leading to issues around mental health and poor educational outcomes,' she wrote.[4] This resonated with me. I remember, as a youngster at my predominantly white grammar school in leafy, middle-class Surrey, sitting through a lesson on immigration. The ugly and unmediated views that were unexpectedly unleashed by classmates I had hitherto considered to be my friends left me and the only other non-white girl in the class in tears. The teacher was unwilling or unable to challenge the racist rhetoric and bigoted attitudes being bandied around, having given little thought to how, after introducing the topic, it should evolve into a constructive discussion.

Warsi's attempt to contextualise the incident was an exception amidst the barrage of sensationalised column inches and hot takes. The saga was caricatured as yet another battle in the culture wars and sinkholes in discourse around Muslim communi-

ties, as Warsi herself recognised on BBC Radio 4's *Today* programme, saying, 'Unfortunately this matter has been hijacked by
extremists on both sides, to, kind of, create this culture war.'[5]
That she should evoke this trend whereby incidents are framed
as symbolic of a deep cultural schism irrevocably dividing society
is telling. Certainly, the media and various political stakeholders
have decided that culture wars are an unquestionable plague rav-
aging the supposed cohesion of our communities. Just as extremists are said to have jumped on their respective bandwagons in
Batley's blasphemy quagmire, radicals are blamed for playing a
dangerous and intractable game of cultural tug-of-war, which
leaves the apparently sensible middle ground floundering.

But who are these so-called radicals, and what is their agenda?
Their depiction in the media brought to my mind Peter Morey
and Amina Yaqin's study of the intersections between the constructs of masculinity and fanaticism and their culmination in the
ubiquitous 'folk devil' stereotype, this time in the image of a
young, bearded, South Asian, male fanatic dubbed 'Islamic Rage
Boy', his face contorted in hate, spitting bile and oozing 'toxic
masculinity' long before the term had become the zeitgeist.[6]
Islamic Rage Boy became a meme in the post-9/11 online world,
a caricature of the violent Islamist terrorist, filled with vitriol for
anything that represents Western values, and confirming all the
worst prejudices about Muslim men. His face was used entirely
without consent or context, of course, an archetype plastered
online by bloggers and media outlets to illustrate murderous
Islamist rage. But who is the young man in the picture? Born in
Indian-administered Kashmir, he is an activist agitating against
the military occupation there, which has led to several periods
spent in detention. His name is Shakeel Ahmad Bhat, and he
frequently attends protests, notably one against the Danish cartoons that made a mockery of the Prophet in 2005. It was a pho-
tograph taken at this event that led his image to be picked up by

right-wing websites and to go on to adorn satirical merchandise. In a 2007 interview, Bhat told *Guardian* journalist Riazat Butt that although it was 'not nice' to see his face made an object of ridicule, becoming a ubiquitous Islamophobic stereotype was the least of his problems.[7] Living in a securitised region meant his focus was on the material conditions of his family and community, not his 15 minutes of fame in Western popular culture.[8]

The Islamic Rage Boy persona is almost certainly an early iteration of what we now perceive as toxic masculinity, and specifically its associations with Muslim men. The notorious stories of grooming gangs in areas of the North of England such as Oldham and Rochdale saw groups of mostly Pakistani-heritage men befriend vulnerable girls, some as young as thirteen, before coercing them into abusive relationships and passing them around to other men for forced sexual encounters. The scandal exploded onto the news agenda in 2010, amidst cries of a cover up and claims that the failure to act earlier was due to the police's and social services' fear of being labelled racist.[9] The story inevitably impacted South Asian men who had nothing to do with crimes perpetrated by a minority in their communities. Anwar is from a large, close-knit, working-class, Mirpuri family in Keighley and was a teenager when the arrests were made. He told me that he had known an older man in the community who 'was caught up in all that business' but had returned to Pakistan before authorities became involved. 'He was in on the drugs. Doing business selling it and that. There were girls who would hang around 'cause him and his associates threw cash their way, and it [went] from there.' Anwar believed the grooming scandal was exaggerated by racists to leave all the men in his community judged and vilified. 'I would go to white areas and people would look at me like I was out to rape white girls. Taxi drivers had it the worst. They get that much abuse from drunk pricks anyway, and they're decent family men who go mosque. Now they're treated like perverts. That's not dignity. They go for a fare and get told "not Asians" right to their face.'

As recently as April 2023, British Prime Minister Rishi Sunak claimed political correctness was preventing victims of grooming gangs from achieving justice.[10] Meanwhile right-wing Home Secretary Suella Braverman sparked outrage with her dog-whistle remarks to the media that perpetrators of the crime of group-based child sexual exploitation were 'almost all British-Pakistani' men.[11] This is despite a Home Office study finding in 2020 that 'group-based CSE offenders are most commonly White'.[12] Facts are minor details when it comes to the demonisation of Muslim men—something that Anwar's mum, after very reluctantly agreeing to speak with me, agreed with. The offender that Anwar referred to was married to one of her distant relatives. As far as Anwar's mum was concerned, the girls making accusations of grooming and rape were the sort who would have ended up as prostitutes anyway. Her defensiveness was unblinking, and her dismissal of the victims a mirror image of the dehumanisation of brown men as nothing more than terrorists/rage boys/groomers. I wondered if her strong desire to blame the victims was an effort to distract from the shame that she felt the accusations had brought upon her family. The urge for self-justification can be overwhelming when you carry the burden of guilt by association.

When I was an undergraduate at the University of Reading, my housemate was sexually assaulted by a Pakistani taxi driver. We lived at Cemetery Junction, an area popular with students due to its large houses of multiple occupancy and reasonable rents. A Pakistani community had settled there since the 1970s, and I blunderingly made efforts to forge links with locals. I gave sporadic lessons—on what subject I don't even remember—to three under-tens who lived in a neat terrace house at the end of my road. On my way to and from campus, I would come across them playing out and found them enchanting, so much so that, seeing their parents one day, I offered to tutor them. Every time I knocked on the door, the eldest child would answer and usher me in excitedly while her mother, with whom I communicated in my rudimentary Urdu, even though she only understood Mirpuri, would hurriedly run to place a toilet roll in the bathroom for me, assuming I didn't use a *lota*.

I was a disaster, as the children were beyond mischievous, and I was clueless as to how to control them, never mind teach them anything. On my third visit, the seven-year-old boy tried to kiss me. His older sister pulled him away and slapped him on the head as they both laughed. I was completely shocked. I couldn't make sense of what had led such a young child to act in that manner. I realised I had no authority over the children. I had been seized by a patronising 'do-gooder' attitude, wanting to connect with people in my area who looked like me, but without really giving it proper thought. I had been driven by a desire to help them when they were doing quite fine already actually, and I had tried to do so without really being equipped with the skills to actually teach them anything. I wasn't even sure I had the sensitivity to be a part of the cultural fabric of their lives, as I had, without even realising, become involved in a power dynamic where I positioned myself above them. In my Black American Literature course, I was studying *Native Son* by Richard Wright,[13] and I thought about Mary, the daughter of the white, wealthy family that the protagonist, Bigger Thomas, worked for. She was friendly and well-meaning, but her over-familiarity made him uncomfortable, leading to tragic results. I too had found the three children adorable and wanted better for them; I thought I knew better than their parents—perhaps I thought I *was* better than their parents. Perhaps I wanted them to be less like their parents and more like me. It was horrifying to realise my hegemonic impulse.

I remembered an unconnected conversation with my landlord, a young, British-born Pakistani man, of somewhat Salafi leanings. He told me that youngsters in the community were out of control because their mothers were from Pakistan and didn't speak English or understand the culture their children were growing up in. This was creating a disconnect between generations and a lack of respect for parents. 'In particular, kids don't respect their mothers,' he told me. Why is it always the fault of the women, I thought to myself. The fathers are out all day working. Perhaps they are taxi drivers, or in the night trade running take-aways and twenty-four-hour convenience stores. Maybe some of them are involved in the drugs trade. They're trying to earn a living for their families, but are they respectful to their wives? Or are they reinforcing misogynistic patterns of behaviour that their children go on to emulate?

I woke up one night to my housemate banging on the front door, and came downstairs as our other housemate let her in. She had been out drinking and got a taxi home. This was before Uber was a thing. Recognising the taxi driver as a friendly, middle-aged man who had driven her once or twice before, she had jumped into the front passenger seat and chatted animatedly during the short journey home. When he parked up outside our house, he told her she didn't need to pay and, pulling out his penis, pushed her head down on his lap and told her she could give him a blowjob instead. She scrambled to get out and ran. As she told us the story, I felt a prickling heat as she described him as a Pakistani taxi driver. When she re-told the story to the police, I felt something I would feel years later when there was a bomb explosion or a stabbing or any suspected terrorist incident. 'Please let it not be a Muslim. Please let the bad man not be from *my community*.' Back then I understood there to be only two communities—the white majority and the rest of us. What is with this shame by association? Does it plague us because we carry around the burden of representation, of collective responsibility? Is it because if one of us lets the side down, we can all expect to be punished, despised, hated? For many, the protesters in Batley had embarrassed 'us' with their Islamic Rage Boy toxic masculinity. Are we secretly asking ourselves why they couldn't be more intelligent, more sophisticated in their response? Was I secretly asking myself why the little kids on the street I lived on in Reading couldn't have parents that were more like me?

What is clear is that localised issues like the protests in Batley became fodder for hysteria around the reporting of incidents which, once fed into a wider narrative of toxic masculinity, speak to a malaise that cannot be discounted. Now we see the prevalence of toxic masculinity has hit headlines, and it has become a fixture in any discussion on contemporary society. But whereas toxic masculinity is assumed to be a relatively new term, the concept has been around for as long as I can remember. In 2012, I was involved in organising the Winter Gathering for the Muslim Institute on 'Men in Islam'. The keynote speaker was Amanullah de Sondy, who was delivering a paper on twentieth-century British-Pakistani masculinity, based on his PhD research.[14] I expect he had arrived in the hope that he would be able to talk through his findings with intellectual giants and would undergo a rigorous and constructive interrogation of his ideas at the Q&A. Unfortunately, one of those assumed giants exuded a certain type of toxic masculinity that held barracking and humiliating a young academic to be an appropriate method of critique. If I remember correctly, at one point he scoffed, 'who is publishing this rubbish'. De Sondy paused, gathered his notes, and with a quiet dignity walked out of the room. Merryl Wyn Davies and I rushed after him with a flurry of apologies as he disappeared into the lift. Some amends were later made and apologies reluctantly offered. The event would become a staple in the folklore of the Muslim Institute's history, and we would chuckle at the fireworks. 'Ah well, this is the entertainment we expect and indulge from the middle-aged characters who make up the Institute's inner circle.' I would laugh along with the others, making excuses and offering platitudes, while deep down knowing that this was not a safe space for those who didn't conform to the rigid notions of masculinity championed by those who claimed ownership over the organisation. De Sondy had attempted to deconstruct the notion that there is one ideal Muslim masculinity, and in that clash, we saw a glimpse into the future.

Since that incident, the concept of toxic masculinity has embedded itself deep into discourse on ailments plaguing Muslim communities.[15] From the Muslim 'manosphere' to Red Pill and incel culture, this worldview has been taking hold in Muslim communities, virtual, real and otherwise. While right-wing activists seized on the phenomenon of the Asian grooming gangs, Islamic Rage Boy and the 'mob' of anti-blasphemy pro-testers to illustrate a threat to 'British values', an exception seems to apply when it comes to toxic masculinity that aligns with the alt-right agenda. Anti-immigration obsession connects to a desire to preserve white, Anglo-Saxon culture from 'creeping Shariah' and the influence of the global south. But such preoc-cupations fall away when perpetrators of toxic masculinity serve as useful distractions from competing agendas.

This is nowhere more evident than in the case of Andrew Tate.[16] A British-American kickboxer, he rose to infamy in 2016 after a brief appearance on the reality television show *Big Brother*. While he was in the *Big Brother* house, video footage of Tate slapping and whipping a former girlfriend surfaced, prompting his removal. He later claimed the incident was consensual, as did she. But what we had seen was a glimpse into the violent misog-yny that characterised his personal life. Tate and other personali-ties, including the likes of Canadian author and commentator Jordan Peterson,[17] use social media to offer advice they claim will empower men around the world. They offer men guidance to succeed in the pursuit of the life goals that they determine every 'real' man should aspire to: accruing wealth and women. They advocate reverting to 'traditional gender roles' that put men in charge, with Tate frequently using degrading and violent language in relation to women, calling them intrinsically lazy, referring to them as the property of men, and declaring that they aren't designed to be independent.

I was alerted to the insidious impact of Andrew Tate in 2019, when I first started thinking about the relevance of notions of toxic masculinity for any discussion of misogyny. His name frequently came up on social media, particularly in niche, now deleted communities on Reddit, where men would spend hours spouting hate against women and blaming them for all their ills. Other than an investigation by *The Daily Beast*,[18] the Red Pill movement and manosphere were yet to grab the headlines they do now. However, when Tate moved to Romania, setting up his now infamous Hustler's University, there was considerable excitement amongst his fans, and his activities and influence seemed to become more co-ordinated.[19] This was soon after Cathy Newman's explosive interview with Jordan Peterson on *Channel 4 News*, in which he refused to acknowledge the existence of a gender pay gap, all while making outlandish claims about gender norms. Despite this bruising interview, Peterson's popularity soared while Newman became a hate-figure on social media, in a campaign she describes in a *Guardian* interview from that time as 'semi-organised'.[20] Tate's Hustler's University was not unlike a pyramid scheme, which incentivised members to recruit more members, who would in turn upload content to recruit even more members, and so on. Although Peterson, who considers himself an intellectual, sees himself as distinct from Tate's brand, it is hardly a stretch of the imagination to assume that Peterson benefits from being perceived as the thinking man's Tate.

Who are the people who occupy the Muslim manosphere? Many of the men whose posts I read online were turbo-boosted by the euphoria of finding a 'safe space' in which they could express their darkest thoughts anonymously and without censure. Most were invested in the 'Red Pill' social movement, which, repurposing a metaphor from the *Matrix* films about waking up to a hidden reality, claims to reveal that women rule the world, or if not women then the 'Matrix', a shadowy elite determined to emasculate men. The men orbiting this realm had complaints that were so vacuous they reeked of cliche. 'Men can't say anything anymore.' 'Men need to learn how to be "real" men again.' There was visceral fear of the #MeToo movement. These were lonely, unhappy men who spoke openly about being rejected by even 'low-value women' who once upon a time would have been grateful for their advances. That women were rebuffing them, or even worse, calling them out, infuriated them.

Not long after making a promise to myself that I would let any person making uninvited sexually charged comments to me know that this was not welcome, I told a man who cat-called me as I was coming out of my house that I didn't appreciate his remarks. I explained that all I wanted to do was go about my business unmolested. 'I know you think it's a compliment, but for me it's really not. I don't understand what gives you the right to make a comment about a woman's appearance, a woman you don't know, who is just going about her day.' He went red and spluttered something. Then he said I looked like his grandma anyway. I burst out laughing, and suddenly Paddy from George Orwell's *Down and Out in Paris and London* came to my mind: 'He looked at women with a mixture of longing and hatred ... A couple of scarlet-lipped old creatures would go past; Paddy's face would flush pale pink, and he would turn and stare hungrily after the women. "Tarts!" he would murmur.'[21] The men in the manosphere remind me of Paddy, and the guy I (perhaps belligerently) decided to 'school' that day. As commentators such as Amia Srinivasan have explored, these men are lonely and feel hopeless and unloved, which leads to a resentment for what they feel they cannot access.[22] They attribute their unhappiness to a rapid social change in the arena of sex and romance. Men speak of being 'involuntary celibates' because of women's liberation and become consumed with the belief it is ruining their lives.

In the years spent researching this book, I've found the dehumanising language used to describe women on the forums of the manosphere deeply disturbing. Almost traumatic. The violence, coupled with growing numbers, engenders confidence and self-righteousness. The hatred directed at so-called feminists and feminism is frightening, while casual racism and homophobia are rampant. The men are mostly anonymous, and only on rare occasions could I identify from their chats that they might be Muslim. However, there was enough Islamophobic content bandied around to suggest that, if they were, they were wilfully turning a blind eye to abuse. How did these heinous views capture the imagination of some Muslim online spaces, culminating in Tate's conversion to Islam and transformation into a poster boy for the Muslim manosphere? There are early clues in the way that their Islamophobia manifests itself, using stereotypical reductive language about Muslims in grudgingly admiring tones.

Such hatred of women has translated into violence. In September 2023, a fifteen-year-old girl was stabbed to death on a London street.[23] The perpetrator was allegedly a teenage boy who became enraged because the girl's friend, apparently his ex-girlfriend, rejected his attempt at a reconciliation. The day after the tragedy, I was talking with Haaniyah Angus, a twenty-five-year-old culture journalist and essayist. In the midst of a crowded room, she confided in me that her mother had recently passed away. The news stung, and I yearned to take away the pain of it all. We went and sat somewhere a little quieter. The *janazah*—funeral—was tomorrow, she told me. Family from Somalia, and across the diaspora were beginning to arrive. As a heaviness hung in the air, we talked about life and death and family and struggle. She spoke about an article she had written, which unearthed that a common theme running through patriarchal cultures was the construction of an ideal of what a man's life should look like: wife, two kids, picket fence, nice house, good job, fancy car. 'That idealised image hasn't existed since my grandparents' days, if ever,' she pointed out. Even so, 'a lot of men internalise this inadequacy growing up, not understanding it's not due to women that they aren't realising this ideal. It's because people can't afford to have those things or live this idealised life.' Haaniyah mentioned the cost of childcare as a huge deterrent to women having children, and that the cost-of-living crisis was leaving couples and individuals unable to save to buy their own home or a top-of-the-range car.

For Haaniyah, the election of Donald Trump as US president in 2016 was a turning point in normalising misogyny, and Andrew Tate represented a continuation of the same boldness to publicly articulate opinions that for decades were socially unacceptable. Figures like Tate are highly popular among younger generations, and teachers have expressed concern at the influence of their views on the behaviour and attitudes of schoolboys towards female staff and pupils. 'People think the Gen Zs [the demographic born between the late 1990s and the early 2010s] are highly progressive, but that's not true,' Haaniyah lamented. 'A fifteen-year-old girl was murdered by a teenage boy who wouldn't take no for an answer, who acted like he was entitled to this girl. You see stuff about this girl being killed and the conversations online and offline about it, and there are people actually saying, "This isn't misogyny, it's a crime of passion!" And I'm like, put two and two together: he killed her because a woman said no to him. What does that say about the culture that we're in, that a man will commit femicide? That's patriarchy, it's misogyny. We can argue semantics all day, but it is what it is.'

Haaniyah linked this misogynistic violence to the dream of the picket-fence life. Men are conditioned to expect their lives to turn out like this, she argued, and feel that women owe it to them to make it happen. When it doesn't, their disappointment turns to blame and anger. And they don't blame the systems that caused their disappointment: capitalism and free-market politics. They blame the easy target: women. 'I see it often when people say, "These girls are so ungrateful, because they want thousands in *mehr* [Islamic marriage dower]." But *mehr* exists to protect women, to provide them a safety net.' Haaniyah divides her time between Saudi Arabia, where her father works, and the UK. 'British Muslims tend to be more conservative, and I think that has a lot to do with poverty, because poverty segregates us as communities. There's nothing wrong with communities staying culturally tied together, but when it's to the point that you're so xenophobic because you don't interact with anyone outside your community, then it's a problem. But that's what poverty and Islamophobia does. If you're being attacked as a community, then you want to stand firm in your version of Islam.' The dehumanisation of Muslim men by right-wing media is predictably a precursor to their rejection of values closely identified with the community dehumanising them. And it is this dejection that the Muslim manosphere exploits.

The Muslim manosphere is comprised of various online communities including YouTubers, influencers, bloggers and forum users. They cater to different audiences, creating content with different emphases—aspirational, material, spiritual, leadership guidance. What unites them, however, is their emphasis on self-improvement, and their belief that feminism denies the innate disposition of man, or *fitrah*, based on their interpretation of scripture and the ideal example of the Prophet Muhammad.[24] As far as they are concerned, modernity has emasculated the Muslim male, to the extent that if he acts like a real man, an alpha Muslim, he stands accused of toxic masculinity.

To understand how much these ideas resonate, I spoke with Muslim men across the UK about toxic masculinity, the manosphere, the Red Pill movement and feminism. I've known Mizan, a community worker and spoken-word artist from Northwest London since he first became active in the post-9/11 landscape. A sensitive and thoughtful individual, Mizan caught my attention with a series of social media posts about Andrew Tate at the beginning of 2023. We met for tea and samosas at Regents Park Mosque after *zuhr* prayers one particularly cold March day. He told me he had very recently lost decades-long friendships over Tate after taking what he considered to be a principled stand when Tate converted to Islam. 'I do feel if you're constantly promoting things that are detrimental to other people, a politics that is racist, then I will cut you off, and that's what I had to do with some Muslim friends,' said Mizan. 'When Tate converted to Islam, all of a sudden there was a whitewashing of his past deeds. I believe that when you convert to Islam, you should acknowledge your past and put some things right. We're living in a time that's very different now. If you put things on social media which have millions of views, even if you change your views of whatever that video was, the fact that video is out there causing damage and still being spread around means you have a responsibility to renounce that video.'

Mizan's close group of male friends had formed when they had all been members of the pan-Islamist political organisation Hizb ut-Tahrir, whose stated aim is the re-establishment of the Islamic caliphate. They had frequently had lively discussions and debates, which were now mostly consigned to social media and WhatsApp chats. The split occurred when Mizan and a small group of men and women began discussing the need to call Andrew Tate to account and demand that he publicly denounce videos of himself in which he had advocated violence against women. Mizan despaired that videos of Tate declaring, 'if your girlfriend is cheating you can slice her with a machete,'[25] were still available, and that he had made no declaration since becoming Muslim that he no longer held those views, which were, after all, inimical to the teachings of Islam. The pushback Mizan got from his friends shocked him. 'My friends were privately messaging me, saying, "Oh, he's a Muslim now, give him time." I was like, time for what? It doesn't take time to renounce views and say that stabbing women with a machete is wrong. It doesn't even take a conversion to say that. It's common decency as a human being, no matter what.'

Mizan soon realised that these debates were being replicated everywhere online, in WhatsApp group chats, in private groups on Facebook, and on Twitter. In closed groups with private settings, he was discovering what many of his mostly male friends really thought. What's more, some of the same individuals were making public statements that bore no resemblance to their private comments. When he confronted his friends about the disparity between their public and private chats, he was told it was because they couldn't say what they really thought anymore because 'woke', politically correct society was policing men, particularly Muslim men. I've heard this idea repeatedly in my research. In fact, I've been hearing this from the most unexpected quarters for much of the past twenty years. 'You can't say what you think anymore.' It strikes me that the word 'woke', which originates from African-American discourse, merely means to be alert to racial prejudice and discrimination. That it has become a pejorative term to imply censorship, a foot-soldier in the war against freedom of expression, is testament to those firmly ensconced at the top of the hierarchy of power, and their resistance to any disruption of their monopoly. Words matter. Our use of language is not without responsibility. At what point is freedom of expression more important than freedom from harm? Images of the protesters at the gates of Batley Grammar School spring to mind. Are they driven by a frustration that men cannot say what they want to say anymore? Are they the poster boys of the anti-woke agenda? In this alliance of so-called anti-liberal movements, where is their outrage when their alt-right allies express racist and Islamophobic views? Does the greater goal demand they turn a blind eye?

Adam, from Bradford, is a single man in his late twenties and works in hospitality. He considers himself to be quite open-minded but feels that Tate has been monstered. He says he's watched a lot of videos by Tate and others and finds there are some generally helpful pieces of advice that he gives to men. Adam describes his family as conservative, observing strict gender segregation, something Adam finds unhealthy. Tate has stated that men need to be exposed to feminine energy and that women need to be exposed to masculine energy. 'How can Tate be a woman-hater if he says both genders need to be exposed to each other's energy?' Adam reasons. 'He also tells teenagers to be respectful to their parents.' Adam used to spend most of his spare time online, either on social media or gaming. After following Andrew Tate's advice to go to the gym and work out regularly, he feels better about himself. 'Tate's been a positive influence in my life,' he tells me. 'He's saying common-sense things that are really helping men. The problem is ultra-feminists jump on a few things he says. They're thought police. Men just want a chill wife who's gonna get on with your family, look after the house. Not be giving you stress or making demands. But if you say that, you get called a misogynist. Of course, I'm all for women's rights—Islam gave women all the rights, way before any other religion. But feminists have taken it too far.'

This is simplistic, as far as Mizan is concerned. He acknowledges that Tate offers some men practical guidance that pulls them out of a rut. What he objects to are Tate's horrifyingly misogynistic statements and his affinity with spaces in the alt-right, Red Pill, Muslim manosphere. For Mizan, the Muslim manosphere is not just misogynistic but also a deeply political movement. Even the language Tate uses, that of escaping the Matrix, is designed to obscure his positions. When he sets himself up as challenging the elites, some people assume that he's an anti-capitalist, others that he's against oppression, but for Mizan, Tate represents anti-modernity. Ironically, the solutions Tate presents those who also desire to escape modernity are themselves modern. For Mizan, that's the paradox. Tate is the cheerleader for a political movement that blames women for the many things that are in fact failures of capitalism.

It's a very potent distraction, which works, and Mizan thinks he knows why. 'The reality is that the men drawn to this movement aren't just single men who can't get a wife. There are many unhappily married men, or divorced men, and believe me, divorce is very tough on both genders. I can only speak for men, and men are hurting badly—they feel ignored, they feel they get the blame for everything. They can't do or say anything right.' Instead of choosing introspection, healing or therapy, all of which Tate and the manosphere scoff at, many of these disaffected and unhappy men have taken to blaming feminism for their problems. 'I have male friends telling me their wives have developed "a feminist outlook", and I don't know what that means. If she's talking about her rights, that's her rights. Whether you deliver them or not is another matter. The wife does need to have an understanding that living in your own house rather than with in-laws is difficult—there's a cost-of-living crisis. But this is a semi-political misogynistic movement that blames feminism for everything. It's so simplistic but incredibly easy to fall into, because it taps into people's emotions.'

Moral panics, as well as issues that invoke strong feelings in people, have long been exploited to spread fear and suspicion.[26] These emotions are difficult to reason with, since they don't constitute a rational position; instead, they play on a fear of the 'other', in this case a preconceived notion of Western feminism as the root of social ills.[27] As Mizan found with his former friends, trying to debate with people on the basis of how they feel about an issue, rather than on evidence and facts, is a losing battle. Mizan's friends expressed surprise that he was not a fan of Tate given that he too claims to be fighting against the 'elites'. But when Mizan pointed out that Tate was not talking about the multi-national capitalist elites, he realised people were confused as there are multiple definitions of who the 'elites' actually are. He tried to explain to his friends that there was a right-wing version and a left-wing version, a racist version and an anti-racist version. When the right talks about challenging the elites, they're not talking about a system which privileges them or condemns marginalised groups to poverty, but rather about liberal elites. According to Mizan, their problem with these elites is open borders, as they believe liberals are allowing immigrants to come to the West and destroy white culture. Tate's message plays with this hypothesis. His answer to the destruction of white culture is to look to authoritarian and securitised Gulf and Middle East societies. Instead of wanting to take down these elites, he endorses the lifestyles of privileged members of those communities, ignoring the migrant workers, the cleaners and the domestic workers. He valorises Dubai bling, incredibly rich Arabs in huge houses, while completely erasing the workers, the disenfranchised. For Tate, the solution would be to introduce this style of dictatorial regime in the West, as this would clamp down on debates about gender, sexuality and other so-called culture war issues that are getting the manosphere all worked up. However, he neglects to mention that dictatorships would also clamp down on all dissent and anyone who got in their way. Mizan warns that he is probably oblivious as to quite what or whom he is inviting into ascendancy.

I put this to a supporter of Tate, a nineteen-year-old student called Usman. He told me we shouldn't question Tate's sincerity

and dismissed the criticism he had heard about Tate as just conspiracy theories. But for Mizan, who has lost friends and family
members to this ideology, the traction of Tate's views across the
Muslim manosphere gives credence to a misogynistic and racist
Red Pill political movement. Usman is quick to deny that
Muslims can be part of the Red Pill movement, because according to him, it would be un-Islamic to believe in a pill that dictates whether you have access to the truth or not; only God can
wield such power over humans. But the experiences of Mizan and
others reveal that where the Muslim manosphere and the Red
Pill movement unite is their shared hatred of feminism. Mizan
agrees with Usman that there can be valid critiques of feminism
and 'gender ideology', as is the case with any ideology. The
worldview of those in the Muslim manosphere may be distaste-
ful, but Tate's followers insist they are not criminalising communities or policing anyone, and that their message is about
empowering men. At the same time, their ideology erases many
people from the landscape, and that's what Mizan and other critics of Tate find dangerous.

When asked whether Tate and his fellow manosphere inhabitants are misogynistic, the various men I spoke to offered interesting and varied responses. Mizan argues that rather than harbouring an inherent hatred of women, those in the Muslim
manosphere build a system to police women. They construct an
ideal type of woman, who will submit to their authority and
appreciate being looked after. Any woman who falls outside
these boundaries is dismissed as a 'feminist' and subjected to
dehumanising abuse. Both Mizan and Usman do not believe that
the Muslim manosphere in general and Tate in particular are
guilty of misogyny if the latter is defined as hatred of women.
What they accept is that Tate has embraced an Islam-inspired,
Western-style conservatism, whereby binary gender roles are
clearly defined. The problem arises when men and women who

are unable, or unwilling, to fulfil those roles, are viewed negatively. This is what critics of the manosphere find particularly
uncomfortable. Mizan relates it to the Muslim experience. 'It's
the same as when Muslims don't fall into certain boxes—how are
they viewed? The impact of the misogyny of Tate and Jordan
Peterson and their kind is a similar form of otherisation that we
[Muslims] in our communities experience.'

This otherisation is a factor that William Barylo, a sociologist
who has researched the Muslim manosphere, also recognises. He
similarly agrees with Haaniyah that people's mindsets have been
colonised by new forms of thinking that are exclusive to the West,
and that this has spread through dominant culture and into the
collective imaginary since the Trump presidency. 'It's a form of
colonisation, because it's a history of empire and subjects again,
while now empires have no geographical boundaries,' William
explains. Trump, coupled with the backlash against #MeToo,
Black Lives Matter and climate activism, has propelled far-right
narratives into both the public domain and populist governments
across the globe. 'This general misogynistic narrative is a reaction
to all these interrelated social movements,' says William. 'For
some reason the far right has united to agree to be against these
social movements which question the existing social order that
positions patriarchy and male supremacy at the top.'

William believes that segments of the Muslim populations in
the West embrace these narratives, even though they are aware
that the alt-right is Islamophobic and anti-Muslim. This is illustrated by the support that Jordan Peterson enjoyed among many
Muslim men, until Peterson expressed support for Israel.
Muslims aligned to the far right are undoubtedly finding it a
difficult space to navigate. 'However, many people see this as a
force that has more and more power, so they draw parallels
between what they think is their very specific interpretation of
Islam and their cultural norms and these discourses,' says

William. This has resulted, for example, in some Muslims accusing the Black Lives Matter movement of creating *fitnah*, or discord.[28] 'People are trying to bend their interpretation of Islam to fit this movement and find some validation within this dominant narrative,' William continues. This occurs at all ends of the spectrum. William tells me about Muslim travel influencers and travel bloggers who are happy to make money out of a kind of poverty porn featuring Muslims in so-called developing countries. 'I think people who are craving representation in the media or in politics, or financial stability ... are seeking ways to be accepted by those they perceive to have power,' he says. 'Social media is an exacerbation of the currents we are already seeing in the collective imaginary, and I am seeing people just jumping on the bandwagon.'

As far as the eclectic inhabitants of the manosphere are concerned, their work is addressing a genuine concern that society is in moral decline. They see themselves as trying to lift people off this path to hopeless depravity. Yet, at the same time, their positions seem out of kilter with notions of social justice and equity. Jordan Peterson has stated he doesn't believe in systemic racism, and Tate seems to hold a similar view. In an interview with Piers Morgan, Tate was asked what he would do about knife crime. He proposed deporting convicts to an island to give them what he termed 'tough love'. Mizan's former friends lauded this in their group chat. Mizan pointed out that such a plan is nothing more than neoliberal fantasy and does nothing to help marginalised groups. It in fact harms them while making the 'elites' rich. Essentially, what such a policy would look like is the removal of people from predominantly non-white and immigrant communities to privately financed prisons that aren't held accountable by governments or human rights legislation. It would be turned into an industry without addressing the root cause of the problem, something Mizan compares with Prevent counter-terror legislation, which, he explains, ultimately caused serious harm to Muslims.

The reality is that Tate's politics, despite being born of the failures and decline of capitalism, simplistically blames the feminist movement for the breakdown of societal norms and traditions while employing pro-capitalist solutions in a perpetual cycle of disorientation. This can only occur with the complicity of fans of the manosphere. When Tate wrote that reading books is for losers, Mizan posted his outrage in the group chat. At first his former friends were adamant that the comment must have come from a fake account. When they reluctantly agreed that it had in fact been Tate, they sought to excuse his words or find reasons to justify what he said. Eventually, Mizan found dealing with his friends' confirmation bias exhausting, and after a final blow-out where he was accused of being brainwashed by liberal feminism, to which he responded that the adulation of Tate was cult-like, he knew those decades-old friendships had to end for the sake of his mental health.

Why are the views of Tate so widespread now? What is it about our contemporary moment that makes Tate such a runaway success among Muslim men and across wider society? I asked Mizan whether the reason could be that men were experiencing a crisis in masculinity. He replied without hesitating: 'Men have always been lost. If Andrew Tate had been around twenty years ago, he would have had traction even then. This is not some sort of kneejerk reaction to the #MeToo movement, although the #MeToo movement has certainly caused genuine fear. Men are taking the failures of capitalism and blaming the loss of idealised visions of women on feminism, saying it has destroyed the harmony that once existed when each gender knew their place.' Anti-feminist rhetoric about the destruction of gender roles and traditional families harks back to a time that probably didn't even exist. Tate and his ilk are signalling they want to go back in time. But there was no perfect time. 'Yes, in the 1950s traditional families were more prevalent, but the British Empire was also around, and racism was blatant. You want all that too?' Mizan asks. 'You want to go back there because these groups of people [who don't conform to traditional gender roles] are invisible. It's not as if they didn't exist—they were just hidden and suffering the pain of hiding their true selves.'

Men who find sanctuary in the manosphere are vulnerable to such biases because their experience of the other may be limited. If a young man's only perceptions about women are that they are very materialistic and care about nothing except their careers, he might think that this is what feminism looks like. I watched a video of another popular Muslim YouTuber, Ali Dawah, in full flow at Speakers' Corner in Hyde Park. He was debating a seventeen-year-old girl in hijab who had taken exception to his statement that a husband should feel upset if a wife declines to have sex with him. The girl was apoplectic, saying a husband had no right to demand sex from his wife on tap and that it would be misogynistic to feel upset by such a refusal. It was Mizan who had told me about this video. It had been forwarded to him by the same friends he had broken contact with. 'Look, a man can't even feel upset. See these feminists,' they had said. 'She's a seventeen-year-old. If you ask any seventeen-year-old girl, she would say the same,' Mizan replied. In his view, the girl was young and opinionated and likely still figuring out her thoughts and ideas, without having the real-life experience to base anything on. Eventually, an elderly woman had become involved in the debate and said Islam grants a woman the right to refuse sex in certain circumstances, such as when she is on her period, and in these cases a husband should not feel upset. Mizan told his friends, 'She [the older woman] is actually the feminist. The seventeen-year-old is being a seventeen-year-old. Ali Dawah is barely a few years older than the seventeen-year-old. This is not a sensible debate and is not about feminism.'

Zaf has just finished his A-Levels and is spending his summer working at an Instagram-famous restaurant in East London until he goes to university to begin a degree in engineering. While he was making my coffee, he was telling his colleague that the criminal charges against Andrew Tate (he was charged by Romanian authorities for rape and human trafficking) were a conspiracy to punish Muslim men for being real men. He believes Tate is right, that women are materialistic and just want to marry a rich guy so they can live like a 'princess'. He said that before he started watching Tate's videos, he was shy around girls, but now he realises they are 'basically dumb'. I was taken aback by his logic and anger. I asked him if that was how he viewed his mother, who was a housewife, and who, like his dad, was born in Bangladesh. 'Of course not,' he replied, but without explaining why. I asked him if he knew any women apart from his mum. He didn't have sisters and went to an all-boys secondary school, but he had two female friends from primary school that he was still in touch with. They were 'cool' and 'just normal', he said, not like the women Tate describes. His female cousins were still young, so he had no strong opinion about them.

Zaf's anger seemed to be directed at the women customers at the restaurant he worked at. 'Look at them, it's embarrassing,' he told me. 'They come only to take photos to put on Instagram. Their conversations are pure gossiping, and 90 per cent don't seem to do anything with their lives except look at their phones or gossip. Hearing them chatting makes me depressed about civilisation. They're airheads, really superficial and fake. They wear hijab but they might as well not bother. Can you imagine being married to a woman like them?' Zaf had formed the most dehumanising and reductive opinions about these women, who he said treated him badly at work. 'They speak to me like I'm a piece of shit because they look down on me. Yeah, I'm a waiter, but they're the ones that don't have any class.' Isn't this the loss of dignity that capitalism's service industry brings about for its workers? Zaf must acquiesce to his customers, with whom he never meaningfully engages, only transactionally interacting with them in a dance of hegemony and power dynamics. This is how othering dehumanises.

My conversation with Zaf reminded me of when I spent four months in Egypt, well before the fall of Mubarak and the 25 January revolution. Keen for a quiet interlude from the beautiful chaos of Cairo, I headed for Dahab. A former Bedouin village on the southeast coast of the Sinai Peninsula, it was a backpacker's paradise. I felt more drawn to places like Dahab, or its nearby sister Basata, than to the machinery of resorts such as Sharm el-Sheikh. Sitting at a cafe at sunset, I heard the call to prayer and asked the owner if there was a nearby mosque that had space for women. He was not expecting this query from me. I was not identifiably Muslim, I didn't speak Arabic (though I was trying to learn!), and tourists were not usually looking for prayer spaces. He directed me to an area at the back of the cafe and said I could perform my *maghreb* prayers there. He watched intently while I did so, perhaps intrigued, perhaps unsure if I really was Muslim. When I had finished (I did not take my time), he said local women didn't traditionally work in the tourist trade as it was not a decent place for them. That encounter makes me think about the way that tourism corrodes local customs, how proud communities such as the Bedouin became dependent on servitude to make a living, and about my complicity in this. I think about Zaf and his contempt for the Instagrammers and influencers who patronise the restaurant in which he works, the women he must serve but secretly despises. I think about Paddy in *Down and Out in Paris and London*, and I think about the young family in Reading, whom I felt such an urge to 'improve' and 'save'.

Yet sometimes, the urge to improve and save can mean the difference between social exclusion and thriving in society. Rakin

Fetuga is head of religious education and ethics at a secondary school in North London. He has worked in education since 2000 and runs an organisation called Save Our Boys, mentoring boys and their families to stay in education and avoid being lured into joining gangs. Working as a learning mentor with disengaged young people, he believes there is an issue with men in general. 'The idea of toxic masculinity has been thrown around a great deal, and there are many great men who feel stereotyped,' he says. 'But there is also an issue in Islam of men not treating women well. It comes from a misinterpretation of Islam where they feel that women are there to serve men, which is not correct. Both men and women are equal in the eyes of Allah. But in some Muslim cultures, they have a view where women are seen as second-class citizens.'

The Andrew Tate phenomenon seems to be pervasive. Walking from the station to my home in Southeast London, I coincided with the end of the school day. As children chattered excitedly around me, I unmistakably heard a small girl, not more than ten years old, mention Andrew Tate. I didn't manage to catch much of the rest of the conversation, as the girl skipped off with her friends. But what a topic of conversation for a youngster. Could she or her friends have watched his videos? Or perhaps her teacher had addressed Tate's views in a lesson. The former kickboxing champion has been a cause for concern among teachers all around the UK. And while schools have strived to tackle misogynistic attitudes towards women and girls for decades, the popularity of Tate has not gone unnoticed, as well as the sexually aggressive language and imagery that has become more mainstream among young boys.

Shazia, twenty-nine, is a teacher. After getting divorced, she moved from London back to the family home where she had grown up in Dewsbury. She joined a teaching agency and did supply work in secondary schools in the area. The behaviour of schoolboys seemed to have become more challenging than she had previously remembered. More than once, she would hear of an incident of a boy being punished for talking casually about rape or being accused of threatening to rape a female teacher or fellow pupil. Each time, she said, the boys would say they hadn't meant to frighten or scare women or girls. Parents would plead that their son had spoken in anger or frustration and didn't realise the gravity of his words. The nefarious influence of social media and YouTube was cited. Typically, young boys were using sexually violent language they had picked up online without fully understanding what the words meant. Once, I was discussing my research on the manosphere with a friend when her nine-year-old son stopped us and proudly explained that he knew all about Andrew Tate and the Matrix. My friend was horrified, but I told her this was not unusual, and she needn't be concerned if she made sure to take the opportunity to speak with her son about the manosphere.

At one of the schools in Dewsbury, Shazia was chatting to a white female teacher who wondered whether the mostly Pakistani-origin Muslim boys at the school were drawn to the likes of Tate because his conservative and misogynistic ideology aligned with traditional Islamic teachings they received in the home. Shazia felt herself bristling against the stereotyping of Muslim communities and at how easy it is to demonise Muslim men. In the early 2000s, I was working as an editor for a disability charity in Croydon in South London, and small talk in the office turned to a boat carrying migrants moored off the coast of Australia that was not allowed to disembark. One of the directors said he understood why Australia would not wish to let these mostly Muslim men into their country, because Muslim men are more likely to be rapists than non-Muslims. I was shocked and humiliated. He was dehumanising Muslim men. Men such as my father and my brother. Men I loved. I made sure to call him out, only for his male fragility to erupt, as he called me over-sensitive and said I was taking things too personally.

Yet, it's hard to deny that the alt-right has found a ripe constituency for its most extreme visions in Muslim communities. This is where we say it's complicated, as Amia Srinivasan writes in *The Right to Sex*. After all, we all think we know what we mean when we talk about intersectionality. But do we?

> To reduce intersectionality to a mere attention to difference is to forgo its power as a theoretical and practical orientation ... any liberation movement that focuses on what all members of the relevant group (women, working class, people of colour etc) have in common is a movement that will best serve those in the group who are least oppressed.[29]

Much has been made of the lack of imagination currently plaguing the left, leading to the haemorrhaging of political and ideological support that is being mopped up by the alt-right. In both the diaspora and Muslim-majority contexts, anti-colonial struggles found a natural ally in radical leftist movements. The secularism of many post-colonial liberation campaigns complicated this synergy, as did atrocities by communist states such as China against religious minorities. However, the impact of 9/11 and the War on Terror proved seismic. Muslim communities found themselves cast as suspect, and once again the left offered solidarity in response. The alt-right began to increasingly view this unity with disdain, orchestrating a moral panic that pitted 'woke' leftists, fanatical Muslims and 'politically correct', self-loathing, anti-Western propagandists against the purveyors of freedom of speech, patriotism and national pride. The culture wars were manufactured, and Muslims took their positions.

The ebbing of popular support to the alt-right among Muslim communities can be somewhat explained by the strong appeal to shared family values. The left may offer political and material relief, but the ideology and values that it promotes will hurt you in the *akhirah*, or afterlife, it is claimed. All that needs to be done is to overlook Islamophobia, as well as the West's invasions, occupations and wars in Muslim societies, for Muslims to join the shared vision of social conservatism. Rakin feels there is a lot of confusion in British society about what it is to be a man, and that there is also what he calls an 'extreme part in the feminist movement which is against men altogether, so slogans like "men are trash" and "fuck-boy" are thrown around'. Girls are outperforming boys in schools, and Rakin believes this is because many of the subjects that boys traditionally enjoyed and thrived in, such as carpentry, metalwork, and design and technology, have been dropped. His view is that the rise of Andrew Tate is because young males are not sure where they fit in. 'They feel they are misunderstood, and they feel society is against them,' Rakin says. Meanwhile, Tate drives expensive cars and isn't afraid to say what he thinks. 'Many young boys are gravitating towards him, especially if they don't have any positive role models in their life.'

The shift in political allegiance can be traced to a crisis in modernity. However, this doesn't explain why right-wing figures such as Andrew Tate are deemed to be the solution. Rakin is of the opinion that social media is instrumental. 'Depression, anxiety and low self-esteem have risen to unprecedented levels since the introduction of [social media],' he says. 'Young Muslims are using social media to create new identities that are different from their parents. Social media is also dangerous because there are so many voices on there. Many young Muslims are gravitating to the Salafi/Wahhabi type of Islam, because many of the largest influencers follow this rigid and problematic form of Islam.'

The crisis in modernity is something that Momodou Taal, a British-Gambian PhD student at Cornell University, who spent seven years studying Arabic and Islamic Studies at Al-Azhar in Egypt, feels is relevant. The Muslim manosphere often comes up for discussion on his popular podcast, *The Malcolm Effect*, and it is here that I first heard him advocating for a Muslim response, rather than the current trend to take the lead from right-wing reactionary sources.[30] Momodou believes that critiques of modernity from Black thinkers are the most effective resource for those struggling with such questions. He argues that the maturity of Muslim communities in the West is limited, and that since we are working through and within modernity, the idea that we can be free of modernity is a myth, as the *deen* (religion) is interpreted through time and place. Abstracting ourselves from the West and modernity can be comforting, particularly at this stage of our uneven development, but it is ultimately a destructive myth for Muslim communities.

Similarly, as part of an event at the Bradford Literature Festival, Hizer Mir explored the article he co-wrote with Sahar Ghumkhor on the Muslim manosphere.[31] Mir explained that this group, dubbed 'alt-wallahs', are not an aberration of our contemporary context. They are the next logical step of an umbrella of thinkers, which includes scholars such as Hamza Yusuf and Timothy Winter (Abdul Hakim Murad), across the Muslim world who believe that a decline in Islamic societies was precipitated when traditional Islam became undermined by influences such as postmodernism, Wahhabism, Marxism and other doctrines they consider corrupting and corrosive. This has morphed into a fixation with the figure of the feminist, and Muslim women are now the focus of this so-called decline. The declinists lament the loss of traditional Islam, or what they view as 'authentic' Islam, and are convinced that feminism has destroyed the family structure, emasculated men, spread chaos and depravity and led to the collapse of Muslim communities.

Online influencers constitute the next logical step. They spout moral outrage on social media for clicks and notoriety. Their followers, who are often detrimentally impacted by the very worst aspects of social media that Rakin highlights, may genuinely believe their arguments that a crisis of masculinities is plaguing the modern world. But, for Momodou, the underlying reasons for this are not simplistic assertions about feminism and women being evil, but about disenfranchisement caused by neoliberalism and capitalism. It is in this way that a Muslim response can bring hope. 'There's not enough of a recognition that Muslims have been decolonised, and that in the colonisation process the whole world order changed,' he tells me. 'How we understand gender and race changed. Modernity changed relations, and somehow people believe that those relations are Islamic.' Momodou suggests that we first ask ourselves what modernity is, what modernity ushered in, and where modernity is located. We can look back now and reasonably argue that 1492 saw the tilt in power from the East to the West, when Christopher Columbus landed in the Caribbean and Muslims were driven out of Spain. What would a response of a conquered people be? For Momodou, the key lies in centring those who are traditionally marginalised.

I think of the Muslim social worker from the community helpline who said she believes there is historical trauma in our communities, which is being passed down. She explained that to have a basic understanding of patriarchy, we need to examine how it is produced by the systems and structures which prop up society. Growing numbers of Muslim men are reaching out to charities, NGOs and social services because they are suffering trauma from structural racism or family dysfunction, many of them already scarred by the dislocation of exile. Previously, they didn't know what to do about it, but now they are able to access the resources available to them and figure out the best way to help themselves. In a cultural context where critical thinking and questioning tradition and conventions are strongly discouraged, men are still looking for quick fixes to their complex problems.

This is one of the reasons why they are rather passively absorbing the messages of the likes of Andrew Tate, or choosing to hit the gym and sculpt their bodies rather than engage in difficult self-reflection.

Fauzia Ahmad, a sociologist researching Muslim families, believes men are just as much victims of the patriarchy as women. 'People have such high expectations in terms of looks, physique, status, and not everyone can live up to such pressures. They put so much emphasis on marriage completing half their *deen*, but aren't thinking about what they need to do to sort themselves out first. If you decide to "do the work" and choose not to follow the path to become a toxic or "manly man", [and if you are] kind and soft-hearted, you are told you are perceived as not a real man.' Women have also been taught to appreciate powerful men and may overlook sensitive and considerate men, she points out. 'There are all kind of other dynamics that are at play with this so-called "gender war". We have the hyper-feminists and the hyper-masculine traits, and it makes me wonder where there is going to be a meeting of the minds. Each gender is so quick to critique the other and to dismiss and denigrate their attitudes. "Feminism" is viewed as a slur in certain circles of Muslim men and women. How we think about Muslim female empowerment, and the language we use to talk about hegemonic masculinity, requires thoughtful discussion without descending into toxicity.'

Fauzia explains that there has been an emphasis on women's experiences, including in her own research, but what she now realises is that there is a lot of sadness among men as well. Many decent men don't live up to the archetypal ideal in terms of looks, income, personality and status, and this leads to a deep depression. Mizan said he has been told by Muslim women that he is not the alpha-male, masculine type of man they would ideally like to marry. Yet he has also been told by Muslim women that all men are trash and that he can't be any different. Some men feel compelled to manage their sense of dysfunction by asserting their power, declaring, 'I am in charge,' while feeling psychologically and spiritually powerless. The Muslim manosphere is quick to exploit this confusion. How can someone feel good about themselves and in control when the structures within which you exist are oppressive? The easiest way to feel powerful is to dominate those perceived to be lower down in the hierarchy: your sister, your wife, your mother. This is indoctrinated. A healthy and empowered woman is confident, knows her worth, and will not stand for that, but she becomes branded a difficult woman, and feminism is deemed the catch-all cause for men's problems. Each camp is speaking to limited audiences, and what is lacking is compassion and humanising the other.

Despite the manosphere's best efforts to convince us otherwise, feminism is a distraction, not the cause. Racism and Islamophobia dehumanise Muslim men, and without recourse to justice and empowerment, the mob, as caricatured in Batley, will have their voices distorted and their attentions re-directed to the easiest targets modernity can apply.

5

YOU ARE GARMENTS FOR ONE ANOTHER

'You were talking about having a career. The Aunty moves five spaces away from you.' 'Your 24-year-old-sister just had her fourth child. The Aunty moves five spaces closer to you.' The figurative Aunty is tracking three marriage-age young women and assessing their suitability for betrothal to eligible young men in this light-hearted board game, where the clue is in the name: Arranged![1] Devised by Nashra Balagamwala, the game explores the machinery surrounding society's attempts to attract the positive attention of matchmakers and therefore secure the best possible spouse for their son or daughter.

Nashra grew up in Karachi, Pakistan, as part of a conservative Memon family. She describes being raised to be exactly the type of girl a matchmaker would consider quality marriage material. But when she actually started being noticed by the all-powerful Aunty-jis, she balked at their attention. 'The first time I was approached by a matchmaker was at my sister's wedding, when I was eighteen years old,' she tells me. 'She greeted me with the whole "you're next", and I quickly switched a ring I was wearing to my wedding finger and pretended I was engaged.' With her older sister married, Nashra found herself thrust into the lime-light and needing to come up with more outlandish reasons to evade meeting potential husbands. At one point she cut her hair short. Another time, knowing that matchmaking aunties fetish-ise white skin, she generously applied bronzer to avoid being prized as fair. 'I just kept playing games in my own head and entertaining myself to make the future look less bleak.'

Buying herself some time, having persuaded her parents not to consider marrying her off until she had turned twenty-one, Nashra went to the US to study. She was taking a game design class in her final year, and her professor encouraged her to devise something she felt particularly passionate about. Nashra had just celebrated her twenty-first birthday and, during a recent visit to Pakistan, had been unexpectedly set up with a suitor. Although he sounded good on paper—well educated, good-looking, respectable family, well presented—she couldn't get over the fact that he was a stranger. The topic of arranged marriages was at the forefront of her mind. Feeling that her entire life was a cat-and-mouse-chase with the matchmakers, she thought it seemed a perfect concept to base a board game on. All she needed to do was use all the crazy things she had done, or wished she had done, to evade the matchmaker.

The idea took off. Although it was met with some disapproval from extended family members in Pakistan, Nashra made clear that her aim wasn't to attack the institution of arranged mar-riages. 'I'm not against the idea of an arranged marriage. The problem is when it comes with unreal expectations,' she says. 'In a place like Pakistan, which is conservative, there are a lot of instances where men and women aren't even allowed to be friends. How are they supposed to find a marriage partner in that case?' Nashra recalls a comedy sketch where a family goes to a girl's house and cross-examines her, asking what her qualifications are, what her hobbies are, if she can cook, sew, make tea and clean.

When it comes to scrutinising the boy's qualities, his family's sole response is, 'He has an MBA!' as if that will be enough to satisfy any questions about his eligibility for marriage. This, for Nashra, is where arranged marriages become problematic.

Unfortunately, though perhaps unsurprisingly, Western media initially presented Nashra's board game as a weapon in the fight against forced marriage, linking arranged marriages to gendered violence, acid attacks and domestic abuse. 'I had tried to approach the project from a nuanced perspective, which invited questions about gender roles, society's expectations and individual agency,' she says, 'but initially the media wrote about it with click-bait stories.' Some relatives accused her of throwing Pakistan and their traditions under the bus. 'I was invited to zero weddings that year!' Knowing emotions have a tendency to run high around such issues, Nashra also decided to turn down requests to appear on Pakistani media, with the murder that year of Sabeen Mahmud, a human rights activist and founder of the Karachi-based cafe The Second Floor, very much in her thoughts.[2]

Nashra's nuanced approach acknowledges that arranged marriages are not an automatic pipeline to oppressive situations. It does so without denying that for some women, this can be the case. Irum Ali explains that in many traditional cultures, a good daughter-in-law is mythologised as someone who will make no demands and who will obliterate her sense of self to fit into her family of destination, which is her husband's family. While a good daughter will obliterate her sense of self to fit into her family of origin. Either way, she will not cause problems or be a difficult woman. 'There are nuances and levels to that, and not all families are the same,' Irum says, 'but what is insidious is that even in families that make out they are liberal and empowering of their female members, those expectations are there deep down. That's why I'm passionate about teaching my four-year-old daughter to take up space. My priority is not to be my child's first bully.'

I hear the story of a woman who told her daughter-in-law that wives are like slippers: they are comfortable and indispensable for a period of time, but when they wear out, they can be easily swapped for a new pair. Medina Tenour Whiteman, author of *The Invisible Muslim*,[3] tells me about her research into Sufi *tariqahs* and asks, 'Where are the Rabiahs in these structures?' referring to the influential eighth-century Sufi mystic Rabiah al-Adawiyyah.[4] There is so much emphasis on gentleness and niceness as prized female characteristics, Medina explains, but this is simply not a realistic permanent state for anyone. If a person is unable to express negative emotions, they will break at some point. This is coupled with a tendency to encourage women to marry young, while de-emphasising further education. If there is no forum for debate or discussion through which young women can express thoughts, emotions and ideas, the end result is a flat dialectic. 'With so much emphasis on unity and conformity, it can be hard to find plurality of thought,' says Medina. 'Families in these Sufi *tariqahs* often struggle to deal with dissent or disagreement and celebrate a very specific pattern of womanhood, based on purity, marriage, motherhood, being a dutiful wife. Ironically, for people on a spiritual path, this pressure to suppress certain emotions or thoughts doesn't help us to pursue self-knowledge or embody truth.' There are, of course, many Muslim cultural strands that don't revolve around a subduing of the ego or *nafs*. But is there an expectation of marriage in Muslim communities that requires women to mould and contort themselves so they can easily fit into place, quietly and uncomplainingly occupying their designated space, until they have served their purpose, after which they can be cast aside?[5]

Of course, Medina does not claim this is a universal experience. Certainly, Rakaya Esime Fetuga, who belongs to a *tariqah* in Senegal, enjoys considerable autonomy and speaks of the lack of limitations she experienced growing up in Northwest London with the community of Sufi followers of Sheikh Ahmed Babikir to which her parents belonged. It was only when she entered adulthood and thoughts turned to marriage that she realised some men viewed gender roles in ways that surprised her and that centred on expectations that were far from what Allah expected of them. 'What I struggled with was the idea of taking a role of servitude to someone who may abuse their power. I knew I wouldn't be able to accept that,' she says. After hearing Sheikh Babikir, a learned scholar whom she respects deeply, speak on the topic of marriage, Rakaya felt reassured that she was right in her desire for dignity and mutual respect in marriage and that Islam provided this safety for her.

Although Rakaya does not label herself a 'feminist' as defined by Western discourse, and she avoids confrontation where possible, she says she believes in speaking out against anti-women rhetoric and that if this is what it means to be a Muslim feminist, then so be it. For her, misogynistic behaviour and opinions are not Islamic, and therefore it is her duty to correct men who push their un-Islamic views while claiming they are speaking an absolute Islamic truth. Ultimately, these encounters have led her to seek sanctuary and solidarity with her sisters. 'My default is to retreat back into women-only spaces and talk things through. Some people may argue that by doing that, it doesn't inspire change, but I feel like not everybody has to be the person of change. Sometimes you need your echo chambers and places to refuel, which can inspire those who are more suited to it, to take on the fighting work.' Rakaya has seen some of her sisters in *tariqah* married to brothers who are in the same *tariqah* but who may live in a different country and have connected via the *tariqah*. Although it is not usual for a sheikh to decide a couple should marry and not give them any say in this, Rakaya explains that for most *murids*, or disciples of a sheikh, it would be viewed as a great show of trust and honour to be matched by a person for whom one has immense respect and love. But for many this would be difficult to contemplate.

Fauzia Ahmad has written extensively since the 1990s on how 'arranged marriage' is presented as a trope to illustrate the 'otherness' of British Muslim communities.[6] Caricatured as diametrically opposed to so-called 'love marriages', where couples meet without the facilitation of an 'Aunty-ji', there is frequent slippage between definitions of forced and arranged marriage, with the homogeneous brown woman viewed with pity for her oppression at the hands of the patriarchy. Fauzia's interest in Muslim women and marriage started when she was doing her PhD on the experiences of mostly South Asian Muslim women and their higher education influences and cultural and religious identities. One of the key motivating factors that her research identified was that women were encouraged by their parents to go to university for practical reasons such as securing a job and independence. At the same time, there was also an expectation that graduating with a degree would guarantee they would secure a 'quality' husband. This would come up time and time again in Fauzia's research and led to her interest in marriage. She wondered what happened to those women who thought that getting a degree would bag them husbands worthy in the eyes of society, meaning men who were educated to degree level, who earned a good salary, and whose attitudes around modernity would be in alignment with theirs. The women spoke about their desire to live a married life that balanced religion and culture, and about wishing to marry a man who had the soft skills they themselves developed when they were at university. As Fauzia explored this, she began to see that women were finding it difficult to secure such matches. They weren't meeting the men they thought they would meet at university, and even if they did, these men didn't seem interested in their age group, or were rather conservative, or were aware they could end up marrying someone 'back home'. The women's expectation then became that they might meet someone when they started working. That didn't work out either, as they were either meeting very secular men who they felt would not fit the expectations of their religious family, or the men they considered good-quality catches were simply not in the same field and so they weren't meeting them. At the same time, family networks were loosening or no longer operating as efficiently as they used to. The expectation that parents would find partners for their children in their social or family networks was no longer a guarantee. With parents realising their circles couldn't help them find anyone suitable, they were delegating the responsibility of finding a match to their children, with haphazard results.

From the 2000s, the internet became a place where young people would look for a partner. Fauzia explains: 'We've seen the change in search patterns that were parentally led, where parents were putting ads in papers and consulting matrimonial agencies, to online-based systems where individuals were putting their own profiles up and engaging people through emails and phone calls, and now everything is mediated through apps. Additionally, we've gone from family-oriented marriage events to events where parents might come as guardians, but now very few parents actually attend, so many people are attending marriage events alone.' This shift in generational approaches to getting married, from traditional notions of an arranged marriage to what Fauzia calls 'assisted marriage', where young people meet partners themselves and introduce them to their parents when the time is right and they want to take things forward, has meant a devolution of responsibility from the parent to the child. Some of this has been because parents recognise that they don't have the capacity to know what their children want. 'The upshot of this is that the children do not know either,' says Fauzia. 'This is where there have been lots of problems, because youngsters have been brought up in communities where segregation has been key, and young people have grown up without the experience of speaking to members of the opposite sex from the same religion or cultural group. They are okay at school, university and work, but not equipped to speak to members of the opposite sex for the purposes of marriage.'

Without the necessary communication skills, young people, suddenly given the freedom to start looking for themselves, are at a loss to navigate difficult conversations about marriage with someone they have only just met. 'The discussion becomes very transactional and business-like, because in a first meeting someone is setting out their expectations straight away,' says Fauzia. She describes observing matrimonial meetings where the first thing a woman might say to a man is that she expects her husband to provide the family with a house, and that she would not consider living with in-laws. Her demands are reasonable in her view but may be difficult for many men to meet. Fauzia asks where room exists for compassion and understanding in these initial conversations where people set out their red lines. 'It turns people into commodities. Men do it to women and women do it to men. I'm not putting any blame on either of the genders, because I see it happening both ways—men put expectations on women about giving up a career to have children, for example, or that they must move far from their families after marriage. These sorts of deal-breakers are discussed at an early stage, and even amongst couples who could be compatible, it turns a potential relationship into something that is very commodified.' Each person is thinking in terms of their own checklist and what a potential partner could provide for them and not thinking in terms of compromise.

We are brought up to believe that marrying means completing half our *deen*, and so for many women in particular, this becomes an all-consuming mission.[7] What people don't tend to think about is what they need to do to sort themselves out, work on their issues and become emotionally healthy people. Instead, there is a tendency to think that marriage is the cure for people's traumas and a key to mental wellness. For Fauzia, the realities of modern life are complicated and messy. It is rare for a household to manage on one income, for example. But when people are speaking as strangers, these issues become intractable. Such discussions are awkward and difficult at the best of times, even more so between people who have just met. At one marriage event, she witnessed a practising Muslim women saying that not only did she expect a husband to provide a home, but she would only accept a Shariah-compliant mortgage. The man she was speaking to knew he wouldn't be able to fulfil these demands, so the interaction did not go any further. Where there could be a potential, Fauzia feels it is thwarted, because expectations are unrealistic and there is no room for compromise. 'That becomes the unfortunate side effect for having very high expectations.' She cites fantastically high levels of compatibility as being another common deal-breaker, with men and women quickly rejecting each other because they are convinced someone more compatible is out there that they haven't met yet. 'The increase in the number of matrimonial agencies and events that cater for Muslims of all different levels of practice, ethnicity and professionalism leads to an increase in perceived options. This increase in choice leads to an increase in confusion, causing a commodification of marriage and love.' People armed with their tick-box list of requirements, and with a pragmatic mindset, will tell themselves they will keep attending events and keep searching until they find as near perfect a match as possible. 'That in itself is problematic and leads to people going round and round in circles, getting older, and the onset of panic for women worrying about their biological clock or whose goal was to be married by the age of twenty-five.'

Dating apps have created even more heightened levels of choice and expectation, but this has been coupled by an increase in individualisation. 'While people remain rooted to some cultural or religious reference point and they want to please their families and choose partners their families would be happy with, they are also incredibly individualised and want high degrees of compatibility and have checklists and demands they expect should be met,' says Fauzia. 'The apps merely represent another avenue of searching, and the superficiality of swiping left and right after making an instant judgement based on a picture and a person's brief profile exacerbates this.' In addition, people are nervous when they meet for the first time; they may not present the best version of themselves, and some people take a while to get to know each other, yet many are setting out their demands straight away. For Fauzia, these are not set up as 'a natural conversation that will give people a sense of how well they will get on with each other. There is a lack of compassion in these exchanges.'

However, one friend I spoke to said that her experience of being introduced to prospective marriage partners through the elder or 'Aunty-ji' network led to far worse experiences than meeting via dating apps or through friends. This was because men would present a side of themselves to their elders that completely contradicted the reality of what they were actually about. My friend would only discover this when she met and spoke to them and realised that the go-between who had recommended them did not know them at all. They only knew them as a friend's son or a cousin's wife's younger brother and had no real insight into their character.[8]

Within the remit of what Fauzia terms 'halal relationships', meetings between two people primarily happen with a view to marriage, so dating, in her view, is irrelevant. She finds even talking about halal relationships problematic because doing so suggests some existing intimacy, which, she argues, is often not the case. She doesn't see strict divisions between love marriages, arranged marriages and assisted marriages. Even within what she considers an Islamically defined relationship, people are still hoping for an element of falling in love. 'They are looking for ways to have romance without it crossing boundaries, and don't forget everyone's boundaries are different. For some people they fight against having those emotions; for other people they very easily find themselves open to falling in love. The boundaries are different for individuals but are blurred for everyone, and we can't really talk about strict definitions of arranged and love marriages, which is something the academic literature has done for some time.'

So-called love marriages, it should be remembered, do not necessarily offer automatic protection from abuse. Fatima met her ex-husband on a dating app, and within two months of intense texts and phone calls, they told their Bangladeshi-origin parents they had decided to marry. They had met against the backdrop of the pandemic, so their meetings were not within regular contexts such as restaurants and cafes or social settings. It was just the two of them snatching social-distanced meetups, all of which added to the twenty-nine-year-olds' fervour. He was well-educated and presented himself as liberal and progressive, saying his parents were not all that practising. His family had all the trappings of luxury with a big house, flashy cars and designer clothes. Fatima's parents were from a working-class background and were far more traditional and practising. When they found they had distant relatives in common, they were happy an extended family connection would reassure their parents. He had told her that if he hadn't met Fatima, he probably would have married a non-Asian as he was not a typical British-Bangladeshi guy. She hadn't even thought twice at his suggestion of moving in with his parents. She had grown up accepting this as standard after marriage. Besides, he was an only son, and his sisters were all married and had moved out. He told her it would only be for a year or two anyway, while they saved up to buy their own place.

Almost as soon as they married, the emotional and psychological abuse and controlling behaviour began. Fatima recalls that in the month before their wedding, her ex-husband did everything he could to pursue her; they talked about everything, and she felt understood, accepted and cherished by him. But as soon as they were married, he did everything he could to control her and her identity. She was a confident, gregarious, intelligent young woman with a good job. She thought her upbeat and positive nature was what he had been drawn to, but in fact it just seemed to make him insecure and ignite his fury. Whenever he became angry, he would erupt and scream the house down, whittling her down into nothing with insults and cruel put-downs. He seemed to crave the power he got from tearing her down, and if she cried, it would fuel his fury even more. He would accuse her of cheating on him and would hack into her social media, finances and emails looking for evidence. He would obviously find nothing, but he was convinced she was hiding things from him, such was his insecurity and paranoia. He was a contractor in the corporate sector and understood the reality of the modern working world, but once they married, he demanded she stop having one-to-one meetings with colleagues and forced her to remove all her male contacts from her LinkedIn profile. She tried to appease him, but the more she conceded to his demands, the more extreme they would become. She eventually realised she would never be able to placate his intense jealousy, because ultimately it wasn't about her at all but rather was caused by his crippling insecurity. When she tried to encourage him to get help for his uncontrollable anger or begged him to try couples' counselling to find a way to communicate without resorting to shouting, he would become apoplectic and would tell her he was angry because of her. Like so many men with anger issues, he would claim he had never been angry until he met her and that she was the cause of his anger, and if only she changed her behaviour, he would have no reason to become angry in the first place. But however hard she tried, it wasn't enough to appease his violent outbursts. After marriage, Fatima was working mostly from home, and they moved straight in with his parents. But even though they were together almost twenty-four hours a day, he would demand ever increasing power and control over every aspect of her life. He started saying that as an only son he had a duty to look after his parents and that because of financial difficulties it would be at least ten years until they could start thinking about buying their own place.

On one occasion, Fatima had made a bouquet for her husband's cousin's wedding, and his mother had told her son that his sister needed to make a bouquet and asked if Fatima could organise this. Fatima asked her husband to double-check whether his mum wanted her to make another bouquet, or whether the one she had already made was to be given on behalf of both of them. Fatima had only meant to clarify what they wanted her to do, as she was eager to please and to make her mother-in-law and sister-in-law happy. But her husband's inability to navigate a simple clarification meant that he delivered the question to his mother in a way that she misinterpreted as Fatima complaining. Before long, both her husband and mother-in-law were shouting at her, and as usual, the argument about a minor matter escalated into a screaming match and the hurling of insults. He accused her of being materialistic and claimed she had demanded an extortionate *mehr* (dower) that had financially ruined him and his family. The *mehr* had been decided by her family's elders according to custom and in line with what was acceptable in the community. She had not even been involved in conversations about the amount, and her husband and his family had had every right to decline or negotiate. His family had boasted they had spent £70,000 on their daughter's wedding, and implied that Fatima's family should match that spend. In the event, Fatima's family paid for the entire wedding, saying they would forgo a *walimah*, which is a reception traditionally arranged and paid for by the groom's side. It was only after they were married that Fatima realised she had a very incomplete picture of her husband's personality and background. His work situation was always unstable. His anger issues meant he frequently lost contracts and didn't seem able to hold down a job successfully. It also transpired that he and his parents were heavily in debt. Eventually, they asked her to take out a £40,000 loan to help them, saying the *mehr* had caused their financial problems, and emotionally blackmailed her by saying that if she loved her husband and was a true wife, she wouldn't hesitate.

A couple of months into their marriage, Fatima's husband's yelling and shouting turned into physical abuse. He became fixated on the issue of the *mehr*, which became a metaphorical stick that he would obsess over and beat her with, claiming it was the reason for all his problems. When her mother-in-law witnessed her son being violent with his wife, she dismissed it as just play-fighting and told her that if she told anyone he had hit her, it would only reflect badly on her and that everyone would blame her for provoking him anyway. She kept telling Fatima that as a wife, it was up to her to change her husband for the better, but then became defensive if Fatima suggested her son needed therapy for his issues, as if her parenting was being insulted. Fatima was beginning to feel that she could not endure this marriage, and the double-standards and hypocrisy in the way she was treated began crushing her sense of self. But she knew that if she left so soon, people would say she hadn't tried hard enough to make it work or given the marriage a chance. She also still felt that she loved her husband and was desperate not to give up. Fatima said she became mute. She didn't dare speak, and just focused on trying not to do or say anything to make her husband angry and on doing more for him and his parents to make him happy. But her efforts were never good enough for him, and his anger issues remained unchanged.

Fatima's husband's demands upon her became more and more pedantic. He expected her to set his plate for breakfast, lunch and dinner, every single day and not a minute late, just as his mother had done all his life. If she didn't set his plate exactly as he was used to, he would be furious. Early on in Ramadan, Fatima was so exhausted from working, fasting and cooking that she forgot to set her husband's plate. She called him for *iftar*, the meal to break one's fast, and started eating herself, delaying putting his food onto his plate too early as it would go cold. She listened out for the sound of her husband coming down so she could quickly set his plate, but then it slipped her mind completely. The food was all cooked and was in the pans; all he would have to do was dish his food onto his own plate with a spoon. Yet when her husband did finally come down, he stormed in yelling that she hadn't set his plate and had started eating without him.

Fatima describes her parents as traditional, but when she finally broke down and told them how she had been living, they were the first to tell her that this was not normal. The final straw came a couple of days before Eid. Fatima bought her parents-in-law small Eid gifts and suggested to her husband that they do the same for her parents, as it was their first Eid together. He became angry at the suggestion, again saying that he had financial issues because of the *mehr* that her family had insisted upon. She said she would buy the presents using her own money, and that it could be something very small and inexpensive, even hand-made, since it was the thought that would count. At this point, her husband began screaming in her face, as was his almost daily habit when the slightest thing made him angry. He belittled her and called her names, as usual, raging at her that she was materialistic. This time, Fatima burst into tears, having previously just sat mute while he raged and shouted. Even her mother-in-law, who walked in on the scene, said that the gifts would be a nice thing to do and that Fatima just wanted her husband to make a good impression on her parents. But he kept screaming and humiliating her in front of his parents, and she finally realised she no longer felt safe in that house. Eight months of being yelled and shouted at for the slightest thing became too much. In the last days of Ramadan, she finally made the decision to leave.

Fatima was physically, emotionally and mentally shattered. She prayed *istikharah*, a prayer for guidance,[9] and something within her gave her the courage to leave. She went to her family home and collapsed on the floor, telling her parents everything. With their support she moved out of her ex-husband's home and began researching divorce proceedings via the Shariah court, because her husband refused to give her a *talaq* (divorce). Stuck in a marriage she was desperate to get out of, she turned to Twitter and spoke to scores of women in the same situation as her. Some women she spoke to had also fled domestic abuse, or had partners who were in new relationships and now had families with other women but were keeping their wives in limbo by refusing to divorce. 'Some told of waiting ten years for the Shariah court to grant their divorce, only to be kept getting told to submit to their husband and try to make it work,' Fatima says.

Searching for a Shariah court that values the rights of Muslim women, Fatima was recommended to visit Dewsbury Shariah Council.[10] The process was difficult, draining and long. Fatima was asked to write a statement, which was sent to her ex-husband, who would then respond with his own statement after a month. This would be repeated until both parties had issued two statements each. Her ex-husband's statements were filled with character assassinations and disgusting accusations, while at the same time he was sending her emails, messaging her on social media and waiting outside her place of work, begging her to come back. A Zoom court meeting was then arranged, and both parties were asked to summarise the reasons they were attending. Fatima was offered a *khula*, where a woman gives up her *mehr* in exchange for her freedom. She offered to give up only a portion of her *mehr*, but her husband refused to accept this and demanded to keep it all. The case was then escalated, with a *qazi* (judge) appointed to carefully read through all the statements and decide whether to dissolve the marriage. Within a couple of weeks, she received her certificate stating her *nikkah* had been dissolved.

Knowing that the worst thing you can do to a Muslim woman is cast aspersions on her character, after the divorce, Fatima's ex-mother-in-law called up her relatives and claimed that Fatima had left because she was having an affair with another man. Everyone in Fatima's community understood this wasn't the case, and all it proved was the desperate lengths that her ex and his family would go to in order to salvage their bruised egos.

Fatima sometimes finds herself asking what she could have done to avoid becoming mired in this toxic marriage. But she had asked all the right questions, had done her due diligence, and was completely transparent about who she was and how she hoped their marriage would be. She opened up about her flaws and issues and felt understood and accepted, falling in love with the man that her ex presented himself to be. But sadly, he was completely deceiving her. She could never have imagined he would switch completely and renege on everything they had talked about and planned. Though he wasn't particularly practising, when it suited him he would say that it was his Islamic duty to look after his parents and as his wife it was her duty too. He and his mother would selectively choose parts of Islam that they could use to control Fatima.

What also astonished Fatima was that after her divorce, many people approached her to say that her ex-husband was known in the community for his anger, violence and job instability. It troubles her that nobody thought to alert her family to this, but she thinks this may be because people knew they had met through a dating app and not through a traditional arranged marriage. People might have assumed that she already knew about his past and had accepted it. Now as a divorced woman in the community, Fatima feared she would be judged, but she says the support she has received from people who know her has been heartening. Because of her ex-husband's aggression, unstable personality and attempts to control her, she doesn't know if she will ever be psychologically free of the threat he poses. But she is on a healing journey, drawing comfort from her belief in Allah, and learning lessons from her experience as she rebuilds her life.

One life lesson that Fatima feels she has learned is her questioning of the idea that a Muslim woman's purpose in life is to get married and have children, and that success in life is intertwined with achieving that. Her abusive marriage hasn't ruined her ideals of love and companionship for herself, but she now prioritises her peace of mind and feels that if she doesn't find her spouse in the earthly realm, aspiring to enter *jannah* (heaven) and finding her soulmate there is enough. 'It is hard and challenging to come to terms with the knowledge that some of us may not find our life partners in this world, but I believe there are so many other ways I can lead a fulfilled and rich life, and to find peace in being alone is now just as important to me as seeking a spouse. Someone isn't always written for us, but many other things are written for us, and why should being a wife and mother override all the other joys life can bring us?' She would dearly like to meet someone and re-marry, but having experienced abuse and oppression, she is realistic. She has promised herself she will never put herself through this experience again, and if she does fall in love a second time and get married, it has to be to someone who adds to her life. She will involve their families and seek opinion and guidance from others. 'Other people can see things you may be blind to, or may pick up on the way someone may be interacting with you.'

Marrying again would, of course, bring other challenges, but at the very least Fatima expects a husband who will value her and not treat her as if she is worthless or as if her personality is too much. Moreover, unless a marriage partner grows and evolves with us, she believes that it shouldn't be a radical concept to end a marriage when it is evident the two parties have outgrown each other and are making each other unhappy. 'If we can outgrow friendships, our careers, every aspect of our life, it is realistic that we will outgrow marriage partners as well, and that's okay,' she says. 'Islam allows us to end a partnership if we are unhappy and suffering, and my experience convinces me not only that we have multiple soulmates in this world, but perhaps the energy and comfort that we derive and which gives us meaning is not tied to one person, or any person.' Fatima believes we have no right to criticise other people's relationships, whether they end or endure, as none of us have had the same start in life. 'Human beings are complex. We are all dealing with unhealed trauma and the impact of formative experiences, and the dysfunctional family situations we normalise will always seep into our interactions and how we communicate and navigate intimacy and conflict. It isn't unnatural to end something that oppresses you.'

In Lamya H.'s powerful memoir, *Hijab Butch Blues*,[11] the author is told by her mother about her cousin's husband, who shouts at her in public, confiscated her phone for two weeks, and is suspected to have a problem with alcohol. But when her cousin finally decides to leave this abusive marriage, Lamya's mother's reaction is bewildering.

> One day my mother texts me, *it's imp pls call asap*, and adds a crying emoji. ...
>
> 'Mama, is everything ok?'

'No, I have some very bad news for you ... Your cousin asked her husband for a divorce.' ...

'Mama, no offence, but this is good news. That man was horrible to her.'

'Astaghfirullah. What is wrong with you. He wasn't that bad to her, and even if he was that's not a reason to divorce him.' ...

'How can you say that? You're the one who's been telling me all these terrible stories about this man!'

'Yes, but you're only hearing one side of the story ... She must have provoked him. No one acts the way he did out of nowhere.'

Lamya's mother is determined that there must be another side to the story. A man is not expected to take responsibility for his anger: it must be the woman's fault—she must have caused him to be like this. 'We cannot pass judgement until we hear the other side,' or so goes the traditional argument.

It is acknowledged in Islam that marriage requires hard work and patience, and that is why it is considered half your *deen*. But divorce is not a sin and is entirely permissible, particularly if it is for intractable reasons.[12] Structures have been created to facilitate the considered and measured dissolution of a marriage, because often the enduring of an unhappy situation only serves to create turmoil for the entire dynamic of the family, including any children. The emotional labour that women especially take upon themselves just to maintain this Islamic contract is deeply sad because Islam does not condemn women to unhappiness.

Fatima draws comfort from her faith, but the trauma of her former marriage has prompted a great deal of soul-searching and questioning. She had remained a virgin until her marriage, and in the eight months that she was married to her husband, they only had intercourse three times. He had never fully explained why, and she didn't wish to turn it into an issue, so she normalised this. After she left the marriage and told female family members, she realised this was unusual. She reflects on the fact that she remained pious and chaste until marriage and had spent her life trying to uphold Islamic values and teachings, but she feels robbed of all that she had been brought up to believe marriage would offer her as long as she was a 'good girl'. Other women who have been married and divorced told me they now question the sanctity of virginity, but Fatima will continue to refrain from sex outside of marriage. 'I don't want to think about how I will feel if I did that. Having been brought up to believe that sex outside marriage is a terrible sin, I will feel I've let myself down, even if I now feel disillusioned with the notion of fairy-tale marriages.'

It is not just women who have been divorced or experienced a traumatic relationship who view the prospect of marriage as something which must add to their lives to be worth it. Two single friends in their early twenties, one a third-generation British-Pakistani and the other the daughter of British-Caribbean converts, say to me that they would rather remain single than risk marrying into an abusive situation. I tell them they don't need to decide anything for certain yet, but they remind me that by their age their parents had at least two children each already. Both are from devout, practising Muslim families, which they describe as traditional. They have known each other since primary school, when they attended the same after-school Qur'an class at their mosque in a commuter town in the south of England, and have remained living at home throughout university and the start of their working lives. When I meet them through mutual friends at a wedding, I initially think they have been quite sheltered, socialising only with extended family or with friends from the mosque, where they still actively attend weekly sisters' circles and study groups. Moreover, because of the pandemic, their university experiences have mostly been online, and they seem content to stay local.

But when we talk about their expectations about marriage, the two young women surprise me with the assertiveness of their responses. Both agree that getting married was once very central to their ideas of their future, but since entering their late teens and early twenties, they and their friends have had numerous experiences speaking with men with a view to getting married, which have made them realise they could not settle for someone they were not completely happy with. They have friends who married very young, some barely out of their teens, and most of these marriages, which were introductions, or what Fauzia would describe as 'assisted' marriages, through family or community networks, broke down within a few years.

The two women do not come from well-off families and say they do not need their husbands to be independently wealthy, and they are open to living with in-laws. They aren't high-maintenance women, they insist, but what they have seen from the marriages that have fallen apart around them, as well as through their own conversations with prospective partners, makes them concerned that young men have warped ideas of gender roles and seem to have a desire to dominate and wield power over their wives. They tell me of one friend who got married in her final year of university to someone she had been introduced to but had met only a handful of times. She left her husband within a few months after enduring sexual and physical violence that began almost immediately. Despite attempts at mediation by elders at the mosque who had arranged the introduction, her husband declined to seek help or change his ways, claiming he was simply asserting his rights as a Muslim man. Another of the women's friends, who had grown up constantly being told that she was not the pretty one in the family, agreed to marry a man who was fifteen years older than her, and who she later found out had a long-term girlfriend that he refused to stop seeing. When she gave birth to their first child alone, as her husband was uncontactable when she went into labour, she knew she had to leave or otherwise be destined for a life of misery.

The disillusionment of these young women is striking. Men are trash, they tell me, and they have plenty of evidence to prove it. They are still open to being introduced to suitable partners, they say, but they have zero expectations and have simply placed their faith in Allah. They know that if their only option for marriage were to a man who didn't bring happiness to their life, they would rather stay single. The women's weekdays involve working from home, with evenings and weekends spent volunteering at the mosque, undertaking charitable activities, maybe going to a dessert place with a group of female friends afterwards. They say their devotion to their faith keeps them content and fulfilled. They don't believe in happily ever after. Although in some ways this makes me feel disappointed for them, I am also inspired, because for too long young girls and women have been sold the lie that getting married and living happily ever after is all there is to life.[13]

Irum Ali also questions the idea of a wedding signalling 'happily ever after'. After she divorced her first husband, a few men in her social circle, several of whom were married, assumed she would be open to sleeping with them. She realised that there was an attitude among many men that a divorced woman was 'easy'. The fact that she was single but had previously been married and very likely had sex made her fair game, and without the burdens that would come with seducing a never-married woman who was assumed to be a virgin. 'At some point I had to directly tell these men that they had to stop trying it on,' she says. Irum also found that some of the women in her social circles started to regard her as a threat. Some would make snide comments about how she didn't seem to be 'looking any different' despite her new circumstances, to which Irum would reply, 'He didn't die! I'm divorced, not a widow! What have I lost?' Although Irum describes herself as an atheist who is culturally Muslim, she has a reverence for notions of justice embodied by the example of the Prophet Muhammad. For her, it is important that people understand that there is no shame attached to divorce in Islamic teachings. Marriage is a contract, and each party has the right to end that contract, as set out in the terms of a *nikkah*.[14]

Sexuality is both policed and feared, and it remains an aspect of marriage that Muslim women I spoke to across generations and demographics felt was poorly explained to them. Other than gossiping with friends, many felt they had been extremely naive about what it meant to connect with their sexual selves.[15] Shaista has been married for fifteen years. Sex was something she had giggled about with her friends since she was a teenager, but there was no doubt in her mind that she would remain a virgin until marriage. She and her husband met at their university's Islamic Society in the Northwest of England and decided to marry after graduation. His family were well known in the local Pakistani community, and her parents felt she had made a good match. As the wedding approached, Shaista felt both nervous and excited about the wedding night, but she had done her research and talked to enough married female friends to feel reasonably confident about what to expect.

On her wedding night, however, Shaista found the experience difficult. Her husband wanted to penetrate her as soon as they were alone, and when she found it painful, he thought he just needed to push harder. She eventually asked him to stop, and they agreed to try again the next day, assuming their lack of success was because they were both virgins. The next day's attempt was no better, but a few days later Shaista's husband was able to penetrate her. Yet by then Shaista was traumatised by her experience of sex. Her husband didn't seem to be able to understand why she found it painful, and although he tried to be sympathetic, it became a point of contention between them. Months passed, and sex remained an ordeal and completely without pleasure for her. She asked her husband to spend some time in foreplay before attempting penetration, as she had read that sometimes sex is painful because a woman is not stimulated enough or too tense. But when it came to catering to her needs, he became impatient and complained that over-thinking and trying to get her to relax was leading him to struggle to maintain an erection. Shaista was wracked with guilt. She felt she was letting her husband down and berated herself for being like 'a frigid 1950s housewife'. She had been told that sex for men was a biological urge, and she despaired that she was not fulfilling her duty as a wife, and that instead of giving her husband his rightful pleasure, she was giving him a complex. Her husband sometimes made jokes that he had married an impenetrable woman, and although she knew he didn't mean to be cruel, his comments were deeply wounding.

Eventually, after months of trying everything she could, from using lube to doing her utmost to relax, Shaista focused on just enduring. She pretended she was no longer finding sex painful, and when her husband initiated sex, she lay there, dissociating from her body and willing him to get it over with. She dared not tell anyone as it felt too humiliating to speak about. She had always assumed she would be someone who enjoyed sex and couldn't understand why this wasn't the case. Almost two years into their marriage, the couple had twins, and their sex life subsequently dwindled as they became busy with their children. Occasionally Shaista's husband would initiate sex, but giving birth had changed nothing—she continued to find it excruciating, and he found it difficult to penetrate her. She felt that her husband was disappointed that he had married someone with whom sex was not at all easy. He joked that it was nothing like it was in the films and a million miles away from the porn that he secretly used to watch.

Eight years into the marriage, the twins were at school and Shaista started a part-time job. Over the course of a year, she became close with a male colleague. Office banter and small talk turned into long walks at lunchtime, which then turned into deep, intimate conversations about each other's lives and feelings. Her colleague, a younger Sikh man, was in a long-term relationship but not married. 'Honest to God, I never, ever imagined I would ever have an affair,' Shaista says. 'I wasn't looking for it. I'm too busy with the kids and the house—I was no way looking to get with anyone. It just happened.' Shaista knew her feelings for her colleague were just infatuation, and she felt sure she could stop the flirting before anything happened. But one weekend, she dropped the kids off with their grandmother, who often babysat them and with whom she would stay from time to time, without her husband, for a night. 'I told my mum I had plans to meet some schoolfriends I hadn't seen for a while, and she said she would put the kids to bed. I then met my colleague at his place, and we ended up having sex. I honestly thought I couldn't even have sex because I couldn't easily be penetrated. I actually told myself it wouldn't happen. I even told him, we're no way going to have sex. He thought I was saying I'm not that type of girl and acting coy, but actually I was convinced he wouldn't be able to get it in. We might kiss or what-not, but no way take our clothes off.'

Shaista said that her colleague touched her body in a way that she had never experienced before. 'He would take the trouble to pleasure me and stimulate me and relax me,' she says. 'In fact, he loved doing it.' That night, he used his fingers, performed oral sex on her and eventually penetrated her without it being painful at all, even though she says he was more well-endowed than her husband. 'I couldn't believe it. When he pulled himself on top of me and asked me to guide his penis in with my hand, I was ready for him to hit a wall, but it slowly eased in. It wasn't painful and awful like I was used to. I honestly couldn't believe that sex could be like this.'

Shaista continued sleeping with her colleague for a few more months, before ending the relationship when her mum became suspicious and confronted her. She left the job a short time after. 'To be honest, although I felt guilty, I didn't want it to end. I do love my husband, and there's no way I want to break up our family, but I needed to know if I was abnormal.' Shaista's husband sometimes joked that he was a bit of a saint for putting up with her struggles with sex, and she had been convinced that the problem was with her. 'I hated myself,' Shaista recalls. 'I used to beat myself up about it all the time.' Now, she feels bitter that she suffered for so many years. 'I know I've committed a terrible sin. But I actually can't say I regret it. The affair has let me know that there isn't something terribly wrong with me.'

Shaista's lover opened a door to a sexual self that she never knew could be opened. She had desperately wanted her husband to be the one to go on this journey with her, but he failed to understand her need for sexual fulfilment and how it could improve their sex life, which would, after all, benefit him too. 'My husband would go from first base to fifth base within one minute. He didn't even have patience for cuddling or touching—it was just straight to penetration. And as soon as he was finished, he would roll over and sleep. It really was as cliched as that.' Shaista says she feels unable to understand how her husband, who she says is a good man in many other ways, can be so selfish in this arena. She and her husband still very rarely have sex, and he has no idea about her affair. She is not interested in having another affair, as she describes the fear of being found out as terrifying. Even so, she feels angry at having been cheated out of an enjoyable sex life for years. 'I was always asking him to touch me, hold me, kiss me. A few times I said, let's have a bath together. I had always found the idea of him washing my hair really sexy, but he just couldn't be arsed. All he wanted to do was have sex whenever he felt the urge. Any romance or affection was just too much effort for him.'

When I interviewed the women who run the community helpline, they told me that one of the most heart-breaking scenarios they frequently come across is when a woman is only ever touched by her husband when he wants sex. The Prophet Muhammad was playful and affectionate with his wives, and this is clearly recorded in the Sunnah, yet the neglectful treatment experienced by many Muslim women by their husbands is devastating.[16]

Shaista sought her own path to actualising her sexuality, but it was one laden with risks and the possible breakdown of her marriage if her husband were ever to find out. While many Muslim couples face challenges in their sex life, help is out there if they are able and willing to access it. Amirah Zaky is a certified transformational coach, sex educator and founder of Amirah Zaky Wellness.[17] Having overcome vaginismus—when the vaginal muscles involuntarily tighten during attempts at penetration—and a fear of penetrative sex when she married her husband at the age of eighteen, years later Amirah realised that she could help other women by talking about her experience. As she set about establishing her coaching services, she cultivated a social media presence. Most of her followers are Muslim women, initially drawn from her networks within the British-Egyptian communities in London where she grew up. When Amirah shared a deeply intimate YouTube video about how she had overcome the difficulty and pain she experienced during sex in her first year of marriage, the response was overwhelming. 'People left comments saying, "thank you for talking about this, you've given me hope," or, "please may I contact you ... I need your help."'[18]

Amirah utilised her coaching skills to help those who reached out to understand and resolve their debilitating condition. As demand grew, she realised she was unable to coach every single person who contacted her, so she devised an online course with a video guide providing step-by-step instructions on how women can overcome vaginismus or a fear of sex. She then went on to create another course to help women to experience more sexual pleasure, and most recently a sex education course aimed at children and teenagers, which also helps parents to educate youngsters, in an age-appropriate way, about sex. Amirah teaches women to embrace sexuality in alignment with Islam and what she describes as 'God-consciousness'. Part of practising as a Muslim is about having an awareness of God in your actions, she explains, saying that it is this that she tries to apply in the way she delivers her online sex education content and in her courses. The term 'God-consciousness' also allows Amirah to relate to women of other faiths, not just Muslim women. She hesitates to use 'Islam' in any messaging about her work, as she doesn't want to present herself as an Islamic scholar, feeling that she is not qualified to claim that title. I ask her what she thinks defines her coaching as 'God-conscious', and she replies that it is her intention to deliver sex education in a way that helps a person maintain a close relationship with God. Whereas other sex educators might promote something that, in her opinion, is not in alignment with Islamic teachings, she would not do so. That doesn't mean there are any aspects of sex that are out of bounds in client sessions; Amirah would speak to a client about anal sex or porn, for example, but without promoting these practices. Although some coaches who have been trained by her and who work with her will take on unmarried clients, Amirah limits her work to clients who are married, or about to marry, and who are seeking to resolve sexual difficulties within the context or expectation of what she defines as heterosexual, faith-based marriage.

Amirah is trying to challenge the notion that you can't be religious and still enjoy sex. A common struggle that she finds women come to her about is the concept of chastity, and she often helps her clients to manage their sexual desires. Her approach is to encourage them to access their sexuality, which she believes is from God, in a way that conforms to their beliefs. She has found that it is common among Muslim women to associate sex with shame and negative emotions. In these cases, Amirah encourages clients to reflect on where they first adopted their beliefs about sex, as a step towards helping to reframe the way they view sexual intimacy and pleasure. Many carry negative beliefs about sex because of judgement from their communities and because they were taught that being a good Muslim woman is not compatible with sexuality. Amirah has frequently encountered the mindset that sex is for male pleasure and that all that matters is for a woman's husband to be sexually satisfied. Women do not learn about the beauty of their bodies, except in the context of purity culture or bodily shame, and the female sexual anatomy is associated overwhelmingly with pain, such as during periods and childbirth.[19] This only serves to traumatise women and fills them with dread and shame when it comes to sex.

This is not helped by the lack of education about consent and safeguarding, such as how to teach children boundaries about touching. Irum's parents hired a man from the local mosque to teach her Arabic when she was eight or nine, and by the second lesson he was touching her in a way that made her uncomfortable. She told her parents and they discontinued the lessons immediately, but she says that many other girls she knew had horror stories about abuse and inappropriate behaviour from tutors and even family members and yet were disbelieved. They were told they must have imagined it or that they had misunderstood a hug or an innocent gesture. Often, young girls can't quite understand or articulate how a man is making them uncomfortable, or they might not know how to object. Sexual purity is emphasised in Muslim societies without even being spoken about, but at the same time there is no information about how to be safe or consent, Irum argues. 'Purity culture is intertwined with a culture of silence, and women go into adulthood and marriage with no knowledge of what healthy sexual desire, boundary setting and sexual empowerment really means.'

A hadith frequently used to justify a man's right to sex, even if his wife is unwilling, claims that the Prophet said the angels will curse any woman who refuses to have sex with her husband. For Amirah, this is an example of the way Islamic teachings are taken out of context and used to spiritually abuse women, objectify them and teach them that their sexual rights are subordinate to those of their husbands. In contrast, Amirah believes that 'true' Islam, which she describes as being cleansed of cultural baggage, empowers women as sexual beings. 'True Islam comes from what God teaches, in the Qur'an, through authentic hadith and looking at the life of the Prophet and how he practised his sexuality with his wives,' she says. She hopes that Muslim women will, in this way, be convinced that sex was created for their pleasure too. She believes Islam is a sex-positive religion and that Muslim women should be encouraged to view their sexuality as a part of faith.

In her book *The Right to Sex*, Amia Srinivasan writes about discussing porn in an introductory undergraduate class on feminist theory. Braced for a dismissive attitude towards anti-porn positions, she asked her students:

> Could it be that pornography doesn't merely depict the subordination of women, but actually makes it real? ... Does porn silence women, making it harder for them to protest against unwanted sex, and harder for men to hear these protests? ... Does porn bear responsibility for the objectification of women, for the marginalisation of women, for sexual violence against women?[20]

To each of these questions, all of Srinivasan's students, not only those who were female, resoundingly answered yes. Irum concurs. 'With social media and access to porn, you have a whole generation of Muslim men who watch porn, and once they marry, they think, great, I can do all this stuff to my wife,' she says. 'Then you have the woman who grew up in a purity culture that taught her to be ashamed of her body and who has zero idea of what vanilla, heteronormative, heterosexual, penetrative sex is, let alone all this. So these two come together, and the man expects the woman to be a sexual being.' Purity culture, body shaming, and constant uninvited commentary on a woman's appearance, life choices and every aspect of existence, coupled with unreal expectations of sex and sexuality in the age of social media and porn, prove a toxic blend for our times.[21]

Nuance and intersectionality are key when it comes to contextualising Muslim women's personal lives. Irum was born in Bangladesh to an upper-middle class, well-educated, liberal family belonging to the country's elite intelligentsia. From a young age she travelled widely, living in the UK and other countries as a result of her father's job as an international banker. The majority of British-Bangladeshis and more generally South Asians in the UK migrated from rural areas, so she acknowledges that she occupies a very privileged position compared with migrants who arrived in Britain with next to nothing. When Irum was called a racial slur by fellow pupils at her private primary school in South London in the 1980s, her mother, an English literature teacher who spoke impeccable English, stormed into school the next day and insisted that the headteacher take action. She felt completely entitled to demand consequences precisely because the advantages of language, education and class privilege left her comfortable in her sense of selfhood and cultural identity, something that other first-generation migrant women perhaps didn't benefit from. Irum's parents were so rooted in being Bengali and Muslim that they could not fathom that letting their daughter take part in the school nativity play, for example, could be a threat to her Bengali-ness or Muslim-ness. Irum believes that they lacked the fragility that a lot of British Muslims currently feel with regard to safeguarding their identity against perceived threats from 'outside' that they fear will dilute their Islam.

Irum inherited this confidence. When she met her first husband, who was from a similarly elite background in Bangladesh, and told her parents she wanted to get married, her father said she must be earning her own money as no one should ever be financially dependent on their husband. At the wedding, her father declined to symbolically 'hand her over' to her in-laws, saying that she would always have a place in his household, whether she was married or not. 'Those words from him and my mum gave me wings,' says Irum. 'They gave me the knowledge that I had a home, was loved, and was valued. I was valued not because I was dutiful or did good things, although there was of course intense pressure to do good things. I was loved and supported just for being me.'

But while Irum's family background was radical, liberal and international, misogynistic messaging was still prevalent. The idea that secular or liberal classes are devoid of patriarchy and that misogyny only exists in traditional or religious spaces is a myth. 'There was no question that the emotional labour in a marriage fell on women,' Irum says. 'Making social connections, cooking, domestic labour, all of the organisation—my mother was the pole of the tent that held up the family. The unspoken suggestion was that of course you can be a doctor or engineer, anything, but you are still a woman. In domestic spaces my female cousins and friends and I were not encouraged to take up space.' At a certain age, particularly as they entered adolescence, these same girls were expected to shrink themselves. They were taught to be seen to be good girls, demure, not to be too loud or too much, nor look anything other than perfect, nor be in any way a problem, nor be difficult women. Otherwise, their marriageability would be, God forbid, dented. Marriage was the priority even for career-focused, elite women. After Irum finished university, her dad sat her down at the age of twenty-two and asked her whether she wanted him and her mother to go about arranging her marriage. 'Because this is the time. Between now and the age of twenty-seven, I can do this for you. Don't come to me when you're thirty, because within the structures of our society, that is not the time, and I won't be able to find someone who is worthy of you.'

In fact, Irum fell in love and married someone from the same social class and a similarly liberal and wealthy elite family. They dated and got married. 'On paper he was perfect. It felt as if we could change the world together, and looking back, I got carried away by an ideal.' Reality didn't live up to expectations, and the marriage didn't work out. 'We just weren't meant to be, but people couldn't understand how I could walk away from someone who was seemingly flawless.' People asked Irum if her husband beat her or cheated on her, or whether his family were cruel. But when she told them, no, none of these things, and that he was a good person but they simply weren't compatible, they could not understand at all.

Irum and her husband had only been able to get to know each other by marrying; before then, they couldn't live together or go on holiday together, so getting married was their only option. Irum believes Muslim communities are not honest about the fact that monogamy is a difficult life-choice and not necessarily a natural permanent state for human beings. It is immediately assumed that debates around polyamory and open relationships are an assault on Muslim family values. 'The conversation hasn't even begun in our communities, to interrogate the idea that we can find our partners sexually attractive for the rest of our lives, other than through the lens of male sexuality. Some men who consider themselves liberal and evolved would never entertain the idea of taking a second wife, yet they don't have a problem being unfaithful, or covertly looking at porn. Just be open about it and not so hypocritical.' Those evolved conversations about what monogamy means and what marriage and sexual autonomy mean are just not happening. For Irum, acknowledging her privilege is crucial to understanding the nuance of specific cultural groups. Even within those groups, it's easy to speak about a certain family being more integrated than another family. 'But how is integration defined?' she asks. 'Through class? Status? Education? Who gets to decide?'[22]

Marrying outside the religion is another indicator sometimes used to insidiously signify integration. Irum met her second husband on a dating app in the UK; he is a working-class, Irish atheist, who chose not to convert to Islam. They had a traditional wedding in Bangladesh, but there was no *nikkah*. But more distracting were her aunties comparing her two nuptials. One aunty said, 'You looked so beautiful at your first wedding. You were so thin then and your skin was glowing. You were the perfect bride; you looked like the cover of a magazine.' Irum was stunned by the idea that she would want to be reminded of her previous iteration as a bride, never mind be compared with her ten-years-younger self. She told the woman that she liked how she looked now, thank you, while wondering why on earth this woman felt she had to say this. Although eyebrows were raised that Irum had married someone outside her family's social class and community—and on top of that, he was not even planning to convert to Islam—ironically, this was balanced by group relief that she had at least married again. Her single and divorced friends were pitied by the community, and she was constantly told how lucky she was that she had found 'someone'. Across many Muslim communities in the UK and beyond, the idea that a woman could live a meaningful and fulfilled single life is still alien.

For Irum's parents, who are practising Muslims, what was important was that she had married a good man and that he was open to learning about their religion and culture. They are aware that Irum is an atheist, and although she acknowledges that this causes them sadness, they know there wouldn't be any meaning in imposing belief on her. They accept and respect her path and refer to the Qur'anic verse that says there is no compulsion in religion.[23] For them, faith is internal and not for show. Irum agrees and says that she didn't want her second husband to convert just for the sake of it. 'I didn't want him to do a fake conversion and be some random white guy who gets a Muslim name for a day. I find this really troubling and hypocritical. I'm sure often it is heartfelt, but more often than not, it is this momentary pious, performative declaration of faith.' She asks why, when it is socially acceptable for Muslim men to marry a woman of any of the Abrahamic religions, Muslim women's marriage choices are by contrast so heavily policed. She is also mindful of the religious trauma that her husband and his family experienced growing up in a Catholic context. His father had been unable to be true to his own sexuality in 1970s Ireland. He married and had a family to try to fit in with the social conventions of the time, before eventually getting divorced and, no longer able to bear living a lie, coming out as gay.

But what if marriage to a man is just not what you want? Dildar was assigned female at birth but always knew from a young age that they didn't fit in with the girls, and also that they didn't fit in with the boys, although this was the gender they were more closely aligned with. At primary school in the UK, they wore a boys' uniform and insisted on having short hair, despite their mum's constant attempts to get them to wear pretty dresses and conform to society's expectations of how a little girl should be. It wasn't such a big deal while they were a child, but as soon as puberty hit, people started treating Dildar differently. For example, a close male friend from Dildar's home country suddenly became distant whenever Dildar would visit for the holidays, as it was now inappropriate to be seen speaking to someone of a different gender. For Dildar's parents, who had grown up in a Muslim-majority country and moved to the UK when Dildar was just a toddler, their little girl was now becoming a woman, and this 'dressing up as a boy' phase could no longer be tolerated. Dildar was expected to act like a woman, dress like a woman, and even sit like a woman with their legs crossed, and to adhere to their parents' definition of binary gender roles and gender expression. Dildar remembers feeling very confused, but they lacked the language and tools to fully comprehend the topics of gender and sexuality and so still identified as a woman. 'I felt deeply for women's rights and rejected gender roles in the home. For example, I knew that if I was a boy, I wouldn't be expected to learn how to cook, so I would rebel against my parents' wishes and expectations of helping in the kitchen, to the extent I delayed learning how to make a cup of tea until the age of sixteen. My father remarked that I would make a bad wife and no man would marry me, but those things didn't sound so bad at the time. I used to dream of marrying a girl.' Looking back now, Dildar wishes their parents hadn't assigned gender to cooking, a basic life skill, because as they grew older and wanted to be more independent, their ignorance in the kitchen backfired. 'Little did I know I would be repeating these same patriarchal dynamics with my romantic interests.'

At the age of twelve, Dildar realised that expressing themselves in a 'boyish' way was still what felt natural to them. It wasn't easy, however. 'I remember walking into the girls' toilets with a masculine-presenting appearance, and everybody would scream thinking a boy entered. The basic need to use the toilet became a source of anxiety for me. This experience is echoed by many gender-non-conforming and trans people,' they say. 'Today's hot debates around single-sex toilets forget that in the midst of all this, there are also kids who have never even been introduced to the concept of gender identity, who just happen to dress differently. They too are discriminated against. The fight for trans and women's rights is the same fight. Back then, I didn't even have access to gender-neutral toilets, so I would wait to use the toilet at home.' Dildar, in their head and heart, didn't feel like they could relate to the women around them. The identities 'man' and 'woman' both felt incomplete. 'I felt like a failed version of both genders. I would write over and over in my journals, "Am I a girl? Am I a boy? I'm not man enough. I'm not woman enough. Who am I?"'

Dildar started wearing hijab out of choice when they turned fourteen, and during the next few years they became active in the Muslim community in their school and local area. They surrendered to Salafi Sunni Islam, packaged as true and pure Islam, in an attempt to find meaning and stability in their life, even though it was neither spiritually nor emotionally fulfilling. 'Those black-and-white, unquestioning and uncomplicated "x is a sin, y is not a sin" rules for living life meant I could have a false sense of stability and clarity. It helped distract me from my reality.'

Dildar started practising a very fundamentalist, strict and rigid Islam and threw themselves into community activities. Despite the cognitive dissonance of living in denial of their true self, in some way Dildar found that the community kept them going. 'There was a weird disconnect in my mind that I knew, deep down, my community wouldn't accept me for who I truly was. At one point it felt like one big performance of religiosity, heterosexuality and femininity. But the relations I made within the community, who I viewed as family, kept me going at that time. In many ways, these relationship dynamics echoed my home life. I told myself that as long as I kept certain parts of myself hidden, everything would be fine. But this proved to be very difficult as time went on.'

Emboldened by the knowledge that according to British law their eighteenth birthday meant they were now officially an adult, Dildar decided to mark their legal coming of age by taking off their hijab and cutting their hair short. 'Gender expression is personal and varies. I now know of assigned-female-at-birth people who don't identify as a man or woman, yet wear hijab without feeling like they are contradicting their gender identity, but this wasn't the case for me.' Looking in the mirror, they felt, for the first time in a long time, that the image reflected back to them was their true self.

Throughout university, Dildar continued to try to suppress their authentic self and remained strongly connected to Muslim communities. 'I had no extended family here. I wasn't very close to my immediate family, so I felt I had to find my own family.' Again, Muslim communities seemed to offer the belonging Dildar craved, fulfilling their strong desire to feel less alone. At the same time, it was becoming more and more painful to suppress their authentic self, and they expressed this wherever and however they had courage to, such as beginning to dress in a style that was more evidently queer and discovering that gender expression need not be binary. Increasingly, it felt that the university Islamic Society, which they were now heavily involved with, was struggling to relate to them. 'I think the ISoc members assumed I was a staunch feminist and thought nothing more of it. But even that was becoming problematic as the committee was patriarchal in governance, as this structure was deemed to be Islamic and was often justified by women committee members. After half a year I started to realise—regardless of whether it was intentional or not—that I was a diversity token. The ISoc would encourage me to attend meetings with bodies such as the Students Union, so they could refute accusations of not being inclusive enough. They could just wheel me out and say, look we have a woman with short hair who is very boyish! Yet at the same time they organised a *halaqah*, a religious circle where we meet to learn about Islam, that I attended where it was argued that Muslim women dressing in masculine attire were cursed.' The society's hypocrisy, along with the knowledge that they were only accepted there because they performed a useful role, ticking the diversity box to fend off an Islamophobic union, but would never be allowed to stand for president, was painful for Dildar. The same thing happened outside university too in a Muslim organisation that they joined. 'I knew that their acceptance and love for me was conditional as the culture allowed for casual jokes to be made about queer people during committee meetings.'

Feeling alienated from their Muslim community, but similarly unable to find belonging among the queer society on campus, in part because of internalised homophobia, was difficult. Dildar was well exposed to the Islamophobic climate of the institution where they studied, so they couldn't fathom how they would relate to the non-Muslim, white-dominated queer community members. Wrestling with two worlds that they had been brought up to believe were incompatible, Dildar was unable to make sense of their identity and belonging, and they felt alone. They lived with the anguish of this confusion for much of their adolescence, having never been given the option to identify as anything other than one of the binary genders. Growing up in a patriarchal household, where their father was the provider and designated head of the family and their mother had a very domestic, caregiving role, coupled with an added layer of heteronormative, patriarchal Sunni Islam, was a huge barrier for Dildar to make sense of who they are. Not only were they subconsciously being told that they did not fit in with the family, the community and mainstream society, but also that the Creator, Almighty God, did not accept them. Dildar thought religion was a source of hope and purpose for mankind, but religion was being used against them, and this was incredibly painful. 'For the longest time I couldn't reconcile my identity and my faith. Looking back, I turned against myself. I ended up running ten times faster to my faith, seeking answers. I was desperate to be good and be accepted. I completely erased who

I was and denied my reality. I rejected any hope for love or connection for my authentic self by friends and community, and became a shell of myself.'

Dildar believed that by following what they had been taught was the righteous path and by conforming to cis-heteronormative patriarchy, they were becoming closer to God, but this repression came at an unimaginable emotional cost. 'It felt like I was in conversion therapy at times. It was dehumanising, and I got to the point where I knew I couldn't handle it. I couldn't keep living like this.' They never pursued women romantically, and whenever they developed a crush they mostly remained in denial of their feelings, as it was too painful to want a relationship while having been conditioned to believe that this desire for love and partnership with a woman was unnatural and sinful. 'I could not hold the two together, so I had to forgo the idea of having a partner. This could only go on for so long—I eventually reached a breaking point where I was tired of pretending, pretending that what I was going through was sustainable, pretending that Islam made sense to me, pretending that denying myself the very human need for love was a godly act. The same people expecting me to forgo partnership would never prescribe it for themselves. I dared to finally call myself queer at the age of twenty-two.'

Dildar, desperate for answers, embarked on an intensive course on Islam and gender. 'I learned that queer Muslims had always existed. I learned that women were also leaders of their own [Islamic] schools of thought, beyond the four male Sunni imams we're taught about, and about the historical suppression of women's scholarship. Once fathoming how man-made Islamic law really was, and the extent of diversity we used to have but that had been erased politically, I was prompted to imagine a world where the marginalised voices were heard and centred.' Professor Shabana Mir teaches at the American Islamic College, one of only two Islamic liberal arts colleges in the US, and also teaches Islam and gender, covering such topics. I asked her about her courses, and she referred me to one of her blog posts: 'Most of my Muslim students are eager to understand diverse perspective on religious issues, and have been astoundingly eager to broaden their horizons, even to the point of intellectual discomfort.' She goes on to describe occasional appearances by what she describes as the usually male 'Guerrilla Student', who attempts to shut down critical thinking by throwing decontextualised Qur'anic verses into proceedings.[24]

For Dildar, the course they took was life-changing. 'I remember the moment I really comprehended and internalised that Islamic law goes through the lens of human interpretation, with all the biases, vested interests, the blinding role of male privilege, the norms of the time; this was when we were discussing the assumption that women were passive in sexual nature, a prominent view which was actually from Greek ideology and then written into Islamic law. You see this often, the constant othering of women as if women are another species, how somehow even speaking in public can become a *fitnah*, trial and distress, as a man may be at risk of being seduced by her; the enforcement of gender segregation, especially in prayer, where women were to stand behind the men where they cannot be perceived, and by extension were not allowed to lead prayer. This has all contributed to the sexualisation of women, though those upholding these norms claim otherwise. This of course was an attempt to regulate (read: coddle) male sexual perversion through the control of women's social mobility and public presence. I thought about where queer people would fit into all of this. How do bisexual and gay Muslims navigate these spaces? Did that even occur to the lawmakers of the time?'

Dildar describes their realisation that Islamic law is not purely divine and that it doesn't exist in a vacuum. 'Islam is open to interpretation. It has always been evolving, inspired by its social-political-economic context, with an end goal of justice and peace, that's when everything inside me broke—in a good way. It broke the guilt of not being good enough. It broke the mould that I had been desperately trying to fit into, that I had been taught was a mould created by God that God wanted me to fit into, and only then would God and my fellow Muslims love me. It was like I had been in a deep sleep up until this point, and this knowledge woke me up. It really felt like the beginning of my future, because until then I hadn't even dared imagine a future. It's still a journey, I'm not saying I have all the answers. But since then, I've had so much peace in my heart.'

Dildar read widely, having previously been exposed only to highly hetero-patriarchal, conservative Sunni Islamic scholarship. They continued to study feminist Islamic discourse and made connections with other queer and marginalised Muslims, anyone with an interest in critical thinking. Eventually, they started going to Sufi-led *zikr* sessions, gatherings where God is remembered through collective chants, where they felt awed by how the community was so welcoming and inclusive. 'I usually enter religious spaces riddled with anxiety, with hyper-vigilance, knowing full well that I have celebrity status, in a bad way—all eyes are on me. I hope that people just tolerate me and that would be enough. However, for the first time, here I let my guard down. From the moment I joined, my pronouns were respected, I was addressed with terms of affection, there was no expectation to cover your head, and if I wanted to, I could even wear a *kufi* [a brimless, short, rounded cap worn by many Muslim men]. This was something that caused havoc at home with my parents; however, here it was normal. Prayers were led by women too, and one particular man actually said, "Hey, the men have led a few times already, why don't we have a woman leading the group for *maghreb* prayer?", like it was no big deal. Every time I had prayed, I was so stressed fearing I might have a strand of hair showing, and my prayer would be invalidated, but here, I was worried about the presence of my heart. I quickly realised how places of God were meant to be all along—they were shelters away from the madness of the world. Away from all the "isms". A place of love, dignity and strength for everyone. This experience reminded me of amina wadud's argument about patriarchy being a form of *shirk*, associating partners with God, and how patriarchy creates barriers in people's journey towards the Divine. Where were these people all my life? I found my people, and by extension, home.'

Dildar has found a freedom and autonomy that fits best for them, and they have entered a loving and nourishing relationship with a Muslim woman, whom they may never be able to introduce to their parents. It is clear that this freedom scares people, as so much of traditional Muslim identity is rooted in upholding patriarchal norms. 'My mother says she can accept I am the way I am and that I can't help it, but doesn't accept that God made me this way or that I can act on it.' Dildar's parents choose to cling on to the absolute truth of patriarchal Islam as it offers them stability, but for Dildar, patriarchal Islam was imprisonment, offering only torture and misery.

I first met Dildar at the launch of my dear friend Leyla Jagiella's spellbinding book, *Among the Eunuchs: A Muslim Transgender Journey*,[25] in London in September 2022. We all but feared the launch would have to be cancelled due to the state funeral of Queen Elizabeth II, which was taking place in the same week. Leyla, a German convert to Islam and trans woman, is a scholar of religion working on orthodoxy, heterodoxy, gender and sexuality in Islam and Muslim societies. After being introduced, Dildar and I met on a number of occasions and finally organised the interview for this book on a rainy, humid day at the cusp of summer. After hearing Dildar's powerful testimony that day, I reflected on the fact that I had organised Leyla's launch while I was director of the Muslim Institute. I was told to remove Leyla's event from the Muslim Institute website's home page, such is the current climate of the manufactured culture wars that have made marginalised Muslims easy targets.

Shanon describes how he tried all his life to change, trying not to be gay and to be a 'good' Muslim, but when that didn't work, unlike Dildar, he feared his only choice was to abandon his faith entirely. It was only by reading the Qur'an and really engaging with it that he realised he didn't need to do that. 'Starting from a position similar to amina wadud, that the minute I find something I cannot accept, I will walk away, has allowed me to shed a lot of baggage. Now I don't feel the Qur'an is inferior or superior to any other sacred text. I take them as inevitable constructs in which people are trying to engage with something beyond themselves.' When Shanon first started working with an Islamic feminist organisation in Malaysia called Sisters in Islam, the connections were clear. Misogyny and homophobia have the same root—patriarchy—which goes hand in hand with heteronormativity. It was a no-brainer for him to learn from Muslim women who were claiming Islam for themselves, challenging the rules and conformist readings of Islam that men had constructed in order to uphold patriarchy and consolidate power. Muslim women like amina wadud were undertaking in-depth scholarly research, without seeking the permission of male gatekeepers of Islam. They were challenging notions that the Qur'an sanctions domestic violence, asking what it really says about polygamy and apostasy, and finding empowerment in critical readings and plurality of thought. 'Don't all those things have a bearing on me as well? Because we're talking about our integrity over our bodies. I knew I had so much to learn from Islamic feminism.' It is disappointing that so many women who advocate for women's rights in Islam and who are engaged in deconstructing the Qur'an and hadith when it comes to women don't make the same connections between the struggles of women and LGBT people—or worse, claim that the Qur'an is resolute on LGBT issues.

Halima Gosai Hussain has been motivated to challenge all forms of oppression since she was a teenager. Her mother converted to Islam from Hinduism to marry her Muslim father, so her mixed-religion extended family offered an insight into South Asian communities beyond the Pakistani and Indian Muslim diaspora experience. Halima became an active member of Young Muslims, the youth wing of the Islamic Society of Britain. She recalls becoming disillusioned with mainstream Muslim groups and how they were defined by patriarchy. Frustrated that the women were squeezed into small areas at Islamic talks, unable to see the speaker or address any questions to them, Halima dismantled the make-shift screen separating men from women in protest. This trajectory of disruption, along with her study of Islamic scholarship, led her to lead mixed-gender congregational prayers and become involved with Inclusive Mosque Initiative,[26] an intersectional feminist mosque dedicated to creating inclusive safer places for marginalised Muslims and reviving a rights-based Islam.

Halima also performs *nikkah* ceremonies for those who have been told that a *nikkah* marriage contract can only take place between a Muslim man and a Muslim woman, or a Muslim man and a woman from one of the Abrahamic faiths. She is mainly contacted by South Asian Muslim women who are looking to marry white, non-Muslim men. Initially, they come to her asking whether a *nikkah* is even a possibility, and often it is a surprise to them that this is something Halima is happy to do. 'I'm incredibly proud to support someone who wants to engage in an inclusive approach to *nikkah*, in which women and men have equal agency in this process, and given where we are in the twenty-first century, there is very little reason why Muslim women can't marry non-Muslim men.' In the time of the Prophet, Halima explains, there were issues around the potential erosion of a woman's rights to practise Islam if she married a non-Muslim, because of the relative power and privilege of her male partner and women's reliance on men for financial support. This isn't the case now, as there isn't the same discrepancy in the rights of individuals in the eyes of the state, or in women's earning capacity.

'A lot of this work is being done by Musawah,' Halima says, referring to a global Islamic feminist movement for equality and justice in family law.[27] 'It was discussed by the Muslim Parliament and comes from that point of a Muslim woman being confident in the fact that she can marry whoever she wishes, and it is completely legitimate.' Halima finds that sometimes when a woman approaches her to officiate her *nikkah*, some convincing of family members needs to take place. 'But primarily, they are already there and to them it makes sense. They think it's right that they should be able to have a *nikkah* with a non-Muslim man and they're just desperate to find an organisation or a person who can do that. I feel like we are catching up with where a lot of families already are. You will always find the random uncle who will want to take you aside and lecture you. And I'm not really up for having these conversations because I don't need to be bullied by men who think they have the right to tell me what the right way is, when no one even asked for their opinion.'

Muslim women marrying non-Muslim men is hardly a new phenomenon. Tané is the daughter of a Welsh father and a Muslim Turkish-Cypriot mother. Although she aligns strongly with Turkish-Cypriot culture and her upbringing was informed by many of the Muslim traditions of her mother's side of the family, Tané describes herself as having an alignment with Muslim culture rather than being a strictly religious believer. From a young age, her spiritual connection to ways of being

Muslim translated into an underlying set of values, informed by the religion and culture, that initially shaped Tané's view of the world, developing and evolving as she grew older and more worldly in the multicultural hub of London. She remembers at times, both as a youngster and up to the present day, finding her Turkish-Cypriot relatives somewhat insular, living and interacting with neighbours similar to themselves and not venturing beyond their local area. At the same time, Tané also felt a sense of belonging to an identity that was not solely British, which gave her a deeper affinity with other cultures and communities. Her mother came to the UK at the age of two and grew up in a mixed community in Hackney. Tané describes her grandmother, who made no objection to her daughter marrying outside the community, as particularly open-minded for her generation, having eschewed an arranged marriage at the age of eighteen unlike her peers and having her first child at the age of thirty. For Tané, Turkey and Northern Cyprus have no less or more of a problem with misogyny than the UK. The patriarchy just exists in different manifestations. In the UK, for example, she sees distant relatives in unfulfilling marriages who don't have the agency or financial independence to leave. Cousins who grew up very protected and were told they mustn't date find themselves now at the age of thirty being asked by the family why they aren't married. One cousin is starting to date at the age of forty and is having to navigate that minefield ill-equipped, solitarily, but with growing independence. These factors have prompted many of Tané's extended family members to question long-standing conventions of not dating, bringing about a generational shift that Tané welcomes. The machinery of arranged marriages no longer exists or is effective, so how can men and women be expected to marry without being permitted to date?

Tané never dated anyone Turkish until she spent a few months living in Istanbul, where she met her then partner. Her experiences in Istanbul, as well as her relationship, have prompted an innate reconnection with the values she imbibed when she was young. In Istanbul she was inspired by conversations with men and women who were invested in politics, their society and social issues, and who cared about far more than going out and getting drunk, which seemed to be her experience with friends and boyfriends alike in the UK. Attending her partner's sister's wedding in Turkey, she was struck by the fact that the wedding in no way revolved around alcohol, which she contrasts with the damaging fixation on drinking that exists in the UK. However, Tané wonders whether the lack of dating culture in Turkey, which is mirrored in the experiences of more conservative sectors of her Turkish-Cypriot family in the UK, is limiting for young people.

Could it be that emotional immaturity from not having experienced long-term relationships leaves some men viewing women in a two-dimensional way, which some women then accept and internalise? Add to this that learning about compromise, communication styles, boundaries and respect for each other must be negotiated in public or in constrained physical spaces, as unmarried people tend to still live with their parents.

This means young people often get married very quickly in order to progress in their relationship—something both Irum and Fatima pointed to as factors leading them to marry the wrong person. A friend's twenty-one-year-old daughter has been saying for years that all she wants is to be a wife and mother. She comes from a family of strong women, and interestingly her aunts and other female members of the extended family are almost all single. Now in their forties, they are of the generation that fell through the cracks of an outmoded arranged marriage structure but grew up in socially conservative households that would never have tolerated dating. Despite being accomplished, educated and distinguished women from middle-class families, they did not meet suitable men. My friend's daughter was determined to fall in love at university and has achieved her goal. However, the couple have no realistic road map to build a life together. They are both in full-time education, and her husband will be studying for three more years; they are barely out of their teens and have no jobs, independent financial means or life experience. Yet they have no option to be together other than to get married, something they are set on doing, despite parental opposition, because otherwise their relationship can never move forward.

Fauzia Ahmad has spoken to women who tell her they would welcome the re-introduction of the Aunty-ji, a middle figure who knows them and who can introduce them to suitable marriage prospects via their networks. 'I have seen people try to set up agencies that have a more personalised approach, but often they are limited. They don't have the networks women are looking for and have more women than men, because men are more open to the option of marrying "back home" or claim their right to marry out of the religion, or community, and to women of [other Abrahamic religions], without the kind of social sanctioning experienced by women who do the same.' Fauzia also says that the future will see accomplished women in their fifties, sixties and older who find they are single and may look towards alternative forms of companionship, such as 'companionate relationships', when having children is no longer on the table. They may have spent their twenties and thirties dedicated to the project of trying to get married, perhaps remaining single or getting divorced, and have come to realise that happiness doesn't come from another person but from within. Both women and men who have embarked on journeys of introspection and soul-searching are increasingly coming to the conclusion that Mr Right or Miss Perfect don't exist. Few people think about how they can develop themselves or ask what they can offer in a marriage, rather than what their demands are. 'This is part of the individualisation thesis. We have many problems that don't get talked about,' she tells me.

Another trend that Fauzia has identified is that men and women who may not want to live with their partner full-time are looking to 'living apart together' as an alternative model for their relationships. They are applying this to a Muslim context and entering marriages while still living independently, perhaps maintaining their own homes and lives in different parts of the UK. They may go on holidays together, visit each other and have a committed, intimate relationship in every way, but they remain living largely in separate households. Fauzia doesn't think that Muslim communities are ready to explore those types of relationships and feels we have some way to go before this trend is widespread. 'Marriage is heavily focused on producing children, with women over the age of thirty-five seeing their marriageability drop off, leaving them feeling worthless and upset'. This is one reason why there is a need for companionship marriages, where couples do not have the expectation or pressure to have children but instead seek to grow, develop and enrich their lives and each other through shared intimacy. Currently, there is no halal release for people who are single and older, with unmarried women being told they should settle for being a second wife and be grateful. 'Why should a woman accept being a second wife, that puts her in a secondary position, and not be valued for who she is? A woman should not be made to feel she is a consolation prize or pitied because she is no longer young and fertile,' says Fauzia.

Perhaps the Arranged! board game prematurely sounded the death knell for the Aunty-ji. The notion that you should desire, be compatible with and be in love with your partner, and that this person should be your soulmate for the rest of your lives, is actually quite new. We know that love between spouses has always existed, but the emphasis upon individual happiness was not always the norm. There are many issues with individualism, of course, but these expectations also open up a space for women and queer people to structure our argument for agency.

Individualism creates choice where there was once only painful conformity, and for those who would not or could not conform, that meant exclusion. Deniz Kandiyoti describes this as a patriarchal bargain.[28] Fauzia explains how it involves being able to choose the person we love, and even to marry them, while navigating an oppressive system. After all, within most heteronormative couples today the burden of emotional and domestic labour is still borne by women. Add to this connections to extended family and networks that may be lost by moving away, perhaps to be closer to work opportunities, which becomes a priority in a capitalist system that demands we give our time and labour in order to survive.

Marriage among Muslims is playing out in many different iterations. Why would we want to unthinkingly entrench a system that is enmeshed in patriarchy and heteronormativity? It is important that we celebrate the many ways in which we may be garments for one another. Marriage, with all its flaws, can be beautiful and for many women it is one of the pathways through which to become closer to God. What is crucial, however, is that marriage must never be an imposition. It does not need to be a board game where fate is tied to the haphazard roll of a dice.

AFTERWORD

If you've read this book and are disappointed that there has been no definitive, neat summary of the British Muslim female experience, forgive me if I feel that my mission has been accomplished. The stories that women have shared and entrusted to me speak a truth to power that is entirely theirs. We are far from a homogeneous community, with a singular set of values, opinions, ideas, dreams and desires. We come in all shapes and sizes, the product of all milieus and circumstances.[1] What unifies us, however, is how exceptionalised we are and how exceptionally subject we are to myth and misunderstanding. Objectified, fetishised, scrutinised, judged and policed, we live in a world where everyone feels entitled to an opinion about us. All women suffer misogyny. What Muslim women experience is a multi-pronged onslaught from all sides, demanding that we live up to all the various expectations that have been constructed and are held up as the authentic, actualised, true way of being a Muslim woman. As I interviewed women for this book, I was continuously drawn back to the writings of bell hooks, who describes how Black women are located at the margins of society, invisible to the mainstream, silently existing, without voice, without value.[2] It was hooks who invited those who seek to challenge misogyny to view oppression through the lens of white-supremacist, capitalist patriarchy. The truth is that we live in a world where men are encouraged to take their power from the other, and women are the easiest target. The systems of power within which we must function create the perfect conditions for the art of punching down to thrive, as well as masculinities that discourage men from loving for the sake of loving. Instead, a woman's recognition is predicated on how well she serves, and women's pain comes from being taught to serve.

Where do dogmatic ideas of gender norms originate? Speaking with my dear friend Leyla Jagiella, I asked how we got to this point. Was it due to a denial of the constructedness of what we understand to be Islam? Leyla hesitated before saying that Muslims throughout history have agreed that God revealed the Qur'an and the Qur'an is the word of God. 'But what precisely that means has always been open to discussion. Very early on, we find in both Shia and Sunni sources the idea that maybe the Qur'an that we have in our hands today is not the complete Qur'an, that maybe there were things that were lost. That idea existed in early Islam.' Philosophical and theological questions also arise. 'If this is the word of God, does that mean God speaks Arabic? Is this literal Arabic text from God, or is it that God's expression is something much more sublime, and the process of revelation was filtered through a historically and socially situated mind such as that of the Prophet?' These questions were always debated, and different theological opinions explored. As Thomas Bauer,[3] Shahab Ahmed[4] and other historians have detailed, there was seemingly greater tolerance for ambiguity in pre-modern times, and one would not typically have been cast outside the folds of Islam for exploring multiple interpretations of sacred texts.

If we believe, then we believe religion has a divine origin. But it doesn't require belief or disbelief to concede that all religions have the potential to be abused. It is the upholding of patriarchal norms that, bearing this in mind, might be considered in the context of the history of empire.[5] Muslim empires had an interest in developing an idea of the Qur'an that would shield them from criticism. The colonial reality of empire also shapes our understanding of patriarchal norms that defined idealised ways of being Muslim. Leyla puts it best: 'We inherit two issues—the manipulation through political processes of the Muslim past, and Muslim insecurity as victims of colonial history.'

Is modernity therefore the historic juncture that has triggered this current crisis of misogyny? It seems to have changed our interaction with the sources of religion, certainly. There are those who say we cannot dissociate modernity from coloniality—that modernity has contributed to the separation or transformation of cultures through imposed power structures and ideologies.[6] Others highlight instances of cultural hybridity or syncretism emerging from these encounters.[7] The outcomes in terms of cultural separation or amalgamation are multifaceted. If we look at all the political, economic and social dynamics that have occurred since the Industrial Revolution, we can see these have all been about the division and stratification of society. People are disconnected from each other at every level of society. The poster child of modernity that is social media serves to exacerbate this separation. The World Wide Web was supposed to make us more connected, but now everyone is in their internal worlds, encased in their bubble, deafened by their echo chamber and scared of differences. Instead of a global village, what Zygmunt Bauman calls 'liquid' modernity has rendered us hyper-individualised.[8] We are all in survival mode. And for Muslims, particularly those who face both poverty and Islamophobia, the priority is to pay the bills, deal with discrimination, safeguard their family, keep their head down and power on. Modernity and our economic structures leave people with little or no time to deploy intellectual analysis, to reflect, to contemplate radical action that will improve lives.

People are so caught up in their internal dialogue that they cannot express or listen to each other's pain. So many of the women and men with whom I have engaged in conversations around gender in Muslim spheres struggle to acknowledge each other's suffering. Both men and women are speaking about one another in the most dehumanising and derogatory language. Muslim women who speak out are monstered. 'Difficult women' who demand a seat at the table and refuse to stay quiet have their character assassinated. Men calling women feminazis, women saying all men are trash—vicious name-calling does nothing to foster understanding. All it does is heighten emotions and anger and negates the fact that reactionary attitudes from both men and women are coming from a place of pain.

Compassion and justice are central to Islam, yet they are often missing from conversations within Muslim communities. Leyla reminds me that each phase of civilisation goes through a process of cultural negotiation, but how can we build a social discourse on the principle of the hadith that says we should neither cause harm nor reciprocate harm?[9] Leyla describes the necessity of an education of the heart. 'The debates we are seeing are concerned with outer performances and outer identities. Yet as Muslims, our religion is concerned with our inner spiritual and moral development. Whatever viewpoint I have within these so-called culture wars, if in the course of that debate I lose my inner moral compass because I am getting so angry about the other side, then I have lost something about my faith.'

Misogyny exists in Muslim communities; we can't deny it. But the underlying assumption that it must be so difficult to be a Muslim woman or a Muslim from a sexual minority, because it's Islam, and Islam is so exceptionally terrible, and aren't we brave, is a myth. It is not true that so-called Western societies or countries outside the Global Majority are liberal utopias. At the same time, Leila Ahmed argues that it would also be wrong for Muslims to romanticise the pre-colonial era. Though certainly not exclusive to Islam, patriarchy and heteronormativity also existed in Islamic societies before colonisation.[10] In fact, Muslim women and minorities have a centuries-long history of challenging misogyny and patriarchy, a legacy that is often made invisible.

Islam was a radically inclusive movement at its inception, because it paid attention to all the people who were marginalised in their societies and brought them in. This was ethical Islam. Later generations appropriated the teachings of the Prophet and transformed them into a politicised movement, what Leila Ahmed calls 'establishment Islam', creating a dialectic. It is not about men or women. Patriarchy is a system, and as humans we internalise it, making it our worldview. There's a reason why we cling on to it because there are risks in giving it up—a loss of privileges and benefits that are traded off for the oppressions, Kandiyoti's 'patriarchal bargain' once again. But the idea that Islam is uniquely fraught with misogyny is simply a lazy assertion. As Irum mentioned, so-called liberal sections of society who pity my poor oppressed sisters may wish to look a little closer at the subtle misogyny that saturates their worlds. I have found that some of those who most loudly proclaim their feminist principles and declare their allyship with marginalised communities turn out to be the most misogynistic of men. The violence of male fragility, the volcano that erupts when a woman seeks to point out sexist behaviour, the vociferous denials, demand for apology, protestations and indignation—'how dare you call me a misogynist, don't you know how much I've done for women?'—say it all. The reality of patriarchy is far bigger and so much more insidious. It goes far beyond the stereotype of the racialised male beating his submissive wife.

Know that all the wisdom of the Heavenly Scriptures is in the Qur'an, and whatever is in the Qur'an is in al-Fatihah, and whatever is in al-Fatihah is in Bismillah, and whatever is in Bismillah is in the 'ba' of Bismillah, and whatever is in the 'ba' of Bismillah is in the dot under the 'ba', and I am that dot under 'ba'.

Imam Ali, *Yanabi al-Mawaddah*

NOTES

INTRODUCTION

1. A 2016 report by the House of Commons Women and Equalities Committee found that Muslim women are the most economically disadvantaged group in the UK. See https://publications.parliament.uk/pa/cm201617/cmselect/cmwomeq/89/8902.htm, accessed 21 December 2023.

2. Fatima Rajina, 'Shamima Begum: what the media's fixation on her "Western" clothing means for British women', *The Conversation*, 7 April 2021, https://theconversation.com/shamima-begum-what-the-medias-fixation-on-her-western-clothing-means-for-muslim-women-157281, accessed 21 December 2023.

3. Mariam Khan has written extensively about this. See her work in her edited collection of essays by notable Muslim women writers, *It's Not About the Burqa: Muslim Women on Faith, Feminism, Sexuality and Race*, ed. Mariam Khan, Picador, 2019; and Mariam Khan, 'From mute to menacing: why TV's portrayal of Muslims still falls short', *The Guardian*, 15 October 2020, https://www.theguardian.com/tv-and-radio/2020/oct/15/why-tvs-portrayal-of-muslims-still-falls-short-ramy-bodyguard, accessed 21 December 2023.

4. See Arun Kundnani, *The Muslims Are Coming!: Islamophobia, Extremism, and the Domestic War of Terror*, Verso, 2014; Arun Kundnani, 'Integrationism: the politics of anti-Muslim racism', *Race and Class*, Volume 48, Issue 4 (2007): pp. 24–44; and *The Good Immigrant: 21 Writers Reflect on Race in Contemporary Britain*, ed. Nikesh Shukla, Unbound, 2017.

5. A 2020 survey by Muslim Census revealed 82 per cent of young non-Black British Muslims had witnessed anti-Black racism by family and friends. See https://muslimcensus.co.uk/anti-blackness-amongst-young-muslims, accessed 21 December 2023. A report by the European Union Agency for Fundamental Rights titled 'Being Black in the EU: Experiences of people of African descent', published in October 2023, found 'pervasive and relentless' racism on the rise in Europe, with half of respondents to the survey saying that they have experienced discrimination. See https://fra.europa.eu/en/publication/2023/being-black-eu, accessed 21 December 2023.

6. A 2021 report by the Muslim Council of Britain's Centre for Media Monitoring revealed nearly two-thirds of news media reports depicted Muslims negatively. See https://cfmm.org.uk/resources/publication/cfmm-report-british-medias-coverage-of-muslims-and-islam-2018–2020-launched, accessed 21 December 2023.

7. Fauzia Ahmad has written about Muslim women, marriage, divorce and educational achievement since 2001.

8. Samia Rahman, 'Introduction: Alterations and Convulsions', *Critical Muslim 45: Transitions* (2023), https://www.criticalmuslim.io/introduction-alterations-and-convulsions, accessed 21 December 2023.

9. To learn more about Islamic Liberation Theology and decolonial approaches to Islam, see *The Future of Islamic Liberation Theology*, special issue of *Religions*, Volume 14, Issue 9 (2023), ed. Shadaab Rahemtulla.

10. See Sayaka Osanami Törngren & Jonathan Ngeh, 'Reversing the gaze: methodological reflections from the perspective of racial and ethnic-minority researchers', *Qualitative Research*, Volume 18, Issue 1 (2018), pp. 3–18.

11. See Lila Abu-Lughod, *Do Muslim Women Need Saving?*, Harvard University Press, 2013.

12. See Fatima Mernissi, *Beyond the Veil: Male-Female Dynamics in Modern Muslim Society*, revised edition, Indiana University Press, 1987.

13. See Asma Barlas, *Believing Women in Islam: Unreading Patriarchal Interpretations of the Qur'an*, University of Texas Press, 2002.

14. See Abu-Lughod, *Do Muslim Women Need Saving?*

15. The notions of the white feminist and intersectionality emerged in the work of Kimberlé Crenshaw. See Kimberlé Crenshaw, 'Demarginalizing the Intersection of Race and Sex: A Black Feminist Critique of Antidiscrimination Doctrine, Feminist Theory and Antiracist Politics', *University of Chicago Legal Forum*, Volume 1989, Issue 1 (1989).

16. Audre Lorde, *Sister Outsider*, Crossing Press, 2007 [1984], p. 112.

17. In her writings, Sara Ahmed introduces the concept of the 'feminist killjoy' to theorise how living a feminist life disrupts and creates tension in heteronormative spaces.

18. https://premium-oxforddictionaries-com.libproxy.ucl.ac.uk/definition/english/misogyny, accessed 21 December 2023.

19. https://premium-oxforddictionaries-com.libproxy.ucl.ac.uk/definition/english/patriarchy, accessed 21 December 2023.

20. See Hussein Kesvani's *Follow Me, Akhi: The Online World of British Muslims* (Hurst, 2019), one of the first published works to explore the Muslim manosphere.

21. Alex Barasch, 'After "Barbie", Mattel is Raiding Its Entire Toybox', *The New Yorker*, 2 July 2023. https://www.newyorker.com/magazine/2023/07/10/after-barbie-mattel-is-raiding-its-entire-toybox, accessed 21 December 2023.

22. 'Muslim REACTS—Barbie is NOT what you think!!', @OnePath Network, YouTube, 26 July 2023, https://www.youtube.com/watch?v=dtTWbrGs4xQ, accessed 21 December 2023.

23. Na'ima B. Robert, 'Naima B. Robert vs the Muslim Manosphere', interview with @MahdiTidjani, YouTube, 19 September 2021, https://www.youtube.com/watch?v=ogvoHmOA0jk&t=3372s, accessed 21 December 2023.

24. See amina wadud, 'Reflections on Islamic Feminist Exegesis of the Qur'an', *Reinterpreting the Qur'an in the 21st Century*, special issue of *Religions*, Volume 12, Issue 7 (2021), ed. Roberto Tottoli.

25. Arash Heydari, Ali Teymoori & Rose Trappes, 'Honor killing as a dark side of modernity: Prevalence, common discourses, and a critical view', *Social Science Information*, Volume 60, Issue 1 (2021), pp. 86–106.

26. Audre Lorde, 'Learning from the 60s', speech at Harvard University, February 1982, available at: https://www.blackpast.org/african-amer-

ican-history/1982-audre-lorde-learning-60s, accessed 21 December 2023.

1. IS ISLAM FEMINIST?

1. Myriam Francois-Cerrah, 'The Truth About Muhammad and Aisha', *The Guardian*, 17 September 2012, https://www.theguardian.com/commentisfree/belief/2012/sep/17/muhammad-aisha-truth, accessed 21 December 2023.

2. Sofia Rehman, *A Treasury of 'A'ishah: A Guidance from the Beloved of the Beloved*, Kube Publishing, 2023, jacket blurb.

3. See Aisha Geissinger, 'A'isha bint Abu Bakr and Her Contributions to the Formation of the Islamic Tradition', *Religion Compass*, Volume 5, Issue 1 (2011), pp. 37–49.

4. E. Szanto, 'Sayyida Zaynab in the State of Exception: Shi'i Sainthood as "Qualified Life" in Contemporary Syria', *International Journal of Middle East Studies*, Volume 44, Issue 2 (2012), pp. 285–299.

5. Lara Deeb, 'Emulating and/or embodying the ideal: The gendering of temporal frameworks and Islamic role models in Shi'i Lebanon', *American Ethnologist*, Volume 36, Issue 2 (2009), p. 242.

6. *Ibid.*, p. 242.

7. Bradford Literature Festival, https://www.bradfordlitfest.co.uk, accessed 21 December 2023.

8. Leeds Lit Club, https://leedslitclub.wordpress.com/2019/01/25/welcome-to-leeds-lit-club, accessed 21 December 2023.

9. To learn more about Muslim women's fashion, see the excellent book by Hafsa Lodi, *Modesty: A Fashion Paradox* (Neem Tree Press, 2020).

10. See Suhaiymah Manzoor-Khan and Nabil Abdul Rashid, 'A Conversation About Islamophobia in the UK Since 9/11', *The Guardian*, Podcast, 11 September 2021, https://www.theguardian.com/news/audio/2021/sep/10/a-conversation-about-islamophobia-in-the-uk-since-911-podcast, accessed 21 December 2023.

11. To learn more about how Salafi Islam rose to prominence in the UK in the 1990s and early 2000s, see Sadek Hamid, 'The Development of British Salafism', *ISIM Review*, Volume 21, Issue 1 (2008).

12. amina wadud, *Inside the Gender Jihad: Women's Reform in Islam*, Oneworld, 2006.

13. Fatima Mernissi, *The Veil and the Male Elite: A Feminist Interpretation of Women's Rights in Islam*, Basic Books, 1992.

14. Samia Rahman, 'Changing the Face of Muslim Family Life', *The Guardian*, 8 August 2008, https://www.theguardian.com/comment-isfree/2008/aug/08/religion.islam, accessed 21 December 2023.

15. Jane Gabriel, 'Remembering Cassandra Balchin (24 May 1962—12 July 2012)', *openDemocracy*, 29 July 2013, https://www.opendemocracy.net/en/5050/remembering-cassandra-balchin-24-may-1962-12-july-2012, accessed 21 December 2023.

16. *The Truth About Muslim Marriage*, Channel 4, 2017. See https://www.truevisiontv.com/films/the-truth-about-muslim-marriages, accessed 21 December 2023.

17. See Rajnaara C. Akhtar, Rebecca Probert, Annelies Moors, 'Informal Muslim Marriages: Regulations and Contestations', *Oxford Journal of Law and Religion*, Volume 7, Issue 3 (2018), pp. 367–375.

18. For a fuller exploration of Shariah courts, see Samia Bano, *Muslim Women and Shari'ah Councils: Transcending the Boundaries of Community and Law*, Palgrave, 2012.

19. Register Our Marriage, https://registerourmarriage.org/about, accessed 21 December 2023.

20. Samia Rahman, 'Muslims, beyond the headlines', *The Guardian*, 15 December 2009, https://www.theguardian.com/commentisfree/belief/2009/dec/15/muslims-open-society-institute-europe, accessed 21 December 2023.

21. Shahab Ahmed, *What Is Islam?: The Importance of Being Islamic*, Princeton University Press, 2015.

22. Ahmed, *What Is Islam?*, p. 512, fn. cites Ebrahim Moosa, 'The Debts and Burdens of Critical Islam', in Omid Safi (ed.), *Progressive Muslims: On Justice, Gender and Pluralism*, Oneworld, 2003, p. 125.

23. wadud, *Inside the Gender Jihad*, pp. 189–190.

24. See Mustafa Briggs, *Beyond Bilal: Black History in Islam*, self-published, 2022; and Mohamed Mohamed, Sakinah Lenoir & Saraiya Bah's YouTube series *Black and Muslim in Britain*, https://www.youtube.com/@blackandmusliminbritain8310, accessed 20 December 2023.

25. Maulana Ashraf Ali Thanawi, *Perfecting Women: Maulana Ashraf 'Ali*

Thanawi's Bihishti Zewar, Barbara Daly Metcalf (ed., trans.), University of California Press, 1992.

26. Maulana Abul Ala Maududi, *Purdah and the Status of Women in Islam*, Ishi Press, 2011, p. 6.

27. *Ibid.*, p. 12.

28. *Ibid.*, p. 142.

29. Shanon Shah, 'Name Your Innovation', *Critical Muslim 24: Populism* (2017), https://www.criticalmuslim.io/name-your-innovation, accessed 21 December 2023.

30. Al-Ghazali, *Ghazali's Book of Counsel for Kings*, trans. F.R.C. Bagley, Oxford University Press, 1964, pp. 165–166, available at: https://www.ghazali.org/books/kingcouncel.pdf, accessed 21 December 2023.

31. Al-Ghazali, *Ghazali's Book of Counsel for Kings*, p. 158.

32. Mariya Bint Rehan, 'The Rise of the Muslim Incel: Ideological Victim Blaming and Its Harm to Muslim Men and Women', *Amaliah*, 24 October 2022, https://www.amaliah.com/post/66016/muslim-incel-mincel-red-pill-ideology-islam, accessed 21 December 2023.

33. Sunan Ibn Majah 3998, https://sunnah.com/ibnmajah:3998.

34. Karen Armstrong, *The Battle for God: Fundamentalism in Judaism, Christianity and Islam*, Harper Collins, 2000.

35. amina wadud, *Qur'an and Woman: Rereading the Sacred Text from a Woman's Perspective*, Oxford University Press, 1999, p. 1.

36. Sisters in Islam, https://sistersinislam.org, accessed 21 December 2023.

37. See Scott Siraj Al-Haqq Kugle, *Homosexuality in Islam: Critical Reflection on Gay, Lesbian and Transgender Muslims*, Oneworld Academic, 2010.

38. Leila Ahmed, *Women and Gender in Islam: Historical Roots of a Modern Debate*, Yale University Press, 1993.

39. Jami' at-Tirmidhi 2950, https://sunnah.com/tirmidhi/47.

40. Qur'an, 2:282.

41. Mohammad Fadel, 'Two Women, One Man: Knowledge, Power and Gender in Medieval Sunni Legal Thought', *International Journal of Middle East Studies*, Volume 29, Issue 2 (1997), pp. 185–204.

42. wadud, *Qur'an and Woman*.

43. See Qur'an, 58:1.

44. Remona Aly, 'UK mosques must make space for women—not turn us away', *The Guardian*, 19 February 2018, https://www.theguardian.com/commentisfree/2018/feb/19/british-muslim-women-open-mosque-initiative, accessed 21 December 2023.

45. Qur'an, 58:1–6.

46. Ingrid Mattson, 'Can a Woman be an Imam? Debating Form and Function in Muslim Women's Leadership', paper given at 'Sisters: Women, Religion and Leadership in Christianity and Islam' conference, March 2003, available at: https://ingridmattson.org/article/can-a-woman-be-an-imam, accessed 21 December 2023.

47. Ahmed, *Women and Gender in Islam*.

48. Asma Barlas writes that the Qur'an does not command women to veil but rather commands both men and women to dress modestly. See Barlas, *Believing Women in Islam*, p. 55.

49. Aysha Hidayatullah, *Feminist Edges of the Qur'an*, Oxford University Press, 2014.

50. See amina wadud, 'Can One Critique Cancel All Previous Efforts?', *Journal of Feminist Studies in Religion*, Volume 32, Issue 2 (2016), pp. 130–134; and Fatima Seedat, 'Beyond the Text: Between Islam and Feminism', *Journal of Feminist Studies in Religion*, Volume 32, Issue 2 (2016), pp. 138–142.

51. See, however, a forthcoming collection on interrelated representations of Muslim and Jewish sexuality, *Queer Jews, Queer Muslims: Race, Religion and Representation*, ed. Adi Saleem, Wayne State University Press, 2024.

52. Max Strassfield, 'Turning to the Talmud to Find Gender Diversity that Speaks to Today', *The Revealer*, 6 October 2022, https://therevealer.org/turning-to-the-talmud-to-find-gender-diversity-that-speaks-to-today, accessed 21 December 2023.

53. amina wadud, 'Hajar: of the desert by amina wadud', Feminism and Religion, 17 October 2013, https://feminismandreligion.com/2013/10/17/hajar-of-the-desert-by-amina-wadud, accessed 21 December 2023.

54. *Ibid.*

55. *Ibid.*

56. *Ibid.*

57. 'amina wadud at Raise Your Gaze: Islamic Feminism(s) in Focus #RaiseYourGaze', @inclusivemosque, YouTube, 9 February 2018, https://www.youtube.com/watch?v=_VAgENyj4r4, accessed 21 December 2023.

58. Michael Muhammad Knight, 'Queering the Qur'an', *Vice*, 13 November 2012, https://www.vice.com/en/article/jmvnvk/queering-the-quran, accessed 21 December 2023.

59. Michael Muhammad Knight, *Muhammad's Body: Baraka Networks and the Prophetic Assemblage*, The University of North California Press, 2020.

60. Fadel, 'Two Women, One Man'.

2. THE GAZE OF OTHERS

1. *Channel 4 News* journalist Fatima Manji says it is 'open season on Muslims', *Today*, BBC Radio 4, 20 October 2016, https://www.bbc.co.uk/programmes/p04cl562, accessed 21 December 2023.

2. Suhaiymah Manzoor-Khan contemplates gaze and visibility from the perspective of Muslim women in her book *Seeing for Ourselves: And Even Stranger Possibilities*, Hajar Press, 2023.

3. 'Nadiya Hussain: "I'm not just flying my own flag here, I get to fly my mum's, my grandma's"', *Woman's Hour*, BBC Radio 4, 14 September 2023, https://www.bbc.co.uk/programmes/p0gdnjck, accessed 21 December 2023.

4. Susan Sontag, *Regarding the Pain of Others*, Farrar, Straus & Giroux, 2003; Susan Sontag, *On Photography*, Penguin, 1979; Roland Barthes, *Camera Lucida: Reflections on Photography*, Hill and Wang, 1981.

5. Aminul Hoque, 'Nadiya Hussain: A Baker, a Mother, a Wife, a Celebrity, a Brown Woman, a Muslim, a Social Justice Campaigner... a Leader!', in Melanie C. Brooks & Miriam D. Ezzani (eds), *Great Muslim Leaders: Lessons for Education*, Information Age Publishing, 2023, pp. 273–286.

6. The late Azeezat Johnson, a social geographer and critical race academic, wrote extensively on Black British Muslim women and 'the performance and production of racialised bodies across different spaces', including the impact of anti-Blackness in Muslim communities, and of racism and Islamophobia in academia: Azeezat Johnson, '"You're Othered Here and

You're Othered There": Centring the Clothing Practices of Black Muslim Women in Britain', PhD thesis, University of Sheffield, 2017, p. iii.

7. *Refu(ge)Tree* (2020), written and performed by Hodan Yusuf, was streamed by Same Boat Theater Collective on 25 October 2020.

8. Bradford Literary Festival, https://www.bradfordlitfest.co.uk, accessed 22 December 2023.

9. According to a 2021 report by Bradford Council, over 30 per cent of children in Bradford live in poverty. See https://bradford.moderngov.co.uk/documents/s32833/Hlth16FebDocV.pdf, accessed 22 December 2023.

10. See *Our Stories, Our Lives: Inspiring Muslim Women's Voices*, ed. Wahida Shaffi, Policy Press, 2009.

11. Alan Moore, *V for Vendetta*, Vertigo, 2005.

12. Saman Javed, 'Bleak, hidden and uninviting: It's time to improve women's prayer spaces in UK mosques', *The Independent*, 13 June 2022, https://www.independent.co.uk/life-style/women/womens-prayer-spaces-mosques-islam-uk-b2124674.html, accessed 22 December 2023.

13. Nisa-Nashim is a national Jewish Muslim Women's Network to facilitate understanding between women from different communities, particularly Jewish and Muslim.

14. The UK government's Prevent strategy was unveiled by then Home Secretary Theresa May in 2011. It has been criticised by those who view it as harming Muslim communities. See Areeb Ullah, 'What is Prevent and why is it controversial?', *Middle East Eye*, 8 February 2023, https://www.middleeasteye.net/news/prevent-terrorism-strategy-why-controversial, accessed 22 December 2023; and 'RWUK launches landmark report on the Prevent strategy at the Houses of Parliament', Rights and Security International, 22 September 2016, https://www.rightsandsecurity.org/impact/entry/rights-watch-uk-launches-landmark-report-on-the-prevent-strategy-at-the-houses-of-parliament, accessed 22 December 2023.

15. Islamic Society of Britain, https://isb.org.uk, accessed 22 December 2023.

16. For a thoughtful reflection on race, Islam and white privilege, see

Medina Tenour Whiteman, *The Invisible Muslim: Journeys Through Whiteness and Islam*, Hurst, 2020.

17. 'Anjem Choudary refuses to "abhor" Woolwich attack', BBC News, 24 May 2013, https://www.bbc.co.uk/news/av/uk-22650053, accessed 22 December 2023.

18. 'Newsnight, post Charlie Hebdo attacks', @remonaikramaly, YouTube, 13 May 2016, https://www.youtube.com/watch?v=_L3FoeHZuE8, accessed 22 December 2023.

19. NUMBI Arts, https://numbi.org, accessed 22 December 2023.

20. NUMBI's exhibition 'Somali Museum: Any Space Whatever' ran from 14 June 2023 to 1 October 2023 at Whitechapel Art Gallery, London. See https://www.whitechapelgallery.org/exhibitions/somali-museum-any-space-whatever, accessed 22 December 2023.

21. Ayisha Malik, *Sofia Khan is Not Obliged*, Twenty7, 2015.

22. Ayisha Malik, *This Green and Pleasant Land*, Zaffre, 2019.

23. Ayisha Malik, *The Movement*, Headline Review, 2022.

24. See Yousra Samir Imran's *Hijab and Red Lipstick* (Hashtag Press, 2020), a beautiful, semi-autobiographical novel movingly encapsulating identity, misogyny and empowerment through lived experience.

3. SOLIDARITY WITH MY SISTERS

1. A *lehenga* is a form of ankle-length skirt originating from and widely worn in the Indian subcontinent.

2. A *teep*, or *bindi* as it is called in India, is a dot-shaped adornment applied by women to the centre of the forehead.

3. 'Maike Rosa Vogel—Where We Meet (ft. Konstantin Gropper)', @FUTUREMETORPOLISS, YouTube, 28 July 2014, https://www.youtube.com/watch?v=0NERvokThb8, accessed 22 December 2023.

4. *Whores' Glory* (2011), http://www.glawogger.com/whores-glory.html, accessed 22 December 2023.

5. Michael Glawogger, interview with Kisa Lala, 'Interview: Whoring and Hustling With Michael Glawogger', *HuffPost*, 1 May 2012, https://www.huffpost.com/entry/interview-whoring-and-hus_b_1465709, accessed 22 December 2023.

6. *Ibid.*

7. Saba Dewan, *Tawaifnama*, Context, 2019.

8. Leyla Jagiella discusses this at length in her book *Among the Eunuchs: A Muslim Transgender Journey*, Hurst, 2022.

9. Sunera Thobani, *Contesting Islam, Constructing Race and Sexuality: The Inordinate Desire of the West*, Bloomsbury, 2020, p. 13.

10. Laura Bush, 'Radio Address by Mrs. Bush', Office of the First Lady, 17 November 2001, https://georgewbush-whitehouse.archives.gov/news/releases/2001/11/20011117.html, accessed 5 December 2023.

11. An-Nisa Network, https://www.annisanetwork.org, accessed 22 December 2023.

12. Rafia Zakaria, *Against White Feminism*, Penguin, 2022, p. ix.

13. Fauzia Ahmad, 'Still "In Progress?": Methodological Dilemmas, Tensions and Contradictions in Theorizing South Asian Muslim Women', in *South Asian Women in the Diaspora*, eds Nirmal Puwar & Parvati Raghuram, Routledge, 2003, pp. 43–65.

14. Rumi's Cave, https://www.rumis.org/cave, accessed 22 December 2023.

15. See Rachel Down, 'Album review: Voice Of Baceprot—Retas', *Kerrang*, 14 July 2023, https://www.kerrang.com/album-review-voice-of-baceprot-retas, accessed 22 December 2023.

16. Zakaria, *Against White Feminism*, p. 4.

17. 'The National Intimate Partner and Sexual Violence Survey: 2010 Summary Report', National Center for Injury Prevention and Control & the Centers for Disease Control and Prevention, November 2011, p. 2, available at: https://www.cdc.gov/violenceprevention/pdf/nisvs_report2010-a.pdf, accessed 22 December 2023.

18. See Merryl Wyn Davies's *Knowing One Another: Shaping an Islamic Anthropology*, posthumously re-published by Beacon Books in 2023.

19. Sunan Ibn Majah 3488, https://sunnah.com/ibnmajah:3488.

20. See https://www.mizantherapy.com, accessed 22 December 2023.

4. RED PILLED

1. 'Prophet Muhammad cartoon sparks Batley Grammar School Protest', BBC News, 25 March 2021, https://www.bbc.co.uk/news/uk-england-leeds-56524850, accessed 22 December 2023.

2. Shekhar Bhatia & Martin Robinson, 'RE teacher facing death threats

for "showing Prophet Muhammad cartoons" to students is rugby-loving "burly Yorkshire lad" in his late 20s who spoke of his love for "fantastic" job', *Daily Mail*, 26 March 2021, https://www.dailymail.co.uk/news/article-9405929/RE-teacher-facing-death-threats-rugby-loving-burly-Yorkshire-lad.html, accessed 22 December 2023.

3. Sayeeda Warsi, X (formerly Twitter), 25 March 2021, https://twitter.com/SayeedaWarsi/status/1375128207909851137, accessed 8 January 2024.

4. *Ibid.*

5. Sayeeda Warsi, 'Protests outside Batley Grammar school over Prophet Muhammad cartoon row "not right", says minister', ITV News, 26 March 2021, https://www.itv.com/news/2021–03–25/dfe-accused-of-amplifying-divisions-over-prophet-mohammed-cartoon-school-row, accessed 19 January 2024.

6. Peter Morey & Amina Yaqin, *Framing Muslims: Stereotyping and Representation after 9/11*, Harvard University Press, 2011.

7. Riazat Butt, 'All the rage—victim of US bloggers' cartoon hits back', *The Guardian*, 23 July 2007, https://www.theguardian.com/world/2007/jul/23/india.digitalmedia, accessed 22 December 2023.

8. Arundhati Roy's *Azadi: Freedom. Fascism. Fiction.* (Penguin, 2022) captures the impact of Indian military rule in Kashmir.

9. Shamim Miah, 'The Groomers and the Question of Race', *Identity Papers: A Journal of British and Irish Studies*, Volume 1, Issue 1 (2015).

10. Prime Minister's Office, 'PM to clamp down on Grooming Gangs', 2 April 2023, https://www.gov.uk/government/news/pm-to-clamp-down-on-grooming-gangs, accessed 22 December 2023.

11. Independent Press Standards Organisation, 'Decision of the Complaints Committee—17841–23 Centre for Media Monitoring v The Mail on Sunday', https://www.ipso.co.uk/rulings-and-resolution-statements/ruling/?id=17841–23, accessed 22 December 2023.

12. UK Government Home Office, 'Group-based Child Sexual Exploitation Characteristics of Offending', December 2020, p. 8, https://assets.publishing.service.gov.uk/media/5fd87e348fa8f54d5733f532/Group-based_CSE_Paper.pdf, accessed 13 December 2023.

13. Richard Wright, *Native Son*, Harper & Brothers, 1940.

14. Amanullah de Sondy, *The Crisis of Islamic Masculinities*, Bloomsbury Academic, 2013.

15. Sahar Ghumkhor & Hizer Mir, 'A "Crisis of Masculinity"?: The West's Cultural Wars in the Emerging Muslim Manosphere,' *ReOrient*, Volume 7, Issue 2 (2022), pp. 135–157.

16. Hafsa Lodi, 'This is what Andrew Tate means for women like me', *The Independent*, 11 January 2023, https://www.independent.co.uk/voices/andrew-tate-trial-lawyer-muslim-tweets-b2260083.html, accessed 22 December 2023.

17. Kelefa Sanneh, 'Jordan Peterson's Gospel of Masculinity', *The New Yorker*, 26 February 2018, https://www.newyorker.com/magazine/2018/03/05/jordan-petersons-gospel-of-masculinity, accessed 22 December 2023.

18. Bonnie Bacarisse, 'The Republican Lawmaker Who Secretly Created Reddit's Women-Hating "Red Pill"', *The Daily Beast*, 25 April 2017, https://www.thedailybeast.com/the-republican-lawmaker-who-secretly-created-reddits-women-hating-red-pill, accessed 22 December 2023.

19. Ash Sarkar, 'How Andrew Tate Built an Army of Lonely, Angry Men', *GQ Magazine*, 15 August 2022, https://www.gq-magazine.co.uk/culture/article/andrew-tate-tiktok-fame-men-2022, accessed 22 December 2023.

20. Cathy Newman, interviewed by Nosheen Iqbal, 'Cathy Newman: "The internet is being written by men with an agenda"', *The Guardian*, 19 March 2018, https://www.theguardian.com/media/2018/mar/19/cathy-newman-the-internet-is-being-written-by-men-with-an-agenda, accessed 8 January 2024.

21. George Orwell, *Down and Out in Paris and London*, Victor Gollancz, 1933.

22. Amia Srinivasan, *The Right to Sex*, Bloomsbury Publishing, 2021.

23. Mabel Banfield-Nwachi, 'Hundreds gather at vigil for Elianne Andam a week after schoolgirl's murder', *The Guardian*, 4 October 2023, https://www.theguardian.com/uk-news/2023/oct/04/hundreds-gather-at-vigil-for-elianne-andam-a-week-after-schoolgirls, accessed 22 December 2023.

24. 'The emerging Muslim manosphere', *Heart and Soul*, BBC World Service, 20 May 2023, https://www.bbc.co.uk/programmes/w3ct4pjf, accessed 22 December 2023.

25. Shanti Das, 'Inside the violent misogynistic world of TikTok's new star', *The Guardian*, 6 August 2022, https://www.theguardian.com/technology/2022/aug/06/andrew-tate-violent-misogynistic-world-of-tiktok-new-star, accessed 22 December 2023.

26. Adam Curtis, *The Power of Nightmares*, BBC documentary series, 2004.

27. Sara Ahmed, *The Cultural Politics of Emotion*, Routledge, 2013.

28. Sanya Mansoor, '"At the Intersection of Two Criminalized Identities": Black and Non-Black Muslims Confront a Complicated Relationship with Policing and Anti-Blackness', *Time Magazine*, 15 September 2020, https://time.com/5884176/islam-black-lives-matter-policing-muslims, accessed 22 December 2023.

29. Srinivasan, *The Right to Sex*, p. 17.

30. *The Malcolm Effect* podcast, https://kultural.podbean.com, accessed 22 December 2023.

31. Hizer Mir, Hussein Kesvani & Yousra Samir Imran, 'Alt-Wallahs: The Muslim Manosphere', Bradford Literature Festival, 25 June 2023, https://www.bradfordlitfest.co.uk/event/the-alt-wallahs-the-muslim-manosphere, accessed 22 December 2023.

5. YOU ARE GARMENTS FOR ONE ANOTHER

1. Arranged!, https://nashra.co/arranged, accessed 22 December 2023.

2. Maleeha Hamid Siddiqui, 'Sabeen Mahmud—a profile', *Dawn Newspaper*, 25 April 2015, https://www.dawn.com/news/1178106, accessed 22 December 2023.

3. Medina Tenour Whiteman, *The Invisible Muslim: Journeys Through Whiteness and Islam*, Hurst, 2020.

4. See Rkia Elaroui Cornell, *Rabi'a, from Narrative to Myth: The Many Faces of Islam's Most Famous Woman Saint, Rabi'a al-'Adawiyya*, Oneworld, 2019.

5. Also see Bruce B. Lawrence, *The Bruce B. Lawrence Reader: Islam Beyond Borders*, ed. Ali Altaf Mian, Duke University Press, 2021.

6. Fauzia Ahmad, 'Graduating towards marriage? Attitudes towards

marriage and relationships among university-educated British Muslim women', *Culture and Religion*, Volume 13, Issue 2 (2012), pp. 193–210.

7. See *Half of Faith: American Muslim Marriage and Divorce in the Twenty-First Century*, ed. Kecia Ali, OpenBU, 2021.

8. Also see Laurens de Rooij, 'The Relationship between Online Dating and Islamic Identity among British Muslims', *Journal of Religion, Media and Digital Culture*, Volume 9, Issue 1 (2020), pp. 1–32.

9. See 'Istikhara: The Prayer of Seeking Guidance', Seekers Guidance, 3 July 2015, https://seekersguidance.org/answers/hanafi-fiqh/istikhara-the-prayer-of-seeking-guidance, accessed 22 December 2023.

10. See Homa Khaleeli, 'Inside Britain's Sharia councils: Hardline and anti-woman—or a dignified way to divorce?', *The Guardian*, 1 March 2017, https://www.theguardian.com/law/2017/mar/01/inside-britains-sharia-councils-hardline-and-anti-women-or-a-dignified-way-to-divorce, accessed 22 December 2023.

11. Lamya H., *Hijab Butch Blues: A Memoir*, Icon Books, 2023, pp. 156–157.

12. For a powerful reflection on divorce, see Saima Mir's article 'Divorce, Islam and Me: I will forever be the woman who left two husbands', *The Guardian*, 16 February 2019, https://www.theguardian.com/life-andstyle/2019/feb/16/divorce-islam-me-woman-who-left-two-husbands, accessed 22 December 2023.

13. See Karim Traboulsi, 'All the single ladies: The Arab world's "spinster revolution"', *The New Arab*, 8 March 2019, https://www.newarab.com/features/all-single-ladies-arab-worlds-spinster-revolution, accessed 22 December 2023; also listen to Fauzia Ahmad speak about spinsterhood on *Beyond Belief*, BBC Radio 4, 3 October 2018, https://www.bbc.co.uk/programmes/b0b0ptm3, accessed 22 December 2023.

14. 'Divorce in Islam, How Can a Muslim Woman Get a Divorce According to Shariah?', *Amaliah*, 26 November 2018, https://www.amaliah.com/post/52757/divorce-in-islam-how-can-a-muslim-women-get-a-divorce-according-to-shariah-can-a-muslim-woman-divorce-her-husband-khula-how-it-works, accessed 22 December 2023.

15. See *We Wrote in Symbols: Love and Lust by Arab Women Writers*, ed. Selma Dabbagh, Saqi Books, 2021.

16. See 'Intimacy in Marriage: 9 Things We Can Learn from the Prophet Muhammad', *Amaliah*, 30 November 2021, https://www.amaliah.com/post/57577/intimacy-and-sex-in-islam-and-marriage-how-was-the-prophet-muhammad-with-his-wives, accessed 22 December 2023.

17. Amirah Zaky Wellness, https://www.amirahzaky.com, accessed 22 December 2023.

18. Amirah Zaky, '#ABtalks Untold Stories with Amirah Zaky', interview with @AnasBukhash, YouTube, 18 June 2022, https://www.youtube.com/watch?v=iD8URcLT2Ww&t=2260s, accessed 19 December 2023.

19. See Leila Attachfini's interview of Angelica Lindsay-Ali, 'This Muslim Sex Educator Believes God Wants Us to Orgasm', *Vice*, 4 February 2020, https://www.vice.com/en/article/k7e7z3/the-muslim-sex-educator-who-believes-god-wants-us-to-orgasm, accessed 22 December 2023.

20. Amia Srinivasan, *The Right to Sex*, Bloomsbury, 2021, p. 40.

21. Sara Jafari's *The Mismatch* (Arrow, 2021) offers a fictional account of Muslim guilt around sexual desire.

22. See Khadijah Elshayyal, *Muslim Identity Politics: Islam, Activism and Equality in Britain*, IB Taurus/Bloomsbury, 2020.

23. Qur'an, 2:256.

24. Shabana Mir, 'Deploying Critical Distance in a Religious Academic Context', 9 August 2017, https://www.wabashcenter.wabash.edu/2017/08/dedication-to-the-journey, accessed 22 December 2023.

25. Leyla Jagiella, *Among the Eunuchs: A Muslim Transgender Journey*, Hurst, 2021.

26. Inclusive Mosque Initiative, https://inclusivemosque.org, accessed 22 December 2023.

27. Musawah, https://www.musawah.org, accessed 22 December 2023.

28. Deniz Kandiyoti, 'Bargaining With Patriarchy', *Gender & Society*, Volume 2, Issue 3 (1988), pp. 274–290.

AFTERWORD

1. For anthologies that elevates Muslim women's voices, *The Things I Would Tell You: British Muslim Women Write*, ed. Sabrina Mahfouz, Saqi Books, 2017; *It's Not About the Burqa: Muslim Women on Faith, Feminism,*

Sexuality and Race, ed. Mariam Khan, Picador, 2020; *Cut from the Same Cloth?: Muslim Women on Life in Britain*, ed. Sabeena Akhtar, Unbound, 2021.

2. bell hooks, *Ain't I a Woman?: Black Women and Feminism*, South End Press, 1981; bell hooks, *Feminist Theory: From Margin to Centre*, Pluto Press, 2000 [1984].
3. Thomas Bauer, *A Culture of Ambiguity: An Alternative History of Islam*, Columbia University Press, 2021.
4. Shahab Ahmed, *What Is Islam?: The Importance of Being Islamic*, Princeton University Press, 2015.
5. Sajjad Rizvi & Ahab Bdaiwi, 'Decolonising Islamic Intellectual History: Perspectives from Shi'i Thought, Global Intellectual History', *Global Intellectual History*, 2 February 2023.
6. Walter D. Mignolo, *The Darker Side of Western Modernity: Global Futures, Decolonial Options*, Duke University Press, 2011.
7. Homi K. Bhabha, *The Location of Culture*, Routledge, 1994, p. 10.
8. Zygmunt Bauman, *Liquid Life*, Polity Press, 2005.
9. Sunan Ibn Majah 2340, https://sunnah.com/ibnmajah:2340.
10. Leila Ahmed, *Women and Gender in Islam: Historical Roots of a Modern Debate*, Yale University Press, 1992, p. 67.

INDEX

INDEX

INDEX

Hadith, 11–12, 23, 30, 31
  on *hijamah*, 119
  on renewal, 37
  on sex, 189
  on women, 28
Hafez, Rania, 22
Hajar, 45–7, 67
Hajj, 46, 47
halal relationships, 168
halaqah, 197
Halifax, West Yorkshire, 66
Hamza, Abu, 14
Haroun, Mahamat Saleh, 40–41
Hassan, Riffat, 44
Hawa, 33–4
heart-softeners (*al-raqa'iq*), 11
heavy metal, 106
helplines, 110–18, 156, 185–6
al-Hibri, Azizah, 44
Hidayatullah, Aysha, 43–4, 47–8, 50
hijab, 2, 14, 25, 42–3, 57, 78–9, 81, 84, 105, 196
  as commandment of Allah, 42–3
  objectification and, 76, 78–9, 81, 84, 88
  social media and, 105
Hijab Butch Blues (Lamya H.), 176–7
hijamah, 119
Hinduism, 22, 204
Hizb ut-Tahrir, 14, 139
holistic therapy, 118–21
homosexuality, 31–2, 45, 102, 194, 203–4

honour killings, 6
Hoque, Aminul, 57
Huffington Post, The, 93
Husayn ibn Ali, 12
Hussain, Halima Gosai, 204–5
Hussain, Nadiya, 56–7

Ibn Abbas, 33
Ibn Kathir, 33, 36
Ibn Rushd, 37
Ibrahim, Anwar, 31
iftar, 173
immigration, 133, 143
incels (involuntary celibates), 28, 133, 136
Inclusive Mosque Initiative, 50
individualism, 72–3, 103, 209, 213
Indonesia, 106
Inside the Gender Jihad (wadud), 17, 24
Instagram, 149, 150
interfaith organisations, 75
intersectionality, 46, 98–100, 110, 190
Invisible Muslim, The (Whiteman), 162
Iran, 40
Islamic Rage Boy, 127–8, 132, 133
Islamic Society of Britain, 75–7, 204
Islamophobia, 1, 2, 31, 43, 126, 128, 213
  gender identity and, 198
  manosphere and, 136, 138, 141, 145, 154

INDEX

INDEX

INDEX

INDEX

INDEX

INDEX

INDEX